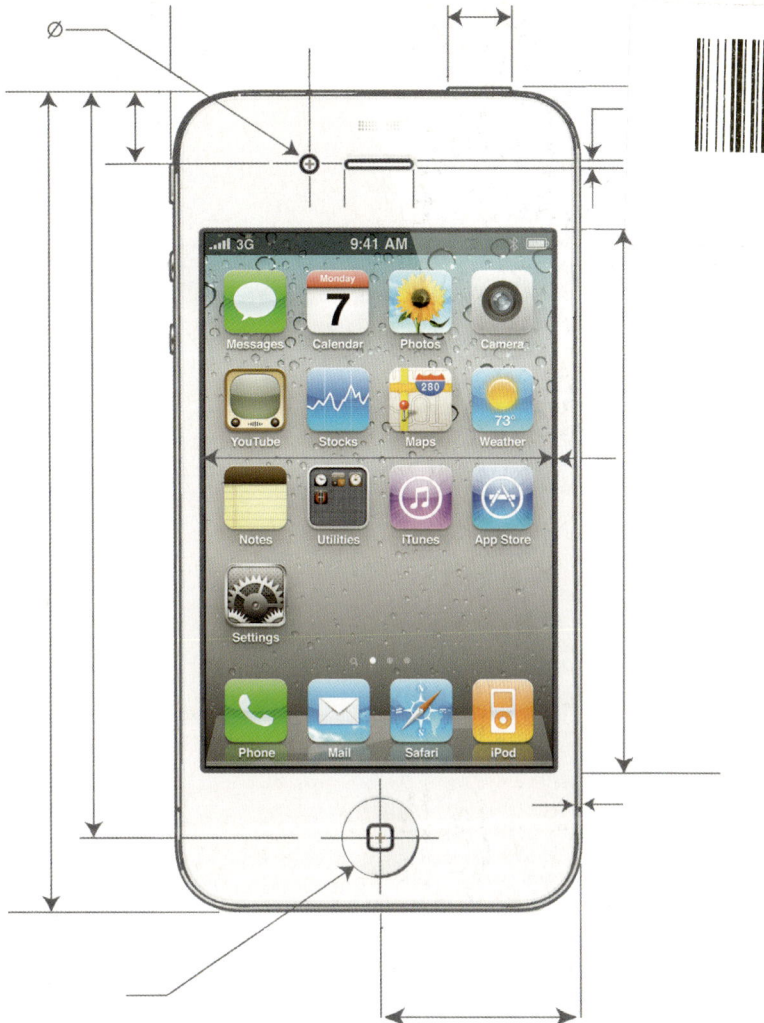

Welcome to iPhone
Tips, Tricks, Apps & Hacks

IF YOU THINK you know everything your iPhone has to offer, think again. Apple's ingenious piece of kit is the smartphone that keeps on giving, and it now has so many uses that it almost makes every other gadget redundant. From the basic functions that come built-in to your phone – such as the camera, calendar and YouTube – to the added extras available through the App Store, your iPhone really opens up a whole new world of usability and functionality.

In this book we will be showing you how to get even more from your iPhone. Starting off with the top 100 tips and tricks to help you in your everyday life, there's then a wealth of tutorials showing you how to record your guitar tracks, test your eyesight, control your TV and much more. You can also learn about jailbreaking, answering all the common misconceptions and showing you how to do it, what the benefits are, plus guides that will help you extend the functions of your iPhone. On top of all that we round up the latest and greatest apps from the App Store, helping you to spend your money wisely.

So if you want to get more from your iPhone and you're ready to see what Apple's device can really do, this is the place to be.

Imagine Publishing Ltd
Richmond House
33 Richmond Hill
Bournemouth
Dorset BH2 6EZ
☎ +44 (0) 1202 586200
Website: www.imagine-publishing.co.uk

Editor in Chief
Aaron Asadi

Production Editor
Jon White

Design
Danielle Dixon, Annabelle Sing

Printed by
William Gibbons, 26 Planetary Road, Willenhall, West Midlands, WV13 3XT

Distributed in the UK & Eire by
Imagine Publishing Ltd, www.imagineshop.co.uk. Tel 01202 586200

Distributed in Australia by
Gordon & Gotch, Equinox Centre, 18 Rodborough Road, Frenchs Forest,
NSW 2086. Tel + 61 2 9972 8800

Distributed in the Rest of the World by
Marketforce, Blue Fin Building, 110 Southwark Street, London, SE1 0SU

Disclaimer
The publisher cannot accept responsibility for any unsolicited material lost or damaged in the post. All text and layout is the copyright of Imagine Publishing Ltd. Nothing in this magazine may be reproduced in whole or part without the written permission of the publisher. All copyrights are recognised and used specifically for the purpose of criticism and review. Although the magazine has endeavoured to ensure all information is correct at time of print, prices and availability may change. This bookazine is fully independent and not affiliated in any way with the companies mentioned herein.

iPhone Tips, Tricks, Apps & Hacks Volume 5 © 2011 Imagine Publishing Ltd

ISBN 978-1-908222-3-29

iPhone
Tips, Tricks, Apps & Hacks
Contents

8 Essential iPhone Tips & Tricks
Discover all the secrets to improve the way you use your iPhone

Tips

- 20 Getting the most out of Safari's advanced features
- 22 Browse the internet privately on your iPhone
- 24 Create a Word document using Quickoffice
- 26 Add your own images to documents in Pages
- 28 Publish your Pages documents to iWork.com
- 30 Dictate notes, texts and emails
- 32 Navigate the world with Google Earth
- 34 Plan a trip using your iPhone
- 36 Take incredible panoramic photos
- 38 Learn to tag a photo location on your iPhone
- 40 Capture passport-style photos on your mobile
- 42 Edit images with Photoshop Express
- 44 Upload and share your favourite photos
- 46 Getting started with iMovie for iPhone
- 48 Edit your iMovie project on your iPhone
- 50 Add a soundtrack to your iMovie project
- 52 Subscribe to videos you want to watch on YouTube
- 54 Broadcast footage of yourself live to the world
- 56 Play and record guitar tracks through your iPhone
- 58 Add and delete locations from Weather
- 60 Sync your iCal with your iPhone
- 62 Improve your fitness using your iPhone

Tricks

- 66 Wirelessly share photos, contacts and messages
- 68 Send photos from your camera to your iPhone
- 70 Transfer media directly to your iPad
- 72 Watch videos using Home Sharing
- 74 Stream audio and video
- 76 Turn your iPhone into a universal remote control
- 78 Share files wirelessly from your iPhone to your Mac
- 80 Use your iPhone as a mouse for your Mac
- 82 Turn your handwriting into text on an iPhone
- 84 Scan documents using your iPhone
- 86 Use your iPhone to scan barcodes
- 88 Translate text and understand foreign signs
- 90 Discover your geographical location
- 92 Identify and purchase a song in an instant
- 94 Test your eyesight with your iPhone
- 96 Measure your heart rate on the move

106 The benefits of jailbreaking
Extend the functionality of your phone with these top tips

Hacks

"Unlock the full power of your iPhone"

Features
100 The secrets of jailbreaking
Everything you need to know about jailbreaking your iPhone

106 The benefits of jailbreaking
The best ways to extend the functionality of your phone

Tutorials
116 Reply to texts without exiting your current app
118 Move multiple applications at once
120 Learn how to launch applications using gestures
122 Fit more apps into your on-screen folders
124 Shrink the icons on your iPhone's screen
126 Get Exposé-style tabs on your iPhone
128 Update your status from any app
130 Enjoy Flash-based content on your iPhone
132 Copy files and connect to your local network
134 Wirelessly transfer data securely over Wi-Fi

152 djay
153 Easy Food, Jamie's 20 Minute Meals
154 Amazon Mobile, In Your Dreams
155 David Gandy Style Guide For Men, Rate Your Life
156 MLB.com At Bat 11, SwingReader Golf
157 Lewis Moody Rugby, Tennis Serve Technique and Tips
158 3D Animation Medical Videos Vol1, BMI/BAI Calculator
159 Human Anatomy Structures
160 Standard First Aid
161 Animation Creator
162 Trimensional, Color Splash
163 8mm Vintage Camera
164 LOVEFiLM UK
165 MyTrend, Facebook Photos Sync
166 Multistatus, Zwapp
167 Word Lens
168 Real Map Plus
169 eWeather HD
170 Ultimate Browser, GoDocs
171 Adobe Ideas
172 Speak It! Text To Speech, CamScanner+
173 Air Video

Apps

138 Redshift – Astronomy
139 Doctor Who Comics, Thriller Books
140 Red Riding Hood Interactive Book, Deadline
141 Dragon Dictation, Audio Memos 2
142 Monarchy The Definitive Guide
143 1400+ Dinosaur Handbook, SkyView-Explore The Universe
144 Beatles Diary
145 BEP360, AR Tattoos
146 PlayStation Official App, Spray Paint
147 Broken Sword – The Smoking Mirror: Remastered
148 Iron Man 2, Plants Vs Zombies
149 Angry Birds: Seasons, Pirates Vs Ninjas Vs Zombies Vs Pandas
150 Samurai II: Vengeance, Lara Croft And The Guardian Of Light
151 AmpliTube Fender

iPhone Tips, Tricks, Apps and Hacks **7**

100 essential iPhone tips & tricks

Essential iPhone Tips & Tricks

Get more from your iPhone by digging deeper into its default apps and unleashing the extra features in the operating system

Despite its name, your iPhone does so much more than letting you make and take calls. If you fancy a trip to the cinema, you can use your groovy gadget to discover the time and location of the next bus, watch a trailer to see which films look good and even make a cinema booking. Your iPhone empowers you by giving quick access to information to help with the little things in life. Indeed, if you leave home without it you may start to feel cut off from the rest of the world!

All iPhones behave identically when you first get them out of the box, but that's no reason for everyone to use their gadgets in the same way. By reading our tips you'll be able to change the way the default apps and iOS behave to make them suit your particular needs. You'll also discover ways to squeeze more functionality out of the default apps and become an iPhone expert.

 **01 Which direction am I travelling in?**
When using the Maps app, you can see your current position on the map as a blue dot. If you're unsure which direction you are walking in simply tap on the compass icon at the bottom left. A torch-style beam will emit from the blue dot, indicating your current direction.

The map can rotate itself to display the direction in which you are walking

100 essential iPhone tips & tricks

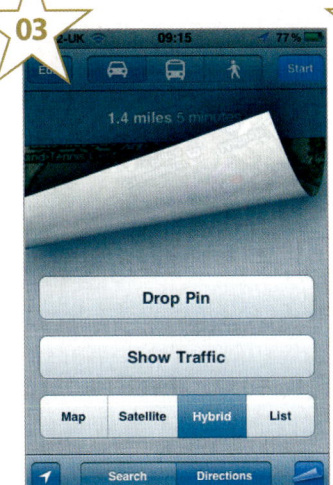

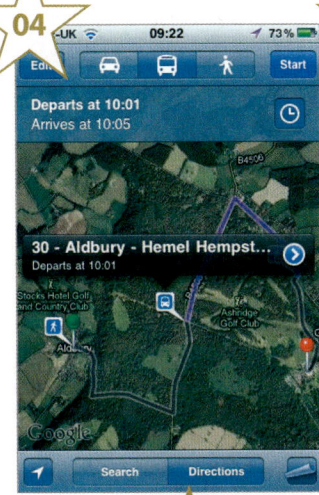

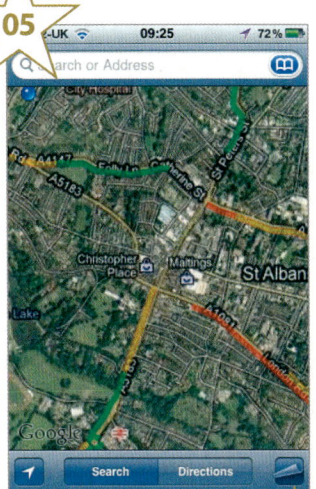

02 Share your location
If you want to rendezvous with an iPhone owning friend, tap the blue arrow by the label that indicates your current location. Choose the Share Location option and then email or MMS a map reference to your friend. They can tap the map's URL link and then view your location as a pin in their own Maps app.

03 Drop a pin
If you can't find a precise location via the Maps app's Search option, you can tap on the curled paper icon at the bottom right and press Drop Pin. Drag the pin to a point on the map, tap the blue arrow and click on the Directions to Here button. The app will then draw you up a route.

04 Get bus times
By default, the Maps app's Directions displays the route and time it'll take you to get to your destination travelling by car. If you click the Bus icon you'll get walking directions to the nearest stop, then see the relevant bus number and departure time to take you to your destination.

05 Instant traffic report
If you're not sure what route to take, tap the Maps app's page curl icon and hit the Show Traffic button. Clear roads will be marked with green, slow moving traffic will appear as amber and real snarl-ups will be highlighted by flashing red lines. You can then plan a faster route.

06 Give turn-by-turn driving directions
The Maps app's Directions menu displays routes as a line from A to B, but this is not suitable for a driver to access safely. Tap on the page curl icon at the bottom right of the screen and choose List to read the directions to the driver in text form.

07 Geotag your photos
Pop into Settings>Location Services. By keeping your Camera app's location service On, the iPhone will geotag each photo that you take. Once you import the shot into iPhoto and go to Places, you'll see your iPhone-captured photos represented by pins on a map.

08 Create big print
If you don't always have your glasses to hand, it can be a hassle having to squint to read small fonts in text messages, notes or emails. Pop into Settings>General and scroll down to Accessibility. Use the Large Text option to make the words in many applications look larger.

09 Count characters
The standard limit for text messages is 160 characters, so long messages may get broken up into several, which can end up being costly especially if the recipient is abroad. Keep tabs on how many characters you're typing via Settings>Message and turning the Character Count on.

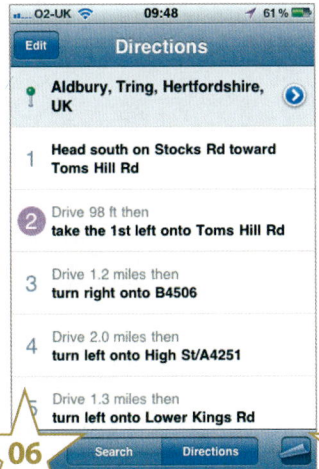

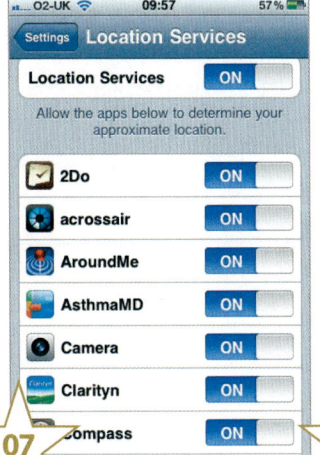

iPhone Tips, Tricks, Apps and Hacks **9**

 100 essential iPhone tips & tricks

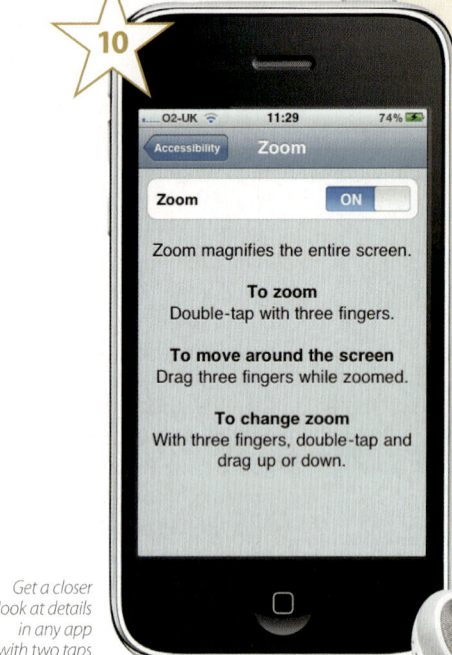

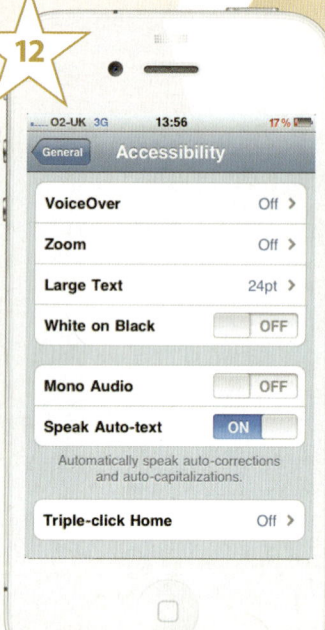

Get a closer look at details in any app with two taps

Avoid those embarrassing auto-corrections

10 Perform a double-tap zoom
For a closer look at your app icons, turn on the Zoom option in the Accessibility menu. A double-tap with three fingers will magnify a particular part of the screen. You can then scroll around the zoomed screen by dragging with three fingers. Double-tap with three fingers to zoom out again.

11 Activate VoiceOver
You can get your iPhone to read out the contents of any screen (including button labels) by turning on the VoiceOver option via the Accessibility menu. But be warned – this will dramatically change the way you interact with the iPhone. This is really handy for listening to a webpage or a book while on the go.

12 Avoid problematic auto-corrections
iPhones correct misspelled words automatically. Unfortunately, it may misunderstand which word you meant to type and replace it with something inappropriate. To avoid this, go to Settings>General>Accessibility. Turn Speak Auto-text On and a voice pronounces every corrected word.

13 Fully close paused or open apps
To see all recently used apps, double-click on the Home button. This will summon the app switcher at the bottom of the screen. Swipe to scroll left or right to see all currently open apps. To quit one, hold a finger on its icon for a few seconds until it starts to wiggle, then click the red circle icon.

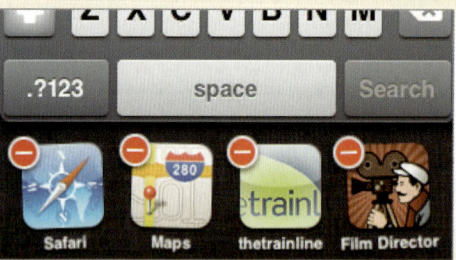

14 Prolong battery life
Tap the Sleep/Wake button to lock your iPhone and save battery power. If find that you keep forgetting to lock it, go to Settings>General>Auto-Lock and reduce the Auto-Lock timer setting to one minute. If you don't need the Bluetooth or Wi-Fi functions, turn those Settings off to save power.

15 Fetch instead of push
Your iPhone regularly chats to the server to find the latest Push Notifications, like Facebook updates or Twitter. This can increase the demands on your battery. Pop into Settings>Mail, Contacts, Calendars and turn Push to Off. You can then fetch data according to a less frequent schedule.

16 Prolong battery life 2
If you want to extend your iPhone's battery life before it goes flat, pop into the General settings, then go to Network and turn off Enable 3G. This may slow down your web browsing experience a little, but if you just want to listen to your iPod then that's an acceptable compromise.

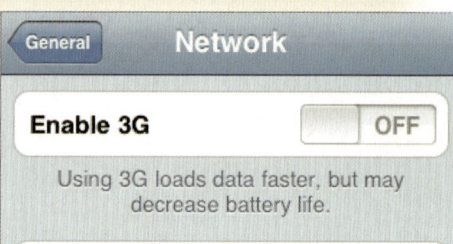

10 iPhone Tips, Tricks, Apps and Hacks

100 essential iPhone tips & tricks

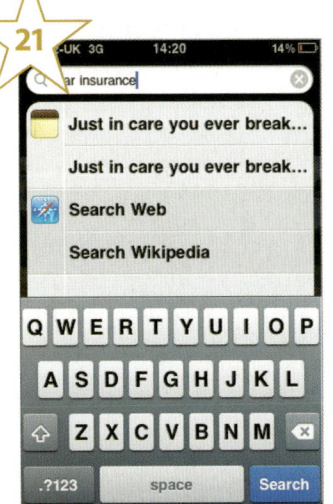

17 Categorise folders
You could spread many apps across 11 scrollable screens, which means lots of finger swiping to find specific ones. Alternatively, hold your finger on an app to make it wiggle, then drag it onto another app to create a folder. Label your folders to store apps by category (like Navigation, Photography and so on).

18 Avoid expensive bills after travelling
When you go abroad your iPhone will search for a new network provider. It may also, however, fetch new data and rack up a big bill. To avoid this, go to Settings>General>Network and turn Data Roaming to Off. This won't affect calls or SMS.

19 Playback control
To start or stop audio from radio apps (like Switcher) you usually need to click their icons and then use their playback controls. Alternatively, double-tap the Home button and swipe to the far left of the app switcher to access playback controls that work for any currently active audio app.

20 Personalise screens
On iPhones running iOS 4 you can personalise your Home screen to display your favourite photo (instead of looking at a boring black background). Choose Settings>Wallpaper. Browse to your Photo Library and pick a shot. You can assign one shot to the Lock screen and one to the Home screen.

21 In the spotlight
If you're after information contained in a specific SMS message or email, it can take ages to scroll through a long list of conversations and contacts. Access the Spotlight Search screen by swiping to the left of the Home screen. Enter a word and Spotlight will search Notes, Mail and SMS messages for your subject.

22 Better keyboard
Compared with an old-school mobile phone's fiddly keypad, the iPhone's touch-sensitive keyboard is easy to use, but you can make it look even wider by rotating the phone from portrait to landscape orientation. To automatically add a full stop and type the next letter as a capital, double tap the spacebar.

23 Even better keyboard
If you own a Bluetooth-enabled Apple Wireless Keyboard, go to Settings>General>Bluetooth. Turn Bluetooth on so that the iPhone is now discoverable, then turn on the keyboard. Once you've paired the iPhone and the keyboard by typing in a PIN code, you can tap out text using the hardware.

24 Create web clips
You can access favourite sites via the Safari app's Bookmark folders, but this can be time consuming. To find a specific site more quickly, browse to it. Hit the arrow-shaped Add Bookmark icon at the bottom of the screen and choose Add to Home Screen. This creates a clickable icon link.

25 Mail me a note
To be automatically emailed a copy of every new note that you make in the Notes app, go to Settings and scroll down to Notes. Change the Default Account from On My iPhone to your MobileMe address. Now notes that you make on your iPhone will appear in your email.

26 Stay up to date
The latest operating systems fine-tune the way the iPhone behaves, which is beneficial for battery life. To make sure that your iPhone's iOS is up to date, connect it to your computer and look in the iTunes Summary pane. Click Check for Updates to discover newer versions of your software.

27 Turn off Auto Brightness
Your iPhone adjusts screen brightness automatically depending on the ambient light intensity where you are using it, but you can manually reduce this and preserve power via Settings>Brightness, turning Auto Brightness to Off.

28 Charge cycle
To help prolong your iPhone battery's life span (the amount of times you can recharge it while maintaining 80 per cent of its original storage capacity), it's well worth charging it to full capacity and then letting it completely drain once a month. This should give your battery a longer life.

iPhone Tips, Tricks, Apps and Hacks **11**

100 essential iPhone tips & tricks

29 Prolong battery life 3
If you're out and about and need to squeeze a bit more life from the battery, you can temporarily disable Location Services. This helps various apps discover where you are so that they can find local amenities like cinemas, coffee shops, the next bus and so on. You can turn this off in Settings>Location Services.

30 Prolong battery life 4
Applying equaliser settings (like Bass Booster) to the iPod app's songs can demand more from your iPhone's battery. To remove any EQ adjustments, go to Settings>iPod>EQ and tap the Off button. If you've added EQ to songs directly in iTunes, you'll need to set the EQ setting on your iPhone to Flat, since the iPhone preserves your iTunes settings.

31 Replace battery
If your iPhone only retains a charge for a couple of hours then this is a sign that the battery is getting old. For £55 plus postage costs, Apple will take your iPhone and replace its battery. Check out the Support section on Apple's website for country-specific information and pricing.

32 Create a more complex passcode
In theory people could guess your iPhone's passcode if it's based on a birthday (or is the classic 0000). For a more complex code go to Settings>General>Passcode Lock. Type in your current passcode and create a new one that mixes numbers and letters.

33 Set up restrictions
To stop your kids using your iPhone's Safari or YouTube apps, go to Settings>General and tap on Restrictions. Tap Enable Restrictions and enter a passcode. You can then turn those apps off so that they are no longer accessible. You can also stop people installing apps on your iPhone.

34 Wiser Wi-Fi
To stop your iPhone automatically connecting to an unknown or suspect Wi-Fi network when you're out and about, go to Settings>WI-FI. Make sure that the Ask to Join Networks option is turned On. You can also save battery life by turning Wi-Fi to Off when you're not using a secure and trusted home or work wireless network.

35 Back up
If you are unfortunate enough to lose your iPhone, you don't have to lose useful information like Calendar entries, photos and notes. Get into the regular habit of plugging it into your computer and syncing it with iTunes to create a backup. This enables you to sync the old iPhone's content with a new one as well.

36 Encrypt your backup
In theory another iPhone user could plug their device into your computer and use iTune's Restore from Backup option to turn his iPhone into a clone of yours. If you're worried, go to the iTunes Summary screen and tick the Encrypt iPhone Backup box. Now you'll need to enter a password before restoring the iPhone from backup.

37 Find a lost iPhone
Make sure that your iPhone is set up to be located by going to Settings>Mail, Contacts, Calendars. Go to Accounts, choose MobileMe and set Find My iPhone to On. Download the Find iPhone app onto an iPad and it can pinpoint your lost iPhone's position on a map.

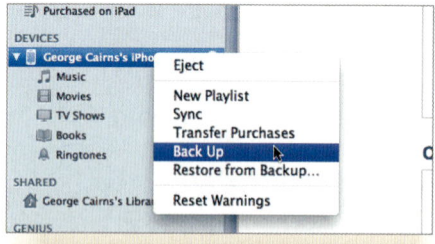

38 Encrypt email
By default your iPhone should encrypt your emails, but it's worth double-checking. Go to Settings>Mail, Contacts, Calendars, then choose an account (like MobileMe). Click on the account email address, hit Mail then choose Advanced. Go to Incoming Settings and turn on Use SSL.

39 AutoFill
It can be a hassle having to type in a password whenever you access a site via Safari. To speed things up go to Settings>Safari. Tap on AutoFill. You can get Safari to access personal details like your name and address by turning Use Contact Info on. Turn on Names and Passwords too.

40 Password protect
If you find it hard to remember multiple passwords then you might find it useful to buy the third-party 1Password app for your iPhone. This enables you to store pertinent passwords for bank, MobileMe or iTunes accounts safely and securely. It can then log you into websites with a tap.

41 Hide text previews
Normally when you receive a text the iPhone displays a preview of its contents, even if the phone is locked. You may not want people to read your personal texts, though, so hide these previews via Settings>Messages, turning Show Preview to Off. Now you'll only be informed that you have a text.

12 iPhone Tips, Tricks, Apps and Hacks

★42 Shake it
Your iPhone's accelerometer enables you to use gestures to control a variety of functions. If you're typing on the move it's easy to make mistakes. It can be a fiddle to try and place the cursor then tap the tiny backspace key to erase an error. By shaking the iPhone you can summon the larger Undo Typing button.

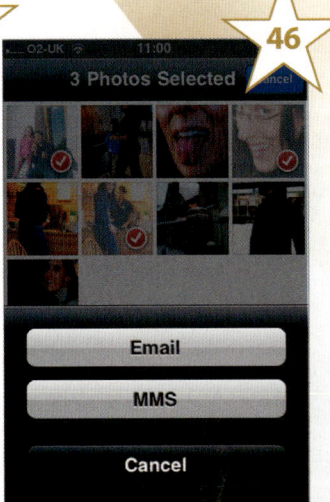

★43 Hard reset
If your iPhone won't unfreeze, try holding down the Sleep button for a few seconds, then drag the Slide to Power Off button. Turning the iPhone back on should fix things. Alternatively, press the Sleep and Home buttons for ten seconds or so until the Apple logo appears.

A hard reset should unfreeze your unresponsive phone

★44 Create a playlist
To create a personalised music playlist, open the iPod app and click the Playlists icon. Tap Add Playlist and give it a name. Click Save then simply scroll through your songs and tap on suitable tunes to add them to your Playlist. You can edit Playlists at a later date to fine-tune them.

★45 Unfreeze an iPhone
Sometimes you may find that your iPhone's screen freezes and won't respond to touch. To get things working again try pressing the Sleep button to make it nod off, then press the same button again to wake the iPhone up and slide to unlock. It should now react to touch as normal.

★46 Batch share shots
As your iPhone is always to hand you'll often end up using it as a photo album and you can share the best images quickly and easily. Simply click the icon at the top right and then tap on the thumbnails of the best photos to tick them. Tap Share and email or MMS them.

★47 Take a closer look
Your iPhone's Camera app has a built-in digital zoom, so you can improve composition and make certain subjects more prominent. Tap the screen and a +/- bar will appear. Slide your finger right along the bar to zoom in, or left to zoom out. This is only available when shooting in Still mode.

★48 Take a screengrab
To get useful information like flight or train details, you often need to perform time-consuming searches via Safari or travel apps. Once you've found the information that you need, press the Sleep/Wake and Home buttons at the same time to save a screengrab to your Photo app's camera roll.

★49 Save web images
If you find a shot via Safari that you want to keep (like a friend's Facebook photo), simply press your finger on the photo for a few seconds and a menu will pop up. By tapping on the Save Image button you can download the shot to your iPhone's Photo Library.

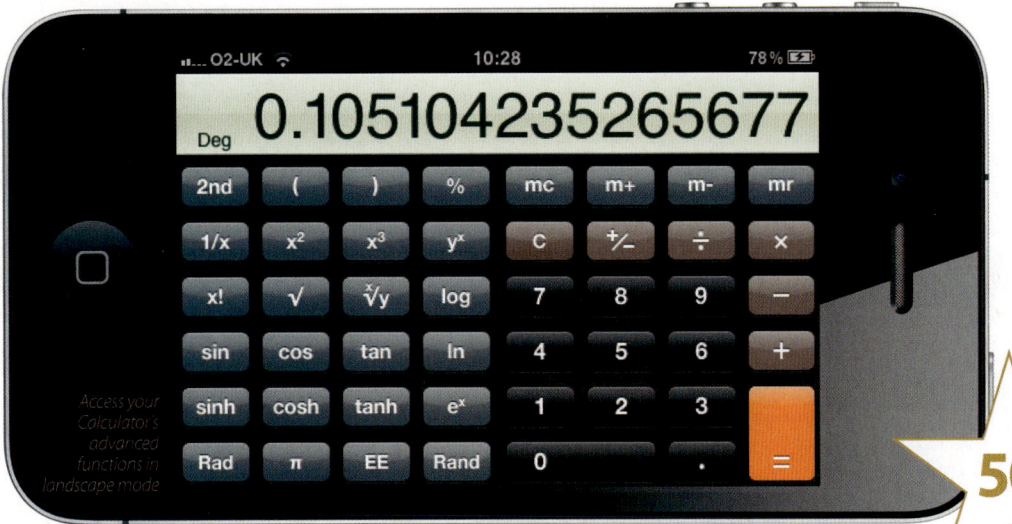

Access your Calculator's advanced functions in landscape mode

★50 Cooler calculator
In portrait mode your Calculator app displays basic functions. While there are plenty of third-party Calculator apps boasting advanced functions, you don't really need them. By turning the iPhone to a landscape orientation you can access its Calculator app's advanced scientific functions, including the option to calculate tangents and cosines!

iPhone Tips, Tricks, Apps and Hacks **13**

100 essential iPhone tips & tricks

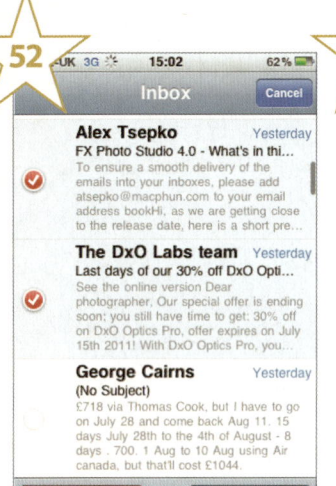

Take a look around using Street View via the Maps app

51 Scroll up quickly
If you're reading a long document it may take multiple finger swipes to scroll back to the top, especially if you've zoomed in for a closer look at the text. To scroll up much more quickly, simply tap the status bar at the top of the screen. This trick works in a variety of apps and saves you precious time.

52 Batch edit emails

To make your mail box less cluttered, tap the Edit button at the top right. Scroll through the mails and highlight each unwanted one. A red tick will appear. You can now batch delete; tap Move to send them to the Trash or Junk mails folders.

53 Faster printing

Instead of syncing images to your laptop and then printing them, print directly from the iPhone. Browse to the picture, tap the icon at the bottom left of the screen and choose Print. You can then select an AirPrint printer and choose the number of copies.

54 Subscribe to calendars

Using the Mac that you sync your iPhone to, browse to apple.com/downloads/macosx/calendars. Download the calendars that you fancy to your Mac's iCal app. Sync your iPhone with your Mac (tick Sync iCal calendars in iTunes).

55 See your contact's location

Tap on a person's full address or postcode in the Contacts app. Maps will automatically open and your contact's name and location will be pinned on a map. You can then plan a route to visit them by tapping on the Directions button.

56 Access Google Street View in Maps

If you want to get a better look at a location pinned on your Maps app, tap on the person-shaped icon to the left of the pin's label. This will take you to a Google Street View map. Swipe the screen or tap the arrows to look around.

57 Lock to portrait

If you're reading a book on the move the iPhone's accelerometer may cause the screen to rotate. To lock the screen to Portrait orientation and stop it rotating, double-tap on the Home button to open the app switcher. Tap the icon at the left so that a lock symbol appears.

58 Call forwarding
If you're going on holiday to an area that has very poor phone reception, you may miss something important, so it's worth forwarding calls to a landline at your holiday destination. Go to Settings>Phone>Call Forwarding. Turn Call Forwarding on and type in the landline number you wish to use.

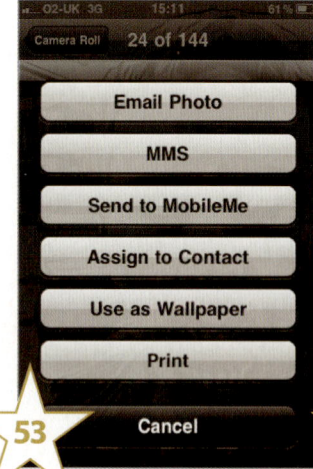

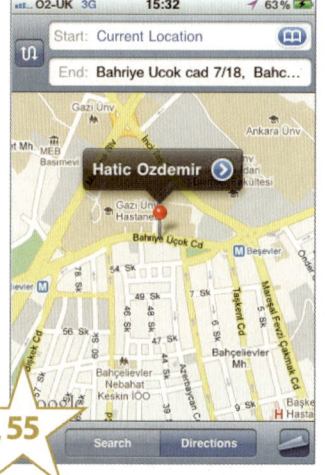

59 Create a Genius playlist
One way to find similar songs in your iPhone's music library is to tap on the Genius icon in the Now Playing screen's top control bar. This will create a Genius playlist containing songs by similar artists. You can save that playlist, or Refresh it for an alternative mix of songs.

14 iPhone Tips, Tricks, Apps and Hacks

100 essential iPhone tips & tricks

★ 60 Push notifications
Many apps use the Push notification service to send information to the iPhone's screen. This can be useful or annoying, depending on the app. For example, if you don't instantly need to know when someone has posted a comment on Facebook, go to Settings>Notifications. Scroll down to Facebook and set Alerts to Off.

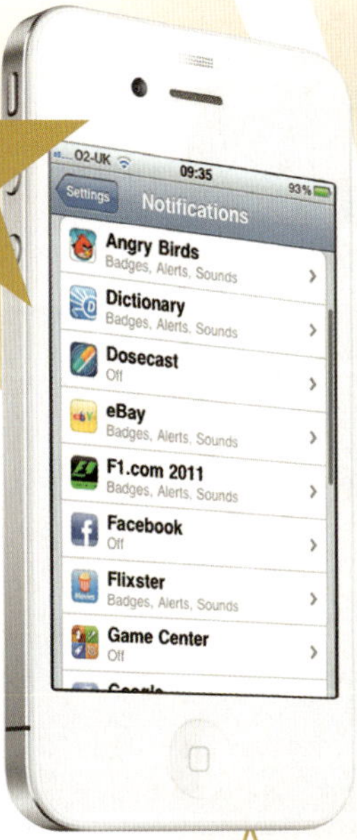

Stop your iPhone vibrating when in silent mode

★ 61 Sync mail
Sync a Google account with your iPhone via Settings>Mail, Contacts, Calendars and tapping on Microsoft Exchange. Enter your account details and choose whether to sync Google Mail, Contacts and Calendars with your iPhone. When asked for server info, pop in **m.google.com**.

★ 62 Complete silence
When in a meeting you can flip the switch on the side of the iPhone to turn off your ringtone. However, the iPhone will still vibrate when you receive a message, and this buzzing can be distracting. Go to Settings>Sounds and in the Silent section, turn Vibrate to Off.

★ 63 Get a new ringtone
Your iPhone comes with 25 different sounds and jingles that you can assign as your ringtone. If you get bored of these, though, you can buy new ones with ease. Go to Settings>Sounds and tap on Ringtone. Scroll to the top of the list and tap the Buy More Ringtones button.

★ 64 Withhold your number
If you want to call someone without them being able to see your iPhone's number, go to Settings>Phone. Tap on the Show My Caller ID option and set Show My Caller ID to Off. You can now call other numbers anonymously.

★ 65 Reorganise your browse buttons
Your iPod app gives you a range of ways to explore your music library. The most useful browse icons are stored in a dock, while others can be accessed by tapping More. To change which icons rest in the dock go to More>Edit. Drag the relevant icons to the dock.

★ 66 Turn off predictive text
The iPhone's attempt to predict what you're typing can be annoying, as you sometimes have to tap on the predicted word to cancel it. To disable this feature, go to Settings>General>Keyboard. Set Auto-Correction to Off. This will disable Check Spelling.

★ 67 Stop shuffling
By default, you can shuffle your iPod app's songs by shaking the iPhone. This is a good way of exploring your music library, but not so useful if you're out for a jog and don't want to shuffle the songs accidentally. To disable this feature, go to Settings>iPod and turn off Shake to Shuffle.

★ 68 Activate Ping
Ping is Apple's social network for music lovers. By turning Ping on in the iTunes app you can like songs via your iPhone or follow other Ping members and discover new sounds. Once Ping is activated you'll see new Ping icons in the iPod app's upper control pane.

★ 69 Add song lyrics to your iPod app
Copy a favourite song's lyrics from the web. In iTunes go to File>Get Info. Click on the Lyrics button and paste in the copied words. Copy the song to your iPhone. Play in the iPod app and tap the album artwork in the Now Playing screen for the lyrics.

★ 70 Quick rewind
When you're listening to a podcast or an audio book you may get distracted and miss an interesting or important bit of information. Tap on the podcast or audio book's artwork to reveal the additional sound controls. Tap on the handy 30-second rewind icon for an instant replay.

★ 71 Control the iPod app via speech
When you're listening to music on the go you might find it more convenient to control your iPod app verbally. Hold down the Home button until the Voice Control screen appears. Say "Play songs by" and choose a favourite artist.

★ 72 Control iPod sound
If you're concerned about damaging your ears with excessive sound levels, you can limit them. Pop into Settings and tap on iPod. Tick Sound Check to automatically limit the maximum level. You can set a maximum level manually using the Volume Limit option.

iPhone Tips, Tricks, Apps and Hacks **15**

 100 essential iPhone tips & tricks

73 View photos by location
When you snap a photo on your iPhone it geotags the shot. To see all the images captured in a particular place go to Photos and tap on Places. Red pins will then appear in the map. Tap on a pin to see how many photos are associated with it and tap the pin's label to view the pictures and video clips that have ben geotagged.

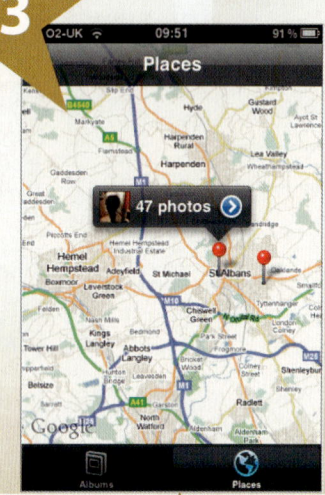

74 Send a message to a group
You can send a single text message to more than one person. In the Messages app, tap the New Message icon at the top right. Tap the plus icon, browse through your contacts and tap to add one. Hit the plus button again to add other contacts then compose the message and send it.

75 Send a voice memo
It can be time consuming to tap out a text message. To send a voice memo to a friend via SMS, go to the Voice Memos app and record your message. Click on the Share Voice Memo icon and tap MMS. Choose a contact and simply click send, so your contact can hear your dulcet tones.

76 Trim a voice memo
It can take a few attempts before you capture a fluent voice memo, so you may want to trim a recorded memo instead of totally redoing it. Tap on the blue arrow to the right of a saved memo and tap Trim Memo. Drag the start and end points to shorten it and tick Trim Voice Memo.

77 Label voice memos
You can use the Voice memos app to record ideas for work, or capture an interview to transcribe later. Memos are labelled according to time and date, which makes it hard to identify them. Click on a memo then click in the grey arrow on its info screen. Tick a label from the list.

78 View a slideshow
Instead of swiping through the shots in an album, share it as a slideshow. Tap to view the first shot then hit the Play icon at the bottom to open Slideshow Options. Tap on Transitions and choose a wipe or dissolve. Turn Play Music on and browse to choose a track from your iPod app's music library. Click Start Slideshow and enjoy.

79 Publish to YouTube
Once you've captured a clip via your iPhone you can broadcast it on YouTube without having to sync to your computer. View your movie and tap the Sharing icon at the bottom left. Hit the Send to YouTube button, log in and upload.

80 Trim a clip
Before uploading a video clip to YouTube or sending it as an MMS file, it might be worth giving it a quick trim to reduce the time it takes to upload. While viewing the movie, tap the screen to display the editing controls. Drag the left and right handles inwards to shorten the clip and then simply click Trim.

81 Email a link to your published movie
Once you've used the iPhone to share a video online via YouTube, rustle up some viewers. Log into YouTube and browse to your video. Tap Mail to the right of the playback controls and enter an email address. The link will automatically embed into the mail.

82 Personalise contacts
Get your friend's face to appear when they call you. Go to the Photos app and browse to an appropriate picture of your pal. Tap on the Share icon at the bottom left of the screen and choose Assign to Contact. Browse to their contact details, move and scale the shot and click Set Photo.

83 Discover a stock's performance history
When using the Stocks app, rotate the iPhone to Landscape for a larger graph of a particular company's performance. To see how they performed on a particular day, drag a finger. Drag two fingers for performance over a longer period.

84 Keep tabs on time
If you need to call someone abroad, use the Clock app to see if they'll be at work (or asleep). Tap on the World Clock icon at the bottom left then the plus sign to add a new clock. Search for the nearest city and tap to select it. Now you'll see the appropriate time for that area.

85 Discover your precise co-ordinates
The Compass app can show you the direction that you're travelling in. If you need to give someone your geographical co-ordinates (after breaking down in your car, for example), then you'll find that information at the bottom of the app's screen.

16 iPhone Tips, Tricks, Apps and Hacks

100 essential iPhone tips & tricks

86 Stream a podcast
You may be accessing your favourite podcasts by downloading them to your Mac and PC and then syncing, but you can save time with iTunes by browsing to the Podcasts page. Tap on a podcast's title and it will immediately start streaming to your phone.

87 Transfer purchases

If you buy a song or app via your iPhone, keep it safe by transferring it to your Mac or PC. Connect the iPhone to your home computer and wait for it to be recognised by iTunes. Right-click on your iPhone's icon in the Devices pane and choose Transfer Purchases.

88 Useful information

It can be useful to know how much space you have left on your iPhone without having to sync it to a home computer's copy of iTunes. Go to Settings>General and tap on About. You can see how many songs, videos and apps you've got stored, as well as any remaining space.

89 Faster searches

Spotlight searches every nook and cranny on your iPhone, but to speed things up you can tell it not to bother looking in certain places. Go to Settings>General>Spotlight Search and untick specific categories. You can also drag to rearrange the order of the search result categories.

90 Add a signature

When you send an Email from your iPhone, you'll probably end it with the same signature ("Cheers, John Smith", for example). Get the iPhone to type your signature automatically by going to Settings>Mail, Contacts, Calendars. Tap on Signature and then type in the text field.

91 Add PDFs to iBooks

If someone mails you a PDF (like your flight details) it can be tricky to read in Mail. Tap on the Share icon at the top left and choose Open in iBooks. You can then access individual pages more easily, turn up the brightness and store the PDF on a bookshelf for easier access.

92 Erase all data

If you want to sell your old iPhone it's wise to make sure that all your personal data is securely erased – though don't do this until you've backed up the phone via iTunes. Go to Settings>General and tap Reset. Tap on Erase all Content and Settings.

93 Control Keynote presentations

Keynote lets you show images and graphs on your Mac. The Keynote Remote app lets you advance the slides by swiping your finger on the iPhone's screen. You can also access presenter notes to help you keep tabs on your presentation's content.

94 Share files

By downloading the free Dropbox app onto your iPhone and setting up a Dropbox account, you can access files from the online storage cloud via your iPhone. This enables you to view images, movies and documents without needing to store them on the iPhone.

95 Multitask GPS

When navigating using GPS-based apps, you can do other things like listen to music. The GPS apps will still run in the background and keep updating your position. If the GPS app needs to give directions, the music will automatically dip so that you can hear the app's instructions.

96 No place like home

Your iPhone can have up to 11 Home screens full of folders. When using an app, return to the last Home screen with the Home button. Press it again and you'll quickly scroll sideways to the first (main) Home screen. Press twice rapidly for the app switcher.

97 White on black

By default the iPhone displays black text on a white background. If you do a lot of reading you may find it easier to read white text against black. To get this look, go to Settings>General>Accessibility. Turn White on Black to On and your colours will invert.

98 Triple-click

You can click the Home button once to return to the main Home screen, or double-click to activate the app switcher. You can assign a function to three Home button presses via Settings>General>Accessibility. Turn on Triple-click Home and use it to Toggle accessibility functions.

99 Special characters

Some foreign words require letters that vary slightly, like Ç instead of C. To find and type foreign variants of a particular letter using the iPhone's keyboard, simply press and hold your finger over the letter. New keys will appear showing the variations of that character.

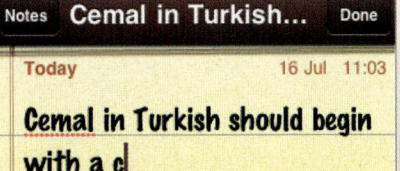

100 Use the Guide

If a particular iPhone feature flummoxes you, then the official iPhone User Guide is only a few taps away. Go to the Safari app and click on the Bookmarks icon at the bottom of the screen. Scroll down and tap on the iPhone User Guide option. Browse for information by clicking on the app's label.

iPhone Tips, Tricks, Apps and Hacks 17

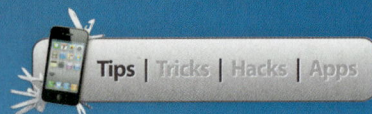

Tips
Maximise the full potential of your iPhone with these step-by-step guides

TOP TIPS
- ✔ Sync iCal
- ✔ Improve fitness
- ✔ Edit in iMovie
- ✔ Tag pictures
- ✔ Plan a trip

20 Getting the most out of Safari's advanced features
22 Browse the internet privately on your iPhone
24 Create a Word document using Quickoffice
26 Add your own images to documents in Pages
28 Publish your Pages documents to iWork.com
30 Dictate notes, texts and emails
32 Navigate the world with Google Earth
34 Plan a trip using your iPhone
36 Take incredible panoramic photos
38 Learn to tag a photo location on your iPhone
40 Capture passport-style photos on your mobile
42 Edit images with Photoshop Express
44 Upload and share your favourite photos
46 Getting started with iMovie for iPhone
48 Edit your iMovie project on your iPhone
50 Add a soundtrack to your iMovie project
52 Subscribe to videos you want to watch on YouTube
54 Broadcast footage of yourself live to the world
56 Play and record guitar tracks through your iPhone
58 Add and delete locations from Weather
60 Sync your iCal with your iPhone
62 Improve your fitness using your iPhone

44 Share your photos with your friends

54 Broadcast yourself live to the world

18 iPhone Tips, Tricks, Apps and Hacks

Tips | Tricks | Hacks | Apps

42 Edit your images with Photoshop

56 Record your guitar tracks on your iPhone

iPhone Tips, Tricks, Apps and Hacks **19**

Tips | Tricks | Hacks | Apps

Getting the most out of Safari's advanced features

Safari is one of the most advanced mobile browsers available. Find out how its features can enhance your mobile browsing experience

Task: Mastering Safari
Difficulty: Beginner
Time needed: 15 minutes

Safari is a well-established internet browser and its intuitive interface means that online browsing is an effortless and thoroughly enjoyable experience, especially when connected to a wireless internet connection.

Pages are rendered quickly and zooming in or out is an absolute breeze. As well as being incredibly easy to use, Safari also has a number of advanced features for more experienced users, most of which are hidden from view.

For example, you can choose exactly which search engine appears in the search bar – with the default Google being interchangeable with Bing and Yahoo! – and whether you want to block pop-ups from constantly firing ads at you. Not only can you save bookmarks, but you can edit and manage them quickly and easily and even opt to create Home screen icons for frequently visited websites. Last, but by no means least, Safari's security settings are second to none and once configured, you can browse the internet safe in the knowledge that the threat from malicious software (malware) and phishing attacks has been minimised.

Step-by-step | Safari Explore Safari's advanced features

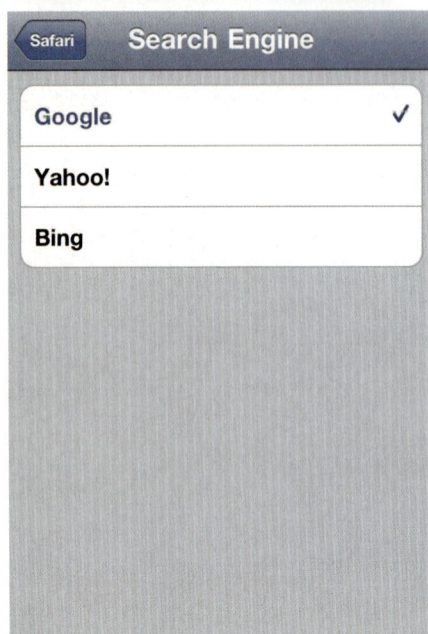

1: Search engine
Safari's advanced features are configured using the Settings icon. Tap Settings>Safari and configure which search engine is used by Safari's search bar.

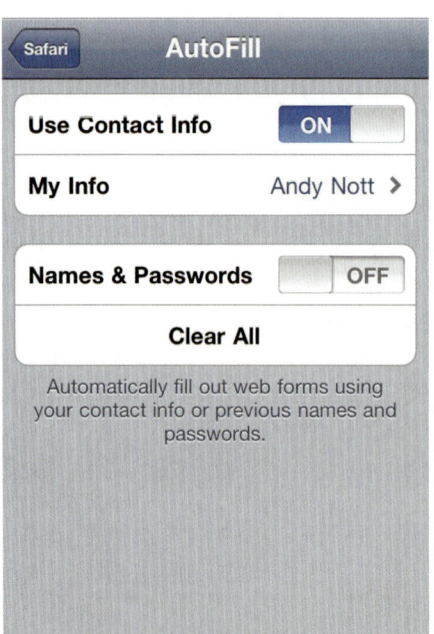

2: AutoFill
Enable AutoFill to automatically complete frequently used data on web forms. Turn off the Names & Passwords option in case of a lost or stolen phone.

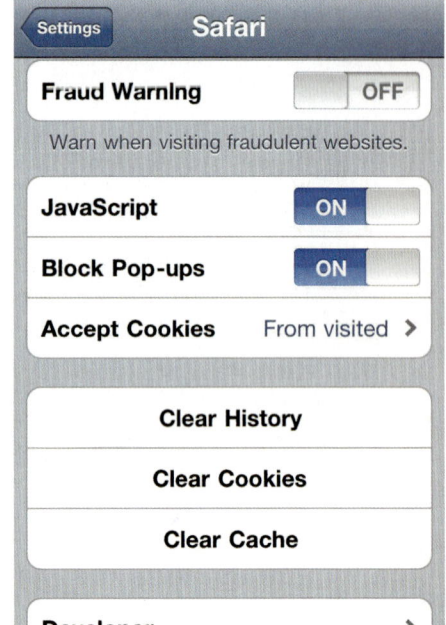

3: Fraud Warning
The security conscious will enable Fraud Warning as this feature notifies you of a site that is logged on Google's database of potentially fraudulent sites.

20 iPhone Tips, Tricks, Apps and Hacks

Tips | Tricks | Hacks | Apps

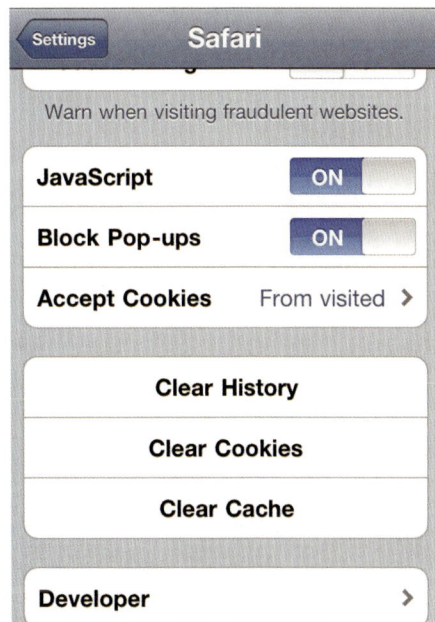

4: Block Pop-ups
Enable Block Pop-ups and any pop-up windows will be blocked. It not only enhances online browsing but also shields you from multiple ads appearing.

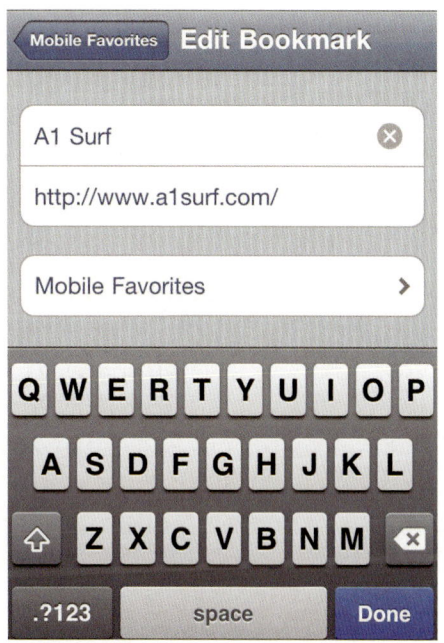

5: Save bookmarks
Bookmark favourite sites with a single tap and you can quickly return to them. Open Bookmarks, tap Edit and you can edit the name and URL of a site.

6: Home screen icon
Create Home screen icons for frequently visited sites. Tap the + icon in the toolbar and then Add to Home screen. Give it a name and then tap Add.

7: Enhanced viewing
For a wider view of websites, rotate your iPhone and use landscape mode. The web page rotates and the column you are reading fills the screen.

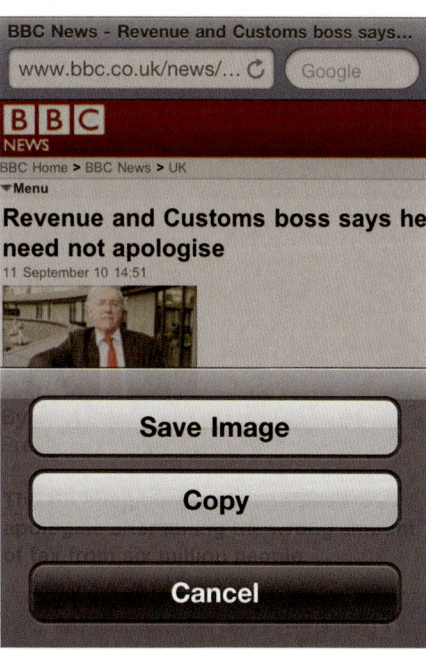

8: Images
Safari also lets you copy and save images. Tap and hold on an image and select Save Image to save it to your Camera Roll or Copy if you want to paste it.

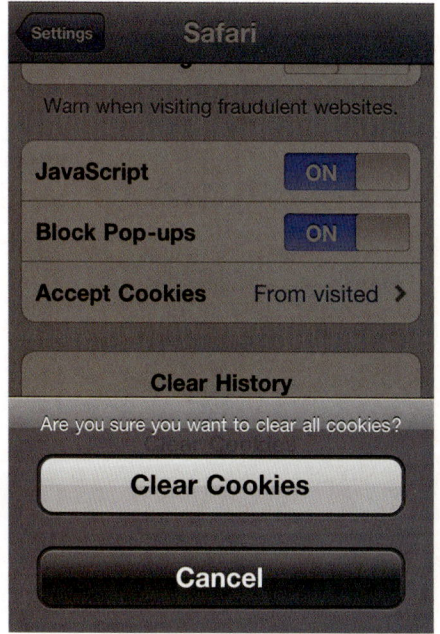

9: Spring cleaning
Return to the Safari settings and clear your browsing history, cookies and cache. As well as ensuring privacy, it will improve system performance.

iPhone Tips, Tricks, Apps and Hacks **21**

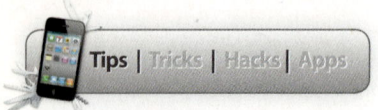

Tips | Tricks | Hacks | Apps

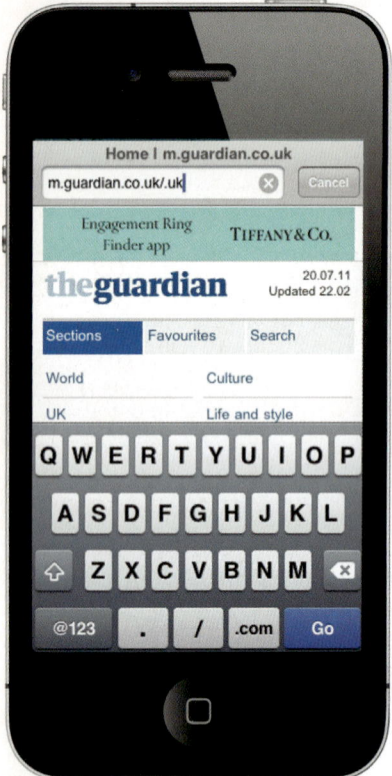

Browse the internet privately on your iPhone

The iPhone's web browser knows where you've been. But what if you don't want people to know which sites you've visited?

Task: Hide your tracks while browsing the web
Difficulty: Beginner
Time needed: 5 minutes

Normally, when you use a web browser on your iPhone or desktop computer, your movements are being tracked. By default every site you visit is recorded in the browser's history, and 'cookies' – little snippets of information – can remember when and where you visited, and what you did when you arrived.

There's a valid reason for tracking your movements – it makes revisiting sites at a later date easier – although you might not want your browsing habits exposed to the world. For example, should you lose your iPhone you wouldn't want your bank information accessed by others.

Many desktop web browsers have a 'privacy' mode where sites you visit aren't stored in browser history and cookies are ignored. However, Safari for iOS 4 lacks that feature and every site you visit is recorded. You can manually clear your browser history, but that requires a consistently diligent approach.

There is an alternative: Full Screen Private Browsing, a free download from the App Store, is a simple, functional web browser. It lacks a 'history' function and doesn't record cookies, so there's no way anyone can retrace your steps.

Step-by-step | Full Screen Private Browsing | Browse the web in private

1: Opening screen
Launch the application to go to a customised Google home page. If you're searching for something, just enter it in the search field.

2: Visiting websites
Alternatively enter the name of the website you want to visit in the URL field. This isn't remembered by the browser – there isn't even a 'Back' button.

3: Reloading pages
The only evidence that a site is loading is the spinning icon at the top of the screen. You can reload the page by tapping the Reload button.

Tips | Tricks | Hacks | Apps

Browsing privately
The main advantages of browsing sites in private

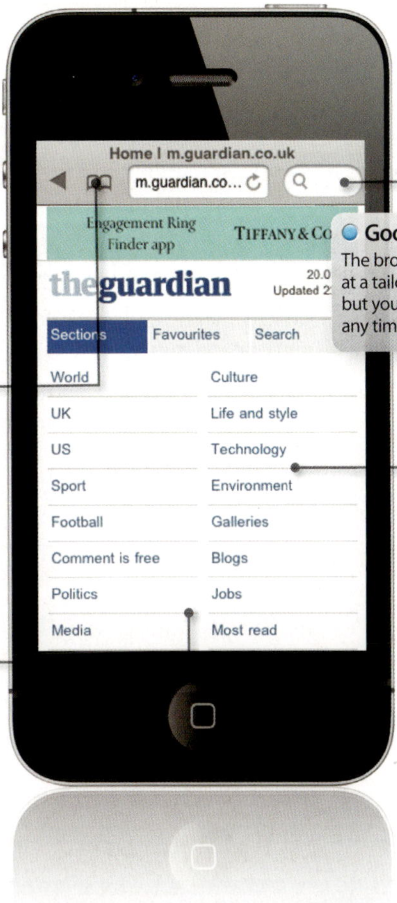

- **Storing bookmarks**
Full Screen Private Browsing doesn't share your existing Safari bookmarks, so you'll need to add your own. Unlike your history, these are stored between browsing sessions

- **A bigger screen**
Full Screen Private Browsing doesn't just offer privacy. The lack of a bottom navigation menu means that the program's viewing area is slightly bigger than Safari's

- **Google searching**
The browser window always opens at a tailored Google search page, but you can also search the web at any time through this search field

- **Safari-like performance**
The program uses the same underlying 'webkit' web engine as Safari, so sites should appear largely the same as they do under Apple's browser

- **Knowledge base**

Secret Safari browsing
You can wipe your tracks in mobile Safari using a special trick. When you've finished browsing, hold down the Sleep/Wake button until you see the Power Off slider. Now hold down the Home button until the Home screen appears.

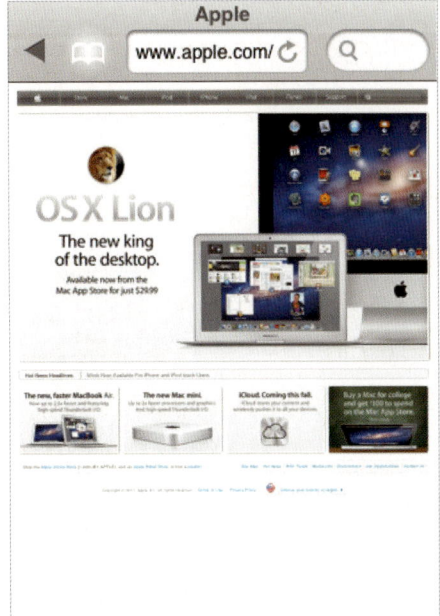
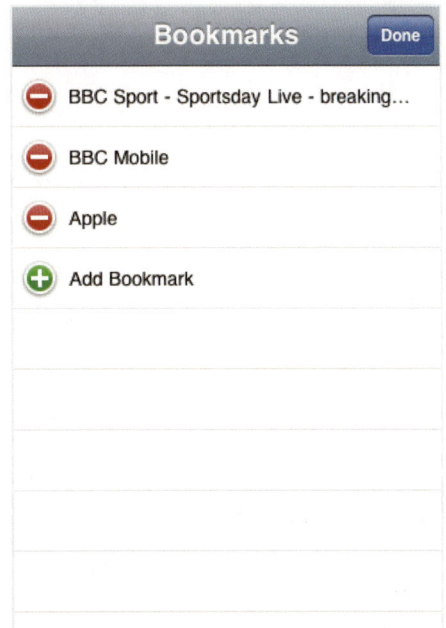

4: Adding bookmarks
You can bookmark favourite sites though, by tapping the Bookmark icon. On the pop-up list, click the 'Add Bookmark' button and then click 'Done'.

5: Managing bookmarks
The site is then added to your bookmark list. Remember that this list is permanently stored, so don't add sites that you want to keep private.

6: Start afresh
When you re-launch the app, you'll see that there's no record of your previous visit. Notice that the start screen is completely clear.

iPhone Tips, Tricks, Apps and Hacks **23**

Tips | Tricks | Hacks | Apps

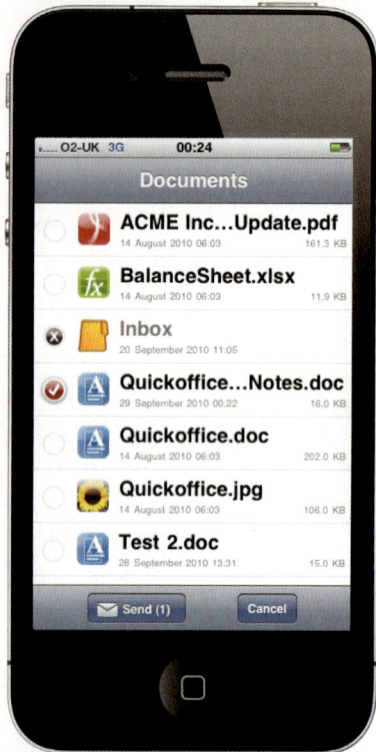

Create a Word document using Quickoffice

The iPhone's compatibility with Microsoft's Office suite has not been its strongest suit. Luckily, Quickoffice is here to help…

Task: Create a Word doc
Difficulty: Beginner
Time needed: 10 minutes

In the world of business, Microsoft Office still reigns supreme as the most widespread word processing and spreadsheet solution. Practically everybody who uses a computer now encounters either Word documents or Excel files. Being able to access, create, edit and export Office documents on your phone is a huge plus, meaning that you can work with files on the go. It's not surprising, therefore, that a strong market has sprung up for Office-compatible mobile apps that can read and edit these files.

Quickoffice for iPhone is one such solution. Available for £6.99 on the App Store, it extends the capabilities of your iPhone to the point where you can create, view, edit and share documents without setting foot in the office. In fact, Quickoffice has such a wide range of functions that we can only scratch the surface in the space allotted here. With this in mind, we're simply going to demonstrate how to pull off one of the more commonly required tasks when using Word, which is to create and save a new document from scratch, that can then be sent out as an email attachment, or transferred over a Wi-Fi network.

Step-by-step | Quickoffice Create a Microsoft Word document

1: Launch Quickoffice
Tap the app's icon on your home screen to launch it. At the bottom of the main screen, you'll find five buttons. Tap the leftmost one to create a new file.

2: Select document type
Tap the button for the type of file you want to create. You can choose between an Excel spreadsheet, a Word document or a plain text file.

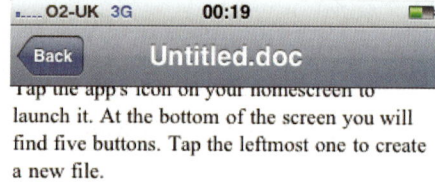

Tap the app's icon on your homescreen to launch it. At the bottom of the screen you will find five buttons. Tap the leftmost one to create a new file.

2.
Select document type
Choose between an Excel spreadsheet, a Word document or a plain text file by tapping the button for the type of file you want to create.

3.
Get typing
Tap the keyboard button in the centre of the toolbar to call up the QWERTY keyboard and type away. When you're finished, tap the 'Done' button.

3: Get typing
Tap the keyboard button third from left in the toolbar to call up the QWERTY keyboard and type away. When you're finished, tap the Done button.

Tips | Tricks | Hacks | Apps

Getting to grips with Quickoffice

We take you even more in-depth on the app's use of text documents

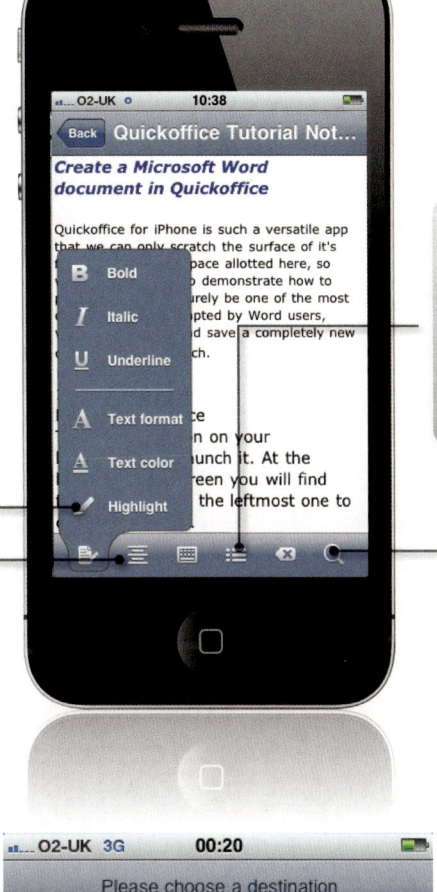

● **Formatting options**
Tap this button to bring up a palette of text formatting options, such as bold, italic or underline, text colour, size and font, and even a text highlighter function

● **Bullet inboard**
This button inserts bullet points to facilitate the creation of bulleted lists. To the right of it is the Backspace button, which works just like the one found on your computer keyboard

● **Knowledge base**
Exclusive selection
Like most other word-processing applications, the text formatting options found in the formatting palette only work on highlighted areas. The iPhone's standard 'double-tap and drag to select' method is used for this, but tapping a block of text quickly three times will highlight an entire paragraph, which can be quite a timesaver.

● **Line it up**
Horizontal text alignment is cleverly handled by dragging a small block of sample text across the screen to reflect where you want your own text to be positioned

● **Zooming in**
Tap the magnifying glass icon to get a word and character count and a search function to track down where key words occur within it

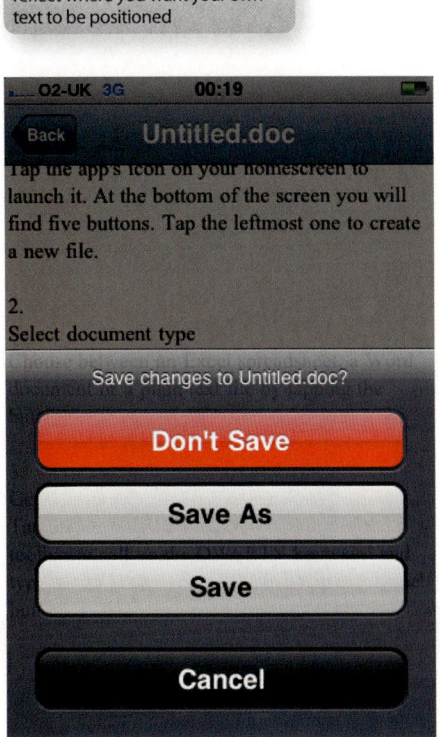

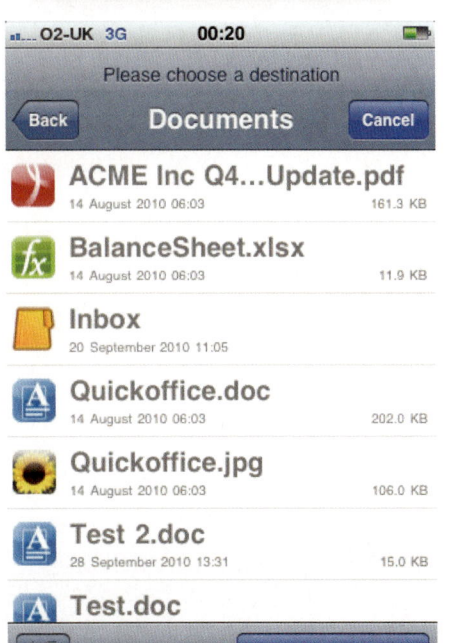

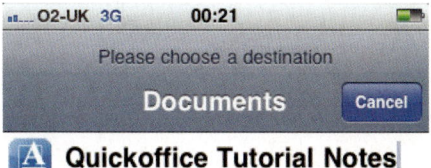

4: Save me, save me
To save your document, first tap the Back button to call up the Save Options screen. Now tap Save As to continue.

5: Select destination
Choose a folder in which to save your file. Tap the folder name, followed by the Choose button. To create a new folder, tap the New Folder button.

6: Name and save
Type a new name for your file and hit Done to save your creation. It will now appear in the list of existing documents in the On iPhone folder.

iPhone Tips, Tricks, Apps and Hacks **25**

Tips | Tricks | Hacks | Apps

Add your own images to documents in Pages

Want to produce a professional-looking document complete with your favourite pictures? It's easy with Pages

Task: Adding images to a Pages document
Difficulty: Intermediate
Time needed: 10 minutes

There are plenty of basic text editors available on the iPhone, but when it comes to producing documents that look as though they have been professionally laid out, there's only one choice: Pages.

Apple has taken the desktop power of Pages from the Mac and squeezed it into the iPhone. It lets you create documents with the ability to add images directly from your Camera Roll, as well as pictures you've synced from iPhoto, making it a fantastic tool for producing good results on the move.

So you could take a picture on the iPhone, edit it with your favourite image editing app and import it into Pages. The superb manipulation features that you can apply to images such as resizing, rotating and moving with your fingers seems much more natural than doing it with a mouse, and can often offer accurate results (although alignment guides are there to help you as you go).

There is also a wide selection of extra effects that you can apply to an image to give it that professional look, including masks to hide part of an image as well as drop shadows and reflections.

Step-by-step | Pages Add images to documents

1: Grabbing your photos
Launch Pages and open the document that you want to add the image to. Tap the Media button at the top and in the next window tap the Media tab.

2: Adding the image
Navigate to the photo you want from the Camera Roll or Photo Library. When you tap the image it will be automatically added to the document.

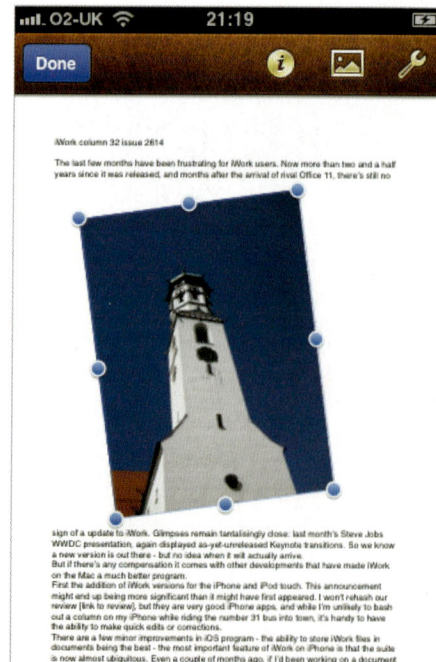

3: Adjusting and moving
Adjust the size by pinching and dragging the image, move it by tapping and dragging the image, or rotate by pinching and rotating.

26 iPhone Tips, Tricks, Apps and Hacks

Tips | Tricks | Hacks | Apps

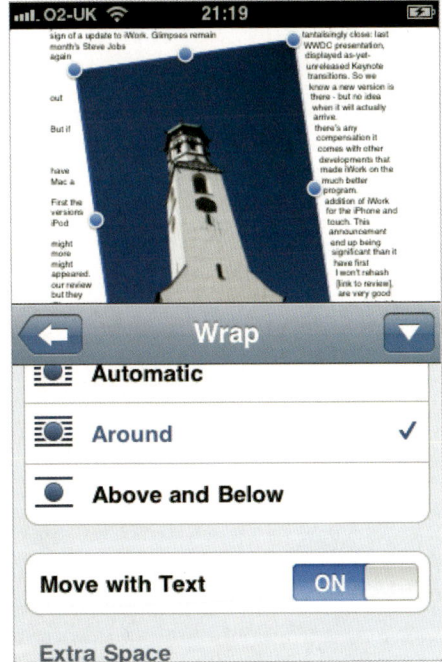

4: Wrapping your text
Click the 'i' button. Under the Arrange tab, tap Wrap and choose one of the Wrap options to adjust how the text will flow around the image.

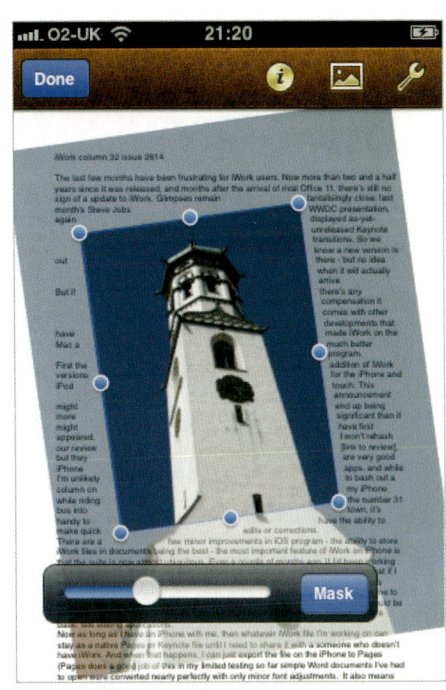

5: Masking things
If you wish to add a mask, select the option and move your finger along the slider to adjust. When you're happy with the results, tap the Mask button.

6: Styling your image
Apply a pre-set style by tapping the Style tab and then tapping one of the six pre-built styles. You can configure an image style with more options.

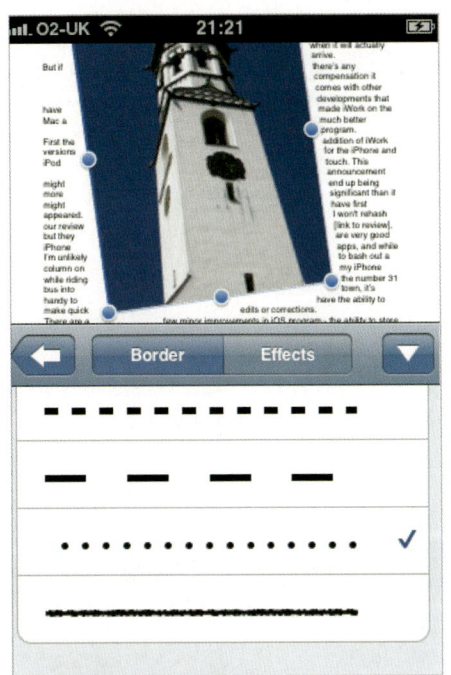

7: Adding a border
To add a border to the image, tap the Borders tab in Style Options to set the colour, width and effect of the border you'd like.

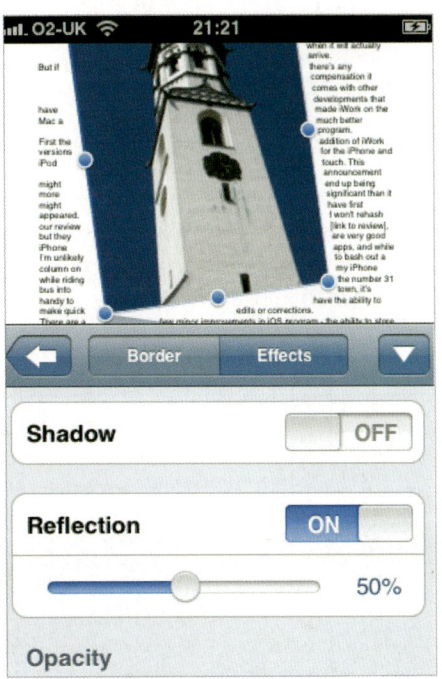

8: Shadow effects
Tap the Effects tab to add up to three more effects to your image: one of four shadow settings, image reflection and setting the opacity of the image.

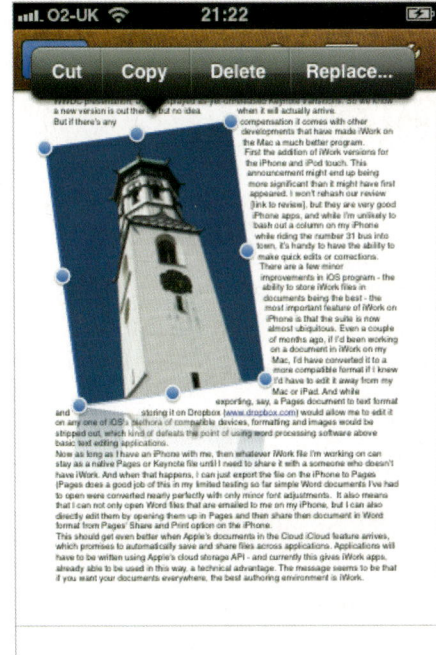

9: Completing the edits
With effects added, tap the downwards-facing icon to return to page view. You can edit the effects by tapping on the image and clicking the 'i' button.

iPhone Tips, Tricks, Apps and Hacks **27**

Tips | Tricks | Hacks | Apps

Publish your Pages documents to iWork.com

Pages makes it easy to share documents online – and a chosen few can collaborate on documents you share via iWork.com

Task: Share a document from Pages to iWork.com
Difficulty: Beginner
Time needed: 5 minutes

All those documents you created in Pages aren't stuck on your iPhone forever. There are several ways to share them with friends or colleagues. You can email them, sync them to a server or copy them to your desktop computer with iTunes. And did you know that you can also store documents on Apple's iWork.com service and invite others to view them?

iWork.com is a little-used collaboration service for iWork applications, which is currently free and in beta. However, it's a surprisingly powerful service. On the iWork.com website, document collaborators can view pixel-perfect previews of your document, and make notes and comments, even simultaneously.

One of the best reasons for sharing your work on iWork.com is that the results are platform agnostic. That means that you can collaborate just as easily with PC users as your Mac friends. In fact, anyone with a web browser can view your files, and those you're sharing the document with can download the file in Microsoft Office and PDF formats, as well as a native Pages file – all with your permission, of course. iWork.com isn't perfect, but it's a great way of sharing your work.

Step-by-step | Pages Sharing a document with Pages

1: Complete the document
When you've finished editing the file you want to share, tap the Settings icon at the top of the document – it looks like a spanner.

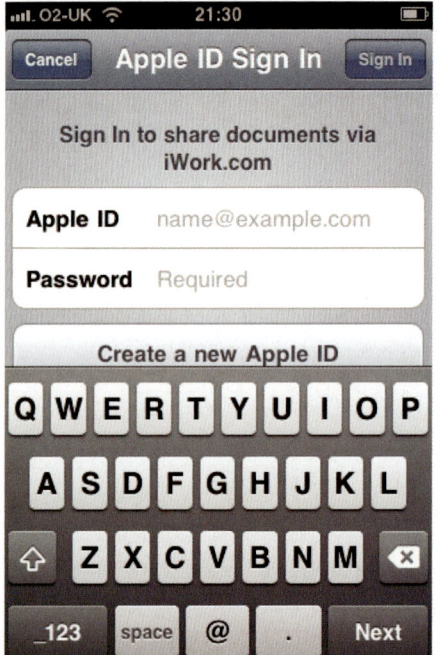

2: Hit the share menu
Tap Share and Print and then select Share via iWork.com. You'll have to sign in using your Apple ID and password before you can share.

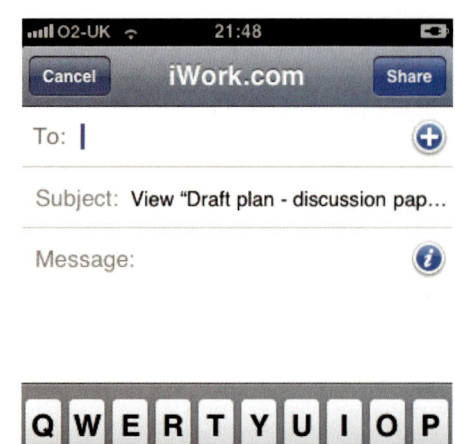

3: Mail's options
Mail will open, and an email has been created with the subject line filled in. Enter the email address of anyone you wish to share the document with.

28 iPhone Tips, Tricks, Apps and Hacks

Tips | Tricks | Hacks | Apps

Setting up a shared file
The many ways you can share a Pages file

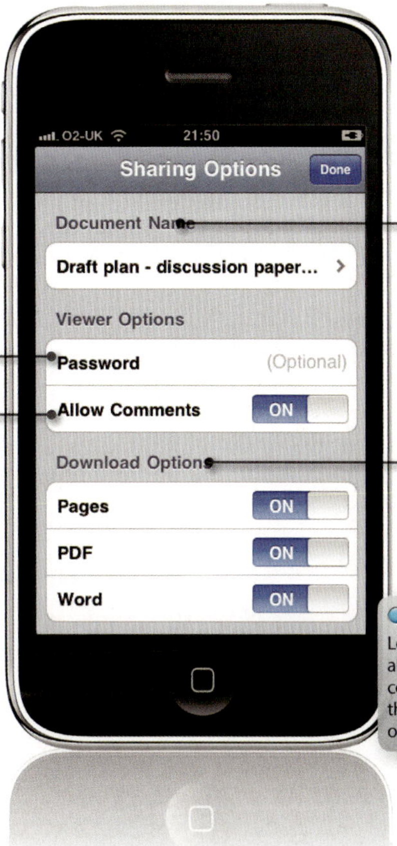

Share any document
Want to share another document? Tap the document name and you can choose from any of the other documents you've uploaded in the past

Knowledge base

Getting started on iWork.com
While you need an Apple ID and password to set up an account at iWork.com, those you're collaborating with don't. They just click the link emailed to them and it should open in a browser, irrespective of the platform they're using.

Password protection
Concerned about security? You can password-protect the shared document to be absolutely sure only your collaborators see it

Commenting
You can comment on shared documents by default, but you can turn this option off if you'd rather keep things clutter-free

PDF, Pages or Word?
Leaving this option unchecked allows the people you're collaborating with to download the file from iWork.com in any one of three formats

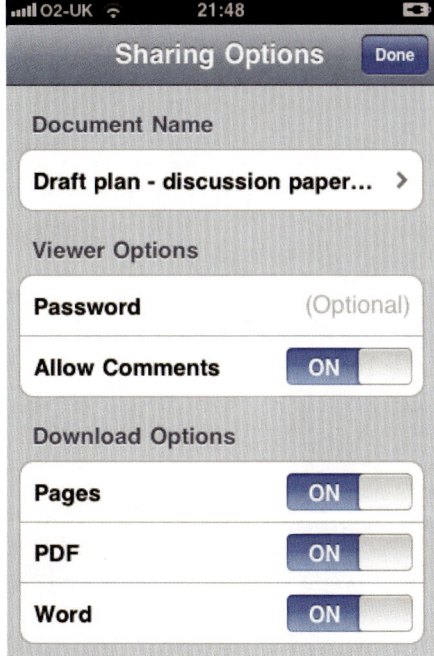

4: Adjusting options
Tap the 'i' icon to set various options, including whether to allow comments on the document and whether viewers can download it. Click Done.

5: Watch progress
Click the Share button and a progress bar shows the upload process. Click the Done button when finished – all users will receive a notification email.

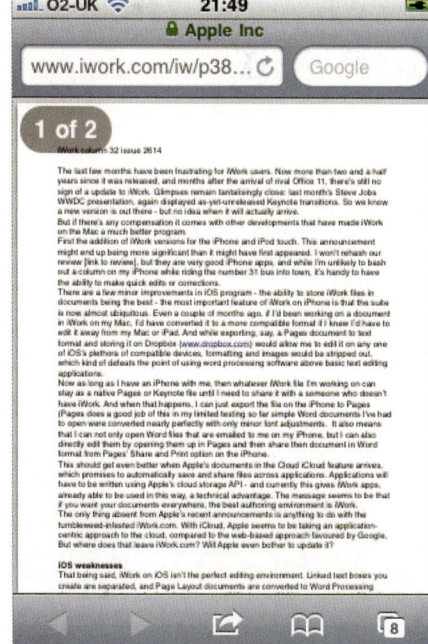

6: View shared document
Viewers who click the link in the email can now see the file on iWork.com in their web browser. It even works on the mobile version of Safari.

Tips | Tricks | Hacks | Apps

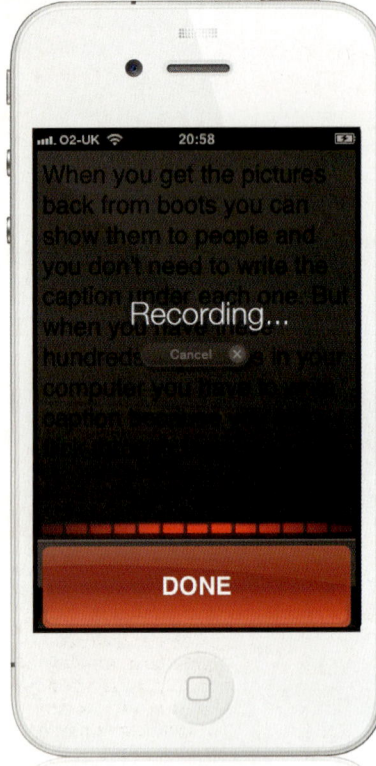

Dictate notes, texts and emails

Give your fingers a rest – you can dictate notes and text to your iPhone using voice recognition software, and the results are surprisingly good

Task: Dictating on the iPhone
Difficulty: Beginner
Time needed: 5 minutes

The iPhone's software keyboard has proven a lot more usable than its detractors originally gave it credit. But there are still times when you'd rather not rely on it to create a quick email or post to your Twitter account on the move. Wouldn't it be good to treat your iPhone as your virtual assistant and dictate your message to it? The good news is that you can.

A free voice recognition app, Dragon Dictation, converts your speech into text. A standalone app, its results can be exported easily to the iPhone's Mail app, or shared with any other iPhone app by cutting and pasting.

If you're thinking that a small, free app might not produce reliable results, you'd be surprised. Dragon Dictation's voice recognition really is impressive. That's mainly because translation is done remotely: you speak into the app, and it's transmitted to the developer's servers, where it is translated to text and sent back to your iPhone. It sounds a roundabout approach, but it's surprisingly fast and accurate. You just need an internet connection for it to work. Here's how to get the most out of spoken text on your iPhone.

Step-by-step | Dragon Dictation | Dictate on the iPhone

1: Set up language and settings
You'll first have to set up your language and other settings. Dragon can import your contacts list for easier recognition.

2: Tap to record
Tap the button to record, and speak clearly and naturally into the microphone for anything up to 30 seconds. The red bars indicate your voice level.

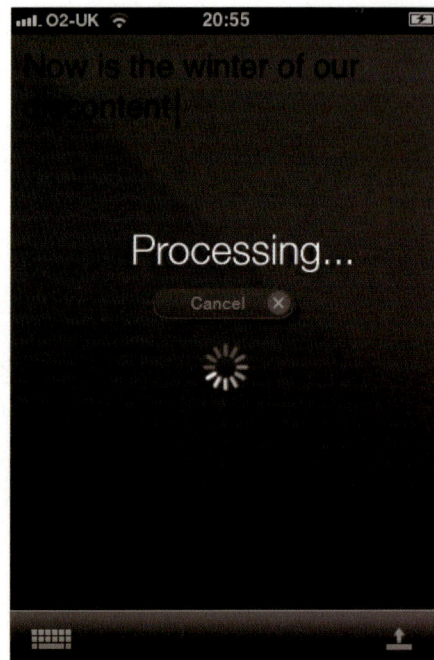

3: Analysing your voice
When complete, click the 'Done' button and, in a second or two, the words you spoke should appear in the editing screen.

Tips | Tricks | Hacks | Apps

Using voice recognition

Here's the inside scoop on voice-to-text

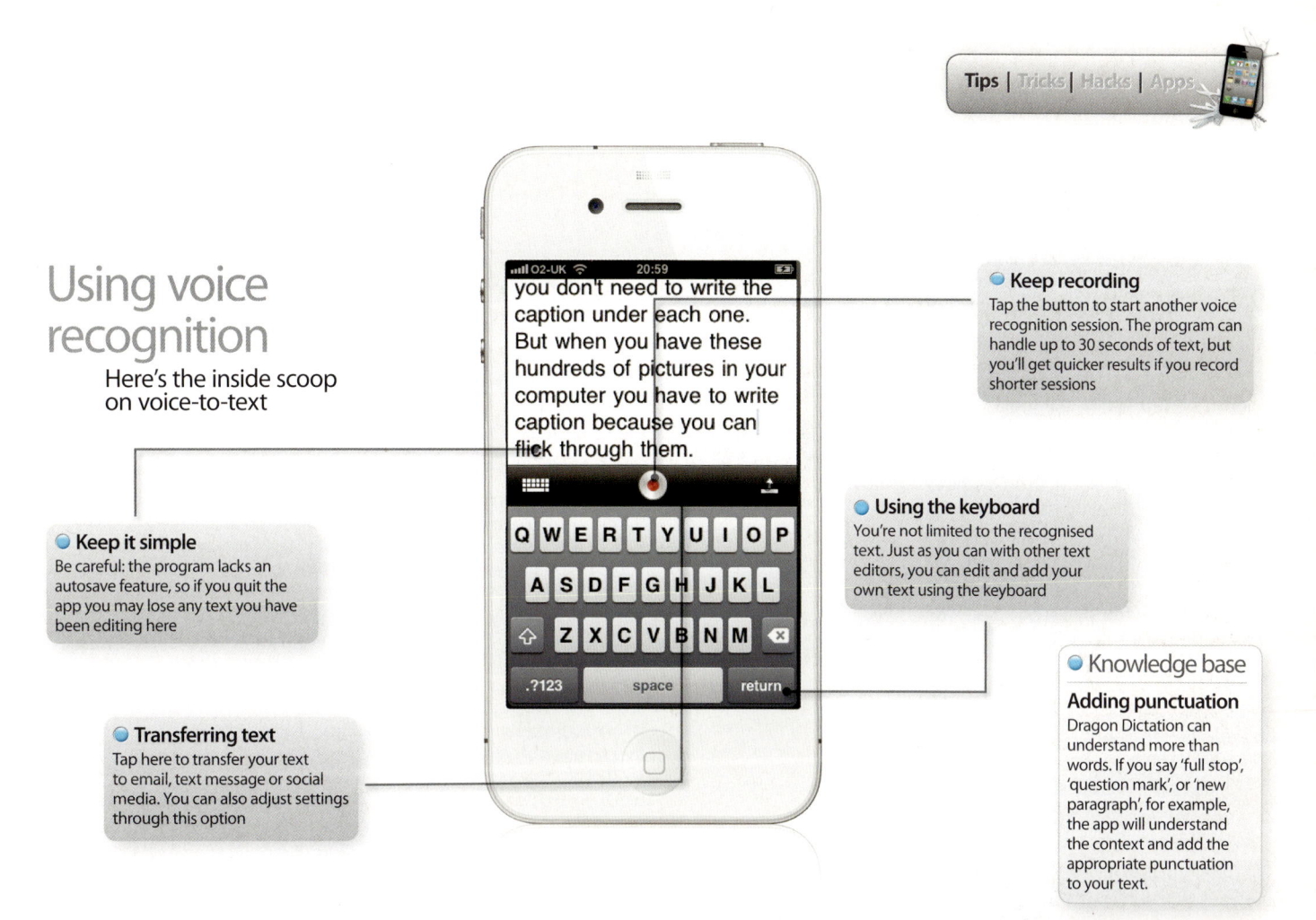

Keep it simple
Be careful: the program lacks an autosave feature, so if you quit the app you may lose any text you have been editing here

Transferring text
Tap here to transfer your text to email, text message or social media. You can also adjust settings through this option

Keep recording
Tap the button to start another voice recognition session. The program can handle up to 30 seconds of text, but you'll get quicker results if you record shorter sessions

Using the keyboard
You're not limited to the recognised text. Just as you can with other text editors, you can edit and add your own text using the keyboard

Knowledge base

Adding punctuation
Dragon Dictation can understand more than words. If you say 'full stop', 'question mark', or 'new paragraph', for example, the app will understand the context and add the appropriate punctuation to your text.

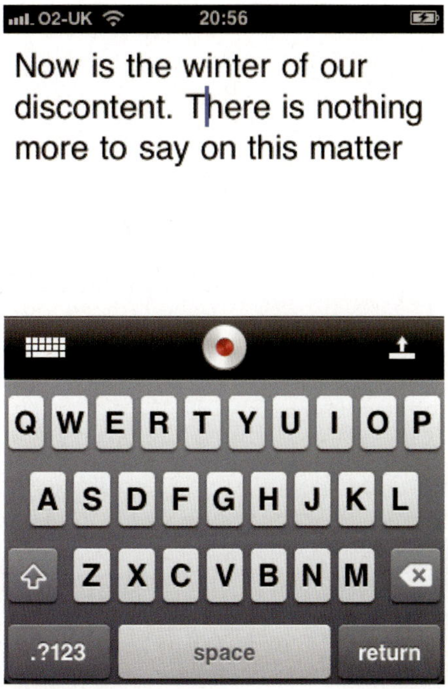

4: Correcting errors
Any mistakes? You can edit the text by clicking the keyboard button on the left to add or remove text, or even paste text via the iPhone's clipboard.

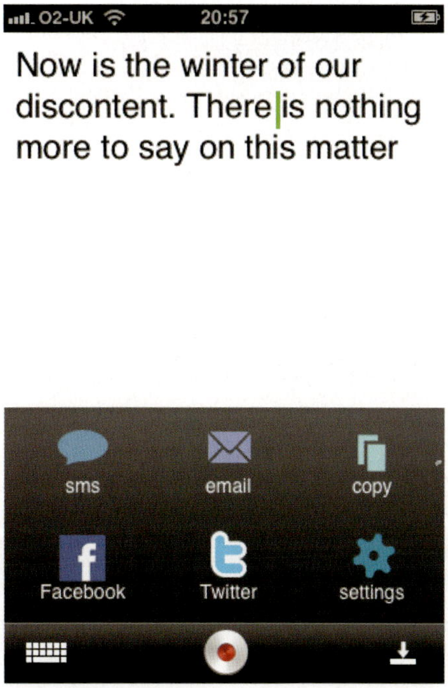

5: Export the results
Tap the button at the bottom right to open up your export options: SMS messaging, email, or the web versions of Facebook and Twitter.

6: Copy and paste
The results are open to just about any app. Tap the Copy button, launch the app you want to add the text, place the cursor in position and double-tap.

iPhone Tips, Tricks, Apps and Hacks **31**

Tips | Tricks | Hacks | Apps

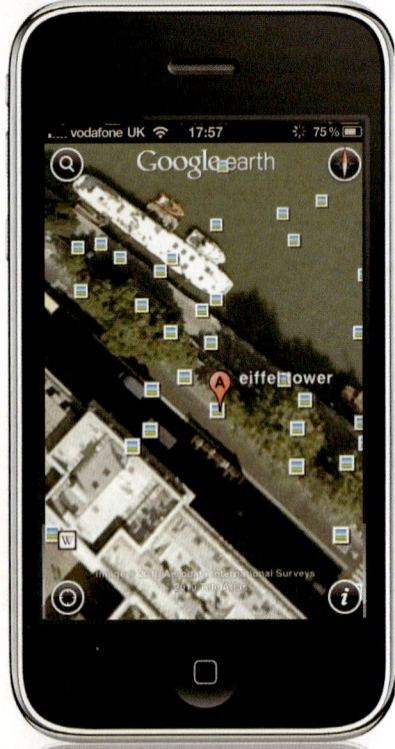

Navigate the world with Google Earth

Google Earth offers a fascinating insight into more of the world than you could ever hope to see in person

Task: Master Google Earth
Difficulty: Beginner
Time needed: 5 minutes

Google Earth is a free solution that offers more than you could have dreamed of only a few years ago. Once you get to grips with how it works you will be flying through any city in the world and learning about the planet we inhabit in a fun and relaxing way. It's not all about far flung places, though, because you can also use it to view your own house and the town you live in, which makes for a somewhat convoluted satellite navigation solution, but one that is sure to give you a more realistic view than any other.

On the iPhone it is based around gestures and knowing these help you get the most from the app. With many extra features built in, it is worth spending some time to explore them because this will help you get even more out of it. It is addictive too and once you start you may find yourself whizzing around the planet every day. In this tutorial we're going to show you how to make the most of the built-in features and where the extra bits and pieces are that come together to make it an app all iPhone owners should have on their phones.

Step-by-step | Google Earth Take a trip around the planet

1: Load it up
Google Earth is available in the App Store for free. Once you have installed it, tap the app icon and you are ready to start.

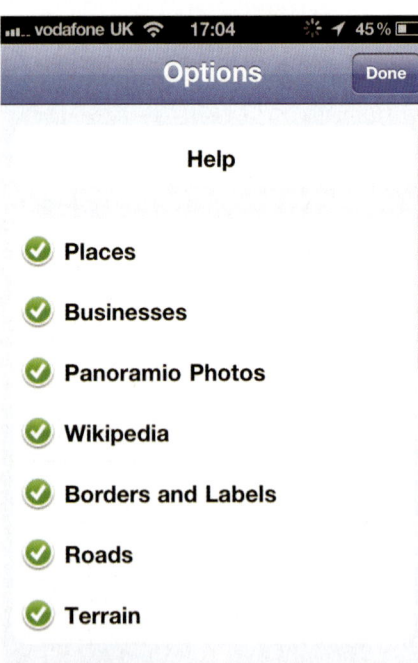

2: What to see
You're presented with your current location, once you've agreed for the app to use it. Tap the 'i' icon (bottom right) and choose what you want to see.

3: Zoom in and out
You can zoom in and out by pinching your fingers together. This works well, but you may experience minor lag when viewing the maps over 3G.

32 iPhone Tips, Tricks, Apps and Hacks

Tips | Tricks | Hacks | Apps

On top of the world with Google Earth

Get to know your planet better with this rather excellent location finder

● **Searching**
This icon takes you to the search screen where you can look up cities, businesses, places and almost anything else you need to find

● **Go home**
This icon takes you back to your current location no matter where in the world you are currently viewing. It is very useful if you need to see what's around you quickly

● **Look north**
You can tap this icon to reset the orientation to north at any time. This is useful if you have been rotating the display with your fingers and have got lost

● **More Detail**
Tapping on any of the on-screen icons will bring up more information such as a photo, Wikipedia article or contact information

● **Knowledge base**

Bring it to life
The Panoramio photo option in Google Earth is a user-generated layer that lets you view photos from all around the world. In some areas, multiple photos are available and new ones are updated every month. You may find that there are too many in a particular area, but you can quickly turn them off in the options if need be.

4: Tilting
Tilting your iPhone produces an even more impressive effect; it will give you a semi-3D view, which you can scroll around with one finger.

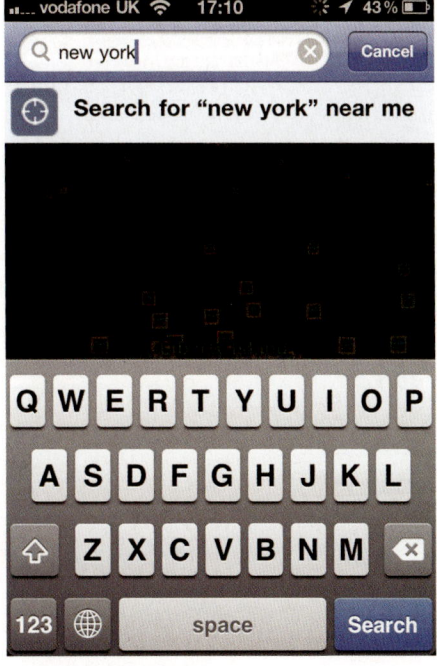

5: Find anywhere
Tap the magnifying glass, top left, to search. For example, type in 'New York' to be taken straight to one of the most famous cities in the world.

By Alan Knox ©

Liberty Island, formerly called **Bedloe's Island**, is a small uninhabited island in New York Harbor in the United States, best known as the location of the Statue of Liberty. The name Liberty Island has been in use since the early 20th century, although the name was not officially changed until 1956. Before the Statue of Liberty, Bedloe's Island was the home to

6: More information
You will notice small square icons on screen that if tapped will bring up further information. Wikipedia, photos and many other sources are supported.

iPhone Tips, Tricks, Apps and Hacks **33**

Tips | Tricks | Hacks | Apps

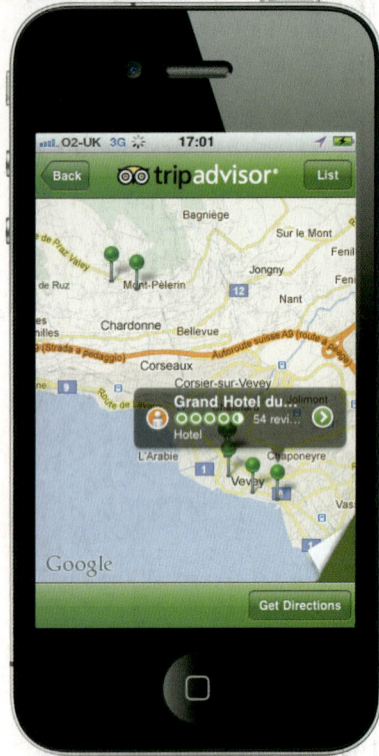

Plan a trip using your iPhone

Looking to get away from it all? With your iPhone in hand, you can make sure you find the best getaways at the keenest prices

Task: Organising travel with TripAdvisor
Difficulty: Beginner
Time needed: 20 minutes

As little as 20 years ago, most of us probably planned our holidays with the help of a high street travel agent. But access to cheap flights and the ability to book holidays directly has enabled us to take control of our travel arrangements. The TripAdvisor website (www.tripadvisor.com) has earned a good reputation as a reliable service for travellers, particularly as it features unbiased reviews and suggestions for destinations all around the world submitted by fellow travellers. Now add to this mix the iPhone, which has made a name for itself as a useful travel companion in its own right.

The iPhone's TripAdvisor app squeezes the website into your pocket by offering a gateway to the same resources as the web version, in a neater format. You can search for local hotels, restaurants and other attractions, and it will even find flights for you. It also offers access to online forums where other TripAdvisor users offer advice and recommendations about holidays and other trips.

Additionally, the iPhone app adds extra power of its own, because it's truly mobile and offers location awareness. That combination can revolutionise the way we travel. In practice, it means you can take the iPhone on a trip and it can interrogate TripAdvisor to find good nearby hotels or recommended restaurants. Once you've used it, chances are you'll find it utterly indispensable.

Step-by-step | TripAdvisor Plan a perfect break

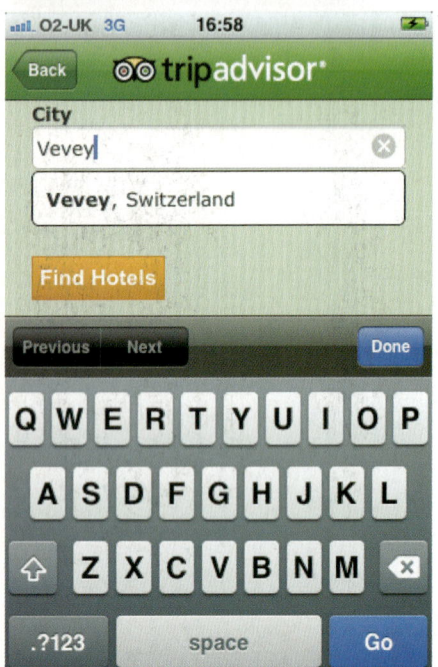

1: A place to stay
Tap the Hotels link and enter the city or address to which you're travelling. TripAdvisor offers a list of suggestions. Tap one and then tap Find Hotels.

2: Cheapest and the best
TripAdvisor searches its database and divides results into hotels and guest houses, ordered by price or rating. The results include a link to book a room.

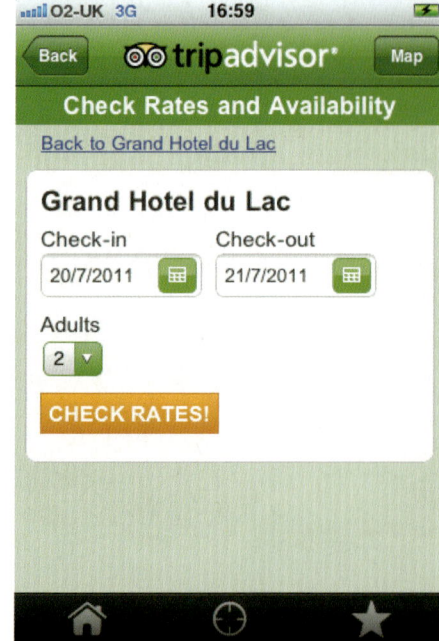

3: Booking the hotel
Tap the 'See on map' button to see where the hotel is, and Check Rates to see price and availability. You can even book the hotel from here.

Tips | Tricks | Hacks | Apps

TripAdvisor travel tips
Getting the most out of the app

General information
Want general information about a destination? Enter its name here and tap the Search icon and TripAdvisor will mine its database for everything about it

Flight control
You can even search for cheap holiday flights. Tap here and enter your travel details and TripAdvisor will search its travel partners for available flights

Travellers' tales
For general research about your trip, visit the TripAdvisor forums. This area offers non-specific advice, tips and chat organised by region or topic

My Saves
It's easy to pick up great travel titbits. If you click the Save button on any pages, the results are stored and can be opened here

Knowledge base
What's the catch?
TripAdvisor is a great free resource – so how does it make money? In two ways: from on-site adverts, as well as through affiliate agencies, such as airlines and hotel booking services, which supply the results whenever you search TripAdvisor.

4: Good local restaurants
You'll be hungry after your journey. On the Home screen, tap Restaurants. Check 'Find restaurants near me now', and filter by cuisine and price.

5: Things to do
To find local interests, tap 'Things to do', choose to find attractions near you and pick a type of attraction. The results are organised by rating or distance.

6: Speak your mind
Tap 'Write a Review' and enter the name of the hotel, restaurant or activity. Rate it based on given criteria and add your own comments to help others.

iPhone Tips, Tricks, Apps and Hacks **35**

Tips | Tricks | Hacks | Apps

Take incredible panoramic photos

You no longer need expensive equipment to capture stunning panoramic shots – a free app will do

Task: Use Photosynth to capture panoramic photographs
Difficulty: Beginner
Time needed: 10 minutes

There was time, not too long ago, when the ability to take gorgeous panoramic images was reserved for kit at the high end of the photography scale. But now it is possible to capture a moment and place in a full panoramic view with just an iPhone and a free app. In this tutorial we talk you through the process of capturing a panoramic image using the wonderful Photosynth app. Essentially, all the hard work is done by the app itself – you simply point your camera at a focal point to start the process, tap the screen and then move your arm while the app itself snaps a string of images to recreate the moment in its own time-coded bubble.

Now you just sit back while the app processes the data, binds all of the shots together and then presents a stunning, vivid image that you can explore in all directions, provided a sufficient amount of images were taken for the app to complete the photographic jigsaw. All of your captured images are then stored in your own in-app library, where you can add in details about the location pictured, share your images with friends or, provided you have a Microsoft Live ID, upload them to Bing Maps, where other users can experience them. So don't delay – start capturing your panoramic world now.

Exploring your panoramic image
Once you have captured your shot, all that's left is to admire it

● **Your shot**
You can swipe to view the full 360-degrees of your captured panoramic shot, the process of capturing which is very easy

● **Edit properties**
You can use your locational data to provide a title, or manually name the shot by tapping the 'Edit properties' option when viewing your shot

● **Knowledge base**
Retaking shot slots
If somebody strays into your sequence as you're capturing your shots then don't be afraid to retake the section of your panoramic image that has been breached. Simply point the camera at the section you wish to amend and then tap the screen to manually snap the segment.

● **Share you image**
Your image can be emailed, posted to Facebook or, if you have a Windows Live ID, submitted to Bing Maps and Photosynth.net

● **Effortless capture**
When you have finished capturing your shot, you can hit Done, after which the app will process the data and sew all the images together

36 iPhone Tips, Tricks, Apps and Hacks

Tips | Tricks | Hacks | Apps

Step-by-step | Photosynth Capture outstanding panoramic shots

1: Launch the app
Upon launching the app, you will be presented with a simple screen of instructions that teach you the basics of using it to take panoramic pictures. It really is ridiculously simple, though.

2: Tap to start
Start off by choosing a main focal point for your sprawling photograph – a point where the 360-degree cycle starts and then ultimately ends – and then tap the screen to capture it.

3: Capture your sequence
Now move your iPhone camera's viewfinder incrementally in any direction and the app will automatically snap the next image in the sequence, provided it is framed green.

4: Frame it right
As you move, point the camera at any 'blank' spaces in the sequence to take the shots required to fill them in. You can manually add shots by tapping the screen at any time.

5: Stitch it up
When you have finished capturing your sequence, tap Done and the app will then begin the process of sewing all of your captured images together into one expansive 360-degree view.

6: Add to library
All the panoramic shots you create on your travels will be stored in your personal library. Tap on an image to open it or tap Edit and press the X to delete the selected image.

7: Scroll image
You can admire your finished shots in all their panoramic glory by tapping on a thumbnail image and then swiping left, right, up or down… any direction you want, really.

8: Add details
When viewing an image, tap 'Edit properties' and you are able to add details such as places (based on your location) and names, as well as view the capture date and time.

9: Share images
Your panoramic shots can be emailed to friends, shared on Facebook or uploaded to Bing Maps and Photosynth.net, where they can be admired and/or criticised by the world.

Learn to tag a photo location on your iPhone

Discover where your images were snapped by turning on your iPhone's Location Services

Task: Turn on Location Services
Difficulty: Beginner
Time needed: 2 minutes

There is no easier way to track the advancement of technology in the last 20 years than through cameras. Years ago, taking a photo involved film, chemists and developing, while praying for a good picture. Now cameras are more accessible and you can snap, edit and sort on the device itself within seconds of capturing your images. What's more, managing your photos and labelling them used to involve scrawling details on to the back of the hard copies, but with your iPhone's Camera app you can get instant records of where each photo was taken by ensuring that the Location Services are activated.

Once you have turned on Location Services for the Camera app, any snaps that you take will be marked as pins on Google Maps, which forms part of the Photos app. So you can pinch to zoom in and instantly see which images were taken where. The only downside of these standard apps is that there is no way to add more descriptive text to the images, such as specific locations. However, there are plenty of free apps that allow you to do just that in the App Store. Enter a search for key words such as 'Photo' and 'Tag' and you should find a variety of apps to suit the need to add more detail to your pictures.

Step-by-step | Photos View the location tags of your photographs

1: Activate Location Services
From your iPhone's Home screen, tap Settings and scroll down the page, select General. Now tap Location Services, then move the slider to On.

2: Switch on Camera
In Location Services is a list of your iPhone apps that use Location Services. Ensure the slider next to Camera is 'On' and return to your Home screen.

3: Launch camera
Launch the camera and take photos. Don't forget to turn the flash on, if required, and then tap the large camera icon to take pictures.

38 iPhone Tips, Tricks, Apps and Hacks

Tips | Tricks | Hacks | Apps

Viewing your tags
Keep track of where your photos were taken

Maps
You can only view the Google Maps in 'classic' format, but you can zoom in and out by pinching the screen

Geotags
The locations of where each of your photos were taken will be marked as pins on Google Maps for easy reference

Switch to album
Options at the bottom of the page allow you to instantly switch between your photo albums and the places where they were taken

Instant access
You can tap on the pins to see which photos were taken at the respective location and switch straight to the album to see them in detail

Knowledge base

Get descriptive
Unfortunately, there is currently no way to add descriptive text to your photos using the standard Camera or Photos apps, but thankfully there are plenty of free apps available that do. Photo Name for example, allows you to take photos and caption them in-app before sharing them with your friends.

4: Open Photos
From your Home screen, tap on the Photos app to open up Camera Roll to see thumbnails. Tap on a thumbnail to see the chosen image in full screen.

5: Go to Places
Tap the Places option on the Camera Roll page for a Google Maps page with pins placed in the locations that all of your photos were captured.

6: View tags
Pinch the screen to zoom in on the pins for map readouts of the locations your images were taken or tap on the pins for a list of the pictures taken there.

Tips | Tricks | Hacks | Apps

Capture passport-style photos on your mobile

It is easy to take passport-style photos on an iPhone, and you can also experience the atmosphere of the photoshoot as well

Task: Take retro passport photos with IncrediBooth
Difficulty: Beginner
Time needed: 5 minutes

In a world dominated by digital cameras and smartphones, it is likely that you have not visited a photo booth in quite a long time. Indeed, the only time most people visit one is to get a passport photo taken when their current one has run out. There is, however, a way to relive the good old days of the photo booth with your iPhone and it is called IncrediBooth. It is a simple application that takes photos, but it has some clever tricks hidden within it and an interface that few apps can rival for personality.

When you consider that the photo booth could bring personality and life to romantic moments and even the mundane passport photo moment, it is far from a bad thing to experience it wherever you are and whenever you want to. There are some practical uses for it, though. You could in theory use the app for documentary purposes, although we would advise checking the rules for submitting photos before you do so. In this tutorial we will show you how to get the most from IncrediBooth and to relive those days when the wait for the photos to drop into the slot was genuinely exciting.

Step-by-step | IncrediBooth Mobile passport photo creation

1: So familiar
Open the app and the interface looks like the interior of an old-fashioned photo booth. Notice the eye level guide next to the main screen.

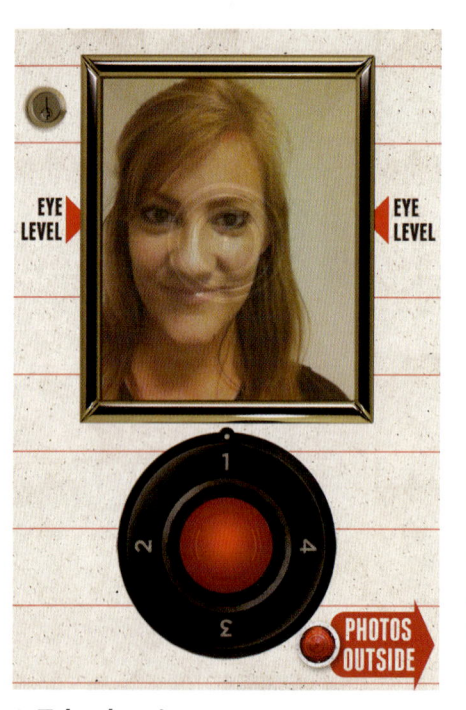

2: Take the picture
To take your first picture point the iPhone at your face and line up your eyes with the level indicator. The app uses the front camera on an iPhone 4.

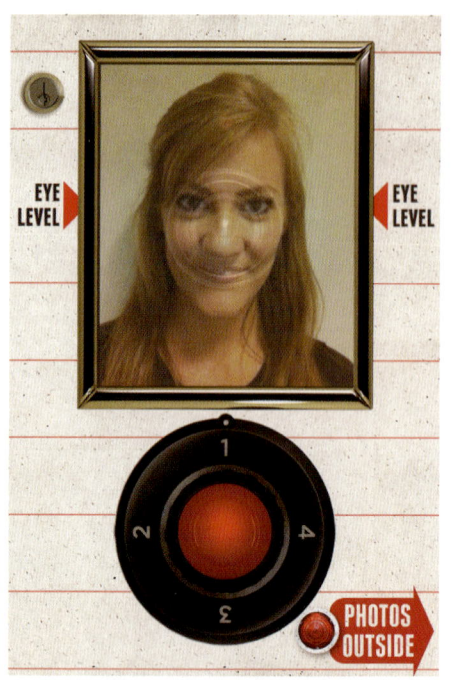

3: The delay
Tap the big red button and the screen flickers with a flashing red light. It does this four times bringing back the tension of staying in the right position.

40 iPhone Tips, Tricks, Apps and Hacks

Tips | Tricks | Hacks | Apps

A beautiful interface

How does IncrediBooth work?

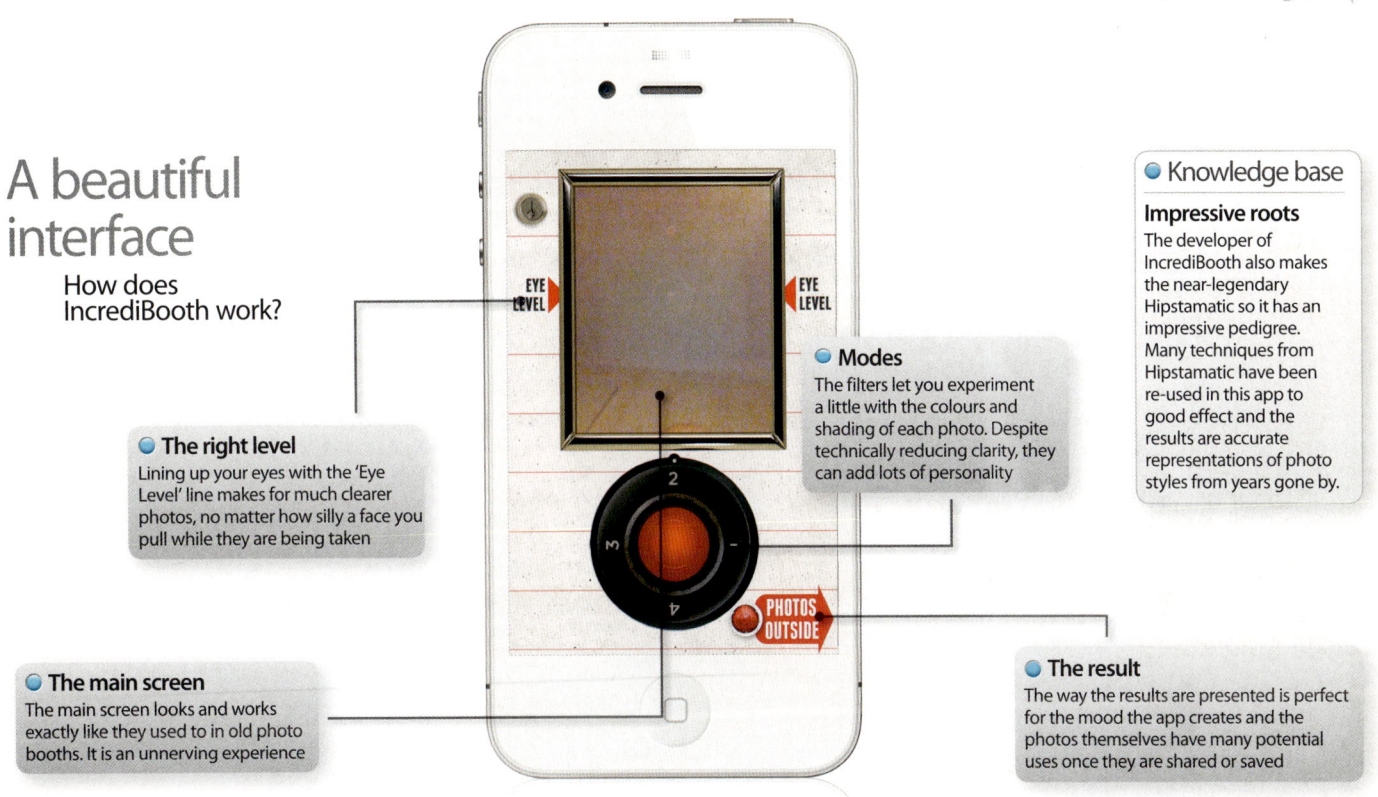

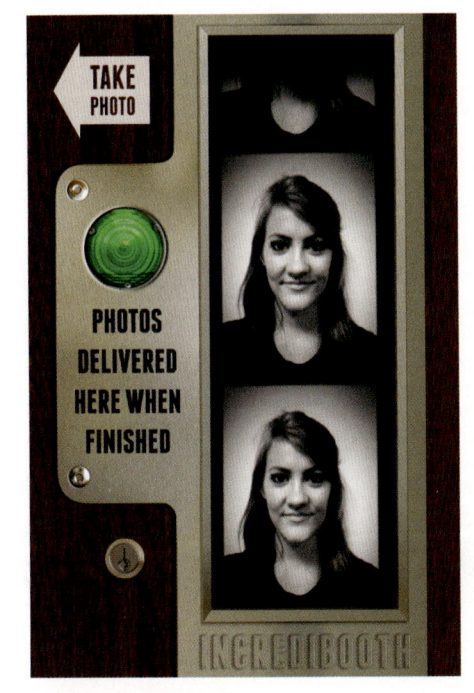

● **The right level**
Lining up your eyes with the 'Eye Level' line makes for much clearer photos, no matter how silly a face you pull while they are being taken

● **Modes**
The filters let you experiment a little with the colours and shading of each photo. Despite technically reducing clarity, they can add lots of personality

● **Knowledge base**
Impressive roots
The developer of IncrediBooth also makes the near-legendary Hipstamatic so it has an impressive pedigree. Many techniques from Hipstamatic have been re-used in this app to good effect and the results are accurate representations of photo styles from years gone by.

● **The main screen**
The main screen looks and works exactly like they used to in old photo booths. It is an unnerving experience

● **The result**
The way the results are presented is perfect for the mood the app creates and the photos themselves have many potential uses once they are shared or saved

4: Developments
Tap the 'Photos Outside' icon and you'll see a strip of four photos, representing a passport strip, and you can scroll through to see each one.

5: Options
When you tap the photo strip you are offered the opportunity to share the photos or trash the strip and to start again.

6: Sharing
You have the option to share your photo strip to Facebook or send it via email. Otherwise you can just save it to your Photo Library.

iPhone Tips, Tricks, Apps and Hacks **41**

Tips | Tricks | Hacks | Apps

Edit images with Photoshop Express

Are you feeling the lack of image editing software on your iPhone? Polish up the photos with this free app from Adobe

Task: Edit images
Difficulty: Beginner
Time needed: 10 minutes

The iPhone's camera, although certainly not the most highly specced, is nonetheless capable of taking some superb photos, which with a bit of basic tweaking often have the potential to be really spectacular. The default factory set of apps doesn't include any kind of photo editing tools, not until iOS 5 at least, meaning that in order to get the best out of the on-board camera, users are faced with downloading a third-party app to do the job for them.

Happily, Adobe – producer of the omnipotent Photoshop – has released a basic iPhone version for this very purpose. Photoshop Express, available free from the App Store, allows you to perform some of the more basic editing techniques, such as cropping, tinting and altering exposure and contrast, and is really easy to use, making full use of the iPhone's touch-screen interface. Here we show you how to get started with it, and how to use it to perform some of the more common functions you might need when tweaking your pics.

Step-by-step | Adobe Photoshop Express | Edit images on your iPhone

1: Launch app
To begin editing, tap the Photoshop Express icon on your home screen to launch the app, then touch the Edit tab at the bottom of the screen.

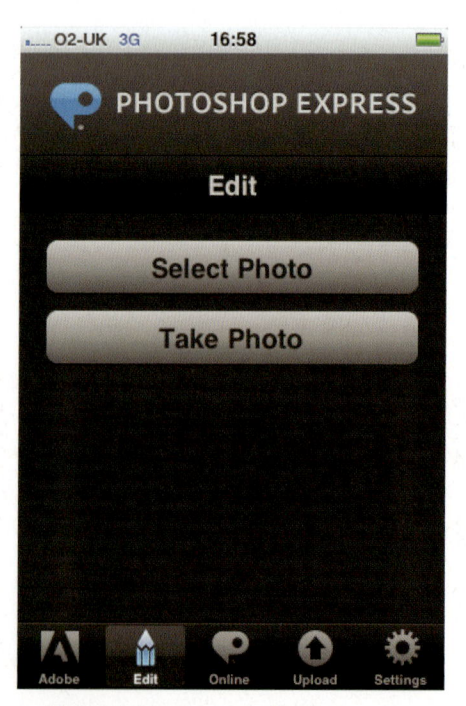

2: Choose import method
Tap Select Photo to use an existing image from your Camera Roll, or take a new one by tapping the Take Photo button to launch the camera.

3: Select photo
From your Camera Roll, tap the thumbnail of the photo you want to edit. It will then appear full screen in the app's main edit window.

42 iPhone Tips, Tricks, Apps and Hacks

4: Crop image
The top-left button has options to crop, straighten, flip and rotate. Select Crop, then drag the corners of the rectangle into place to frame your selection.

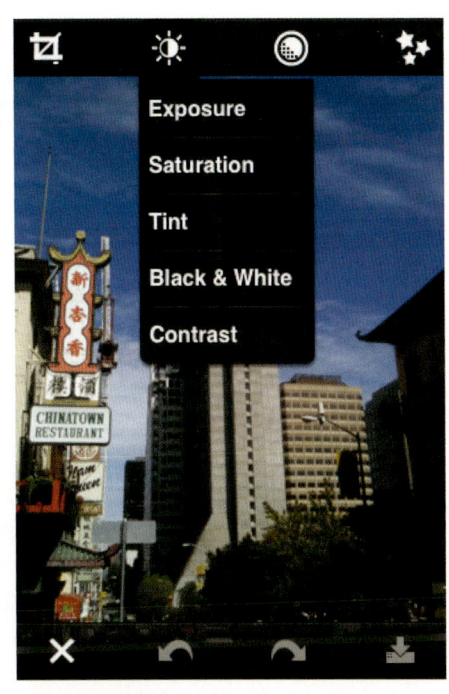

5: Exposure
Exposure, contrast and other adjustment controls can be found under the button pictured. This image needs brightening, so choose Exposure.

6: Adjust exposure
To adjust the exposure, slide your finger left and right across the screen. Left decreases the value, right increases it. Tap OK when it looks correct.

7: Sharpen
This menu pictured contains focus-related controls: soft focus, sketch, sharpen and reduce noise. Select a tool, then slide left and right to make adjustments.

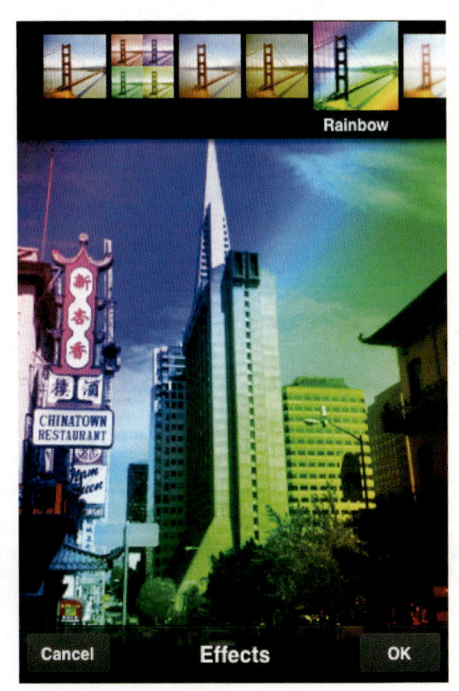

8: Add effects and borders
The starry button in the top right reveals the Border/Effects menu, from which you can choose from a selection of one-touch special effects and borders.

9: Save options
When you're done, tap the bottom-right icon to save. 'Save and Exit' saves a new edited copy to your Camera Roll, leaving the original intact.

iPhone Tips, Tricks, Apps and Hacks **43**

Tips | Tricks | Hacks | Apps

Upload and share your favourite photos

The culture of photo sharing continues to grow and Flickr lets you shoot and upload photos and videos while away from the desktop

Task: Share photos
Difficulty: Beginner
Time needed: 10 minutes

The growth of social networking has led to a sharp increase in the popularity of photo sharing over the last few years. Flickr is arguably the most well-known of the services and this image and video hosting website now hosts more than 4 billion images. As well as being a popular site for users to share and embed personal snapshots, the service is widely used by bloggers to host images that they embed in blogs and social media.

If you're a Flickr user, an iPhone app that connects to the site is a natural extension and the official Flickr app lets you do this and a whole lot more. The most notable feature of the app is the ability to upload images to your account. Whether you choose to take a snapshot with your iPhone's camera or select an existing image from your photo library, uploading is effortless. As a bonus, you can geotag each shot with your current location, add it to a set and assign a level of privacy. iPhone 4 users will be pleased that the app supports HD video uploads and multitasking. This means that your photos will continue to upload in the background while you are performing other tasks.

Step-by-step | Flickr Upload and share a geotagged photo

1: Flickr
Download and install the Flickr app and when you open it, you will see a slideshow that displays images from the site. Now log in to your account.

2: Sign in
Tap on Recent, You or Contacts and you'll go to a one-time authorisation that opens in Safari. Sign in using your Yahoo! ID username and password.

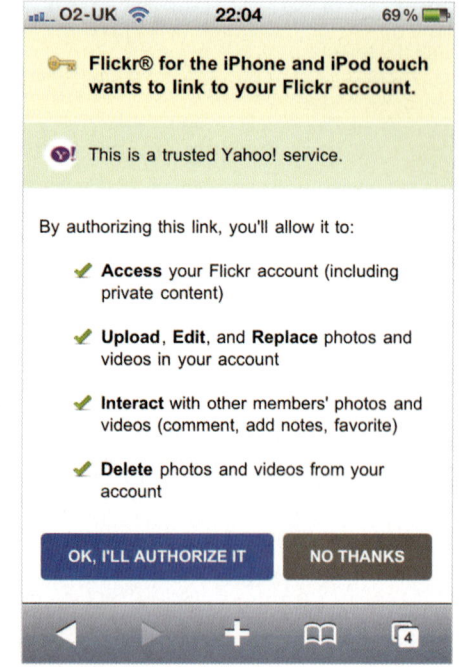

3: Authorise
Tap the 'OK, I'll Authorize It' button and you will have instant access to your Flickr account. You can now perform a range of tasks.

44 iPhone Tips, Tricks, Apps and Hacks

Find your way around Flickr

Get to grips with one of the most popular photo-sharing apps around

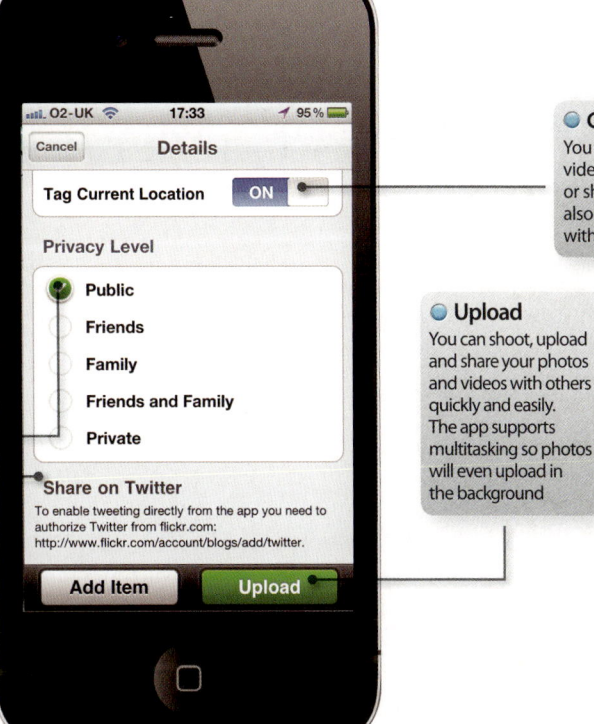

● **Privacy**
The Flickr app does everything you need with simplicity. Setting a photo's privacy level is easy and you can make it private, public or for family viewing only

● **Twitter**
Although a photo-sharing site, Flickr is still a social networking service. Support for Twitter is included and you can enable tweeting directly from the UI

● **Geotag**
You can search for photos and videos, add them to your favourites or share images via email. You can also geotag uploaded snapshots with your current location

● **Upload**
You can shoot, upload and share your photos and videos with others quickly and easily. The app supports multitasking so photos will even upload in the background

● **Knowledge base**

Explore the world
You really can explore the world with the Flickr app. Tap the Search Photos and Videos text box and enter a keyword. Now tap the Q to the left of the box and select All Uploads, From your Contacts or Your Photostream. Refine your search by adding further keywords and very soon you will have access to photos and videos relating to your specific search query.

4: Upload
Now upload an image: tap the upload icon (top right of the screen) and select Upload from Library. Browse until you find an image and enter a name.

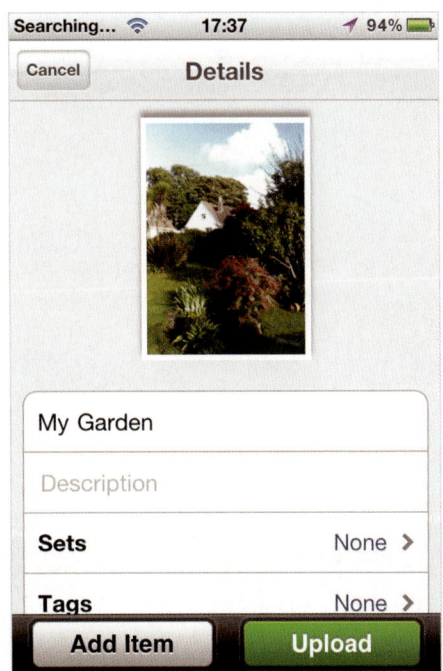

5: Geotag
You can geotag your image by enabling 'Tag Current Location'. Do this and select a privacy level. Tap Upload and it will be uploaded to your account.

6: View image
Tap You to view your collection of photos and you will now see the latest snapshot. You can add a comment, assign it to a set or share it via email.

iPhone Tips, Tricks, Apps and Hacks **45**

Tips | Tricks | Hacks | Apps

Getting started with iMovie for iPhone
Your first steps into a world of mobile movie making

Task: Learn your way around iMovie
Difficulty: Beginner
Time needed: 10 minutes

One of the many great things about Apple software is when we get the opportunity to tell people that it will change the way they go about the process of doing things that had previously been long-winded, difficult to do or had been frustrating. Editing movies could easily be labelled any of the above (even on a Mac) but Apple has, with the power of the iPhone 4, given people the opportunity to negate the need to import and edit on a full-sized computer, and instead given you simple tools to do it right on the device you'll use to capture the footage on in the first place. iMovie for iPhone is not an exhaustive editing suite, and as a result it uses a cleverly worked balance, offering simplicity during use and complexity under the hood when necessary. This tutorial will take you through starting your very first movie, and on pages after this we'll guide you through the entire editing process.

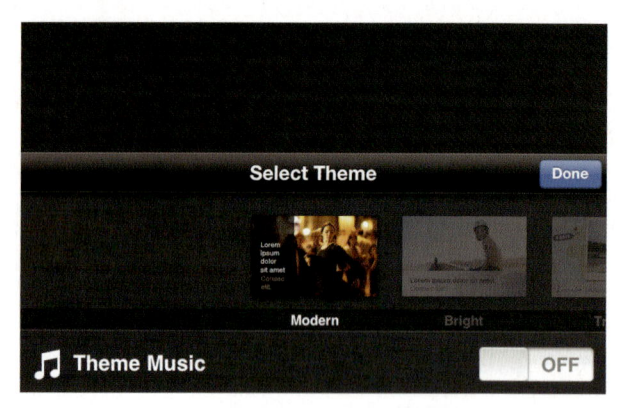

Get to know the iMovie for iPhone app
Learn your way around the iMovie app's layout and controls

Edit window
This is the main window for editing your project. Along the bottom you can see the timeline, and in the main window you can see the point at which the playhead sits

Great quality
You can instantly see during your edit that the footage you have captured is incredibly detailed and easy to see on the new Retina Display. This makes edits easy to accomplish

Knowledge base
The playhead
The playhead is the red line that runs vertically through the timeline. It indicates the place in the timeline that is being showed in the main window. The playhead can be manipulated to help you find places to trim clips and watch them again as you perfect your edit.

Cog
The cog lets you access the settings for the start of the movie. We shall explore this in the next tutorial

Frames
Along the bottom of the edit window you can see the frames of your movie and you can drag the playhead through them as and when you decide to trim each clip

Add footage
Tap this button to be taken to your camera where you can shoot a movie directly into the timeline

Tips | Tricks | Hacks | Apps

Step-by-step | iMovie Create your first movie

1: Open and tap
Open up iMovie. You can do this in landscape and portrait, but we recommend that you use landscape as it offers an easier experience when editing. Tap the plus button to create your first Movie.

2: Themes
You can now pick from one of five Apple themes. These have been specially crafted to offer a cool template that will stitch the project together and give it the slick Apple look.

3: Scroll and tap
Use your finger to scroll through the different themes on offer and then tap on the one you'd like to use in your project. Now tap the blue Done button to confirm your selection.

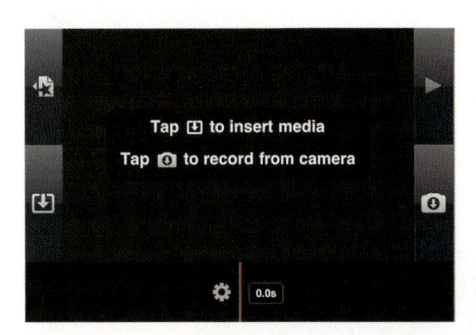

4: Insert
You can now begin to populate your project. Follow the prompt and either navigate to your Camera Roll or hit the other button to record a video right there and then, which will be instantly added to the project.

5: Scroll and pick
If you opt to go to your Camera Roll you will see all of your videos by default. You can scroll through videos, and tapping one will send it into the editing window where you can trim it down to size.

6: Stills and tunes
Along the bottom of the Camera Roll interface there are three tabs, which will allow you to add not only your pre-recorded video but also any photos and music you would like to add as well.

7: Audio pane
In the Audio pane you have the option to navigate through the sections you'll find on your iPod; browse songs by artist, playlist or song name. You can also access the Theme music that is stored in iMovie.

8: iMovie theme music
For some reason Apple has a knack of finding music that just sounds, well, Apple. These are great short bursts of music for you to add to smaller clips. Tap on a song to send it to the edit window.

9: Green bar
Once a music track has been added you can see it as a green bar under your movie footage. There is no option to edit audio in iMovie mobile, so you will have to tailor tracks before importing them.

iPhone Tips, Tricks, Apps and Hacks **47**

Tips | Tricks | Hacks | Apps

Edit your iMovie project on your iPhone
Give your movies the professional touch with titles and transitions

Task: Edit in iMovie
Difficulty: Beginner
Time needed: 15 minutes

One of the things that makes video editing a great creative medium is the ability to add simple but effective elements that can lift random clips from an amateur endeavour to a slick-looking professional project. Titles and transitions can do this job in a matter of minutes, and with the iMovie app on iPhone 4 you can do this on the phone itself. The process is typically simple, but because of the iPhone's screen size you do have to shunt between screens, which can be a little confusing. The system, once you're used to it, can be very quick and very satisfying.

Admittedly, there are a number of limitations to the application and the titles and transitions, so you'll have to get used to working within the parameters you've been given. This tutorial will take you through adding a title and transition to your movie. Once you've mastered it, give all the options a try and see how they suit your movie-making style.

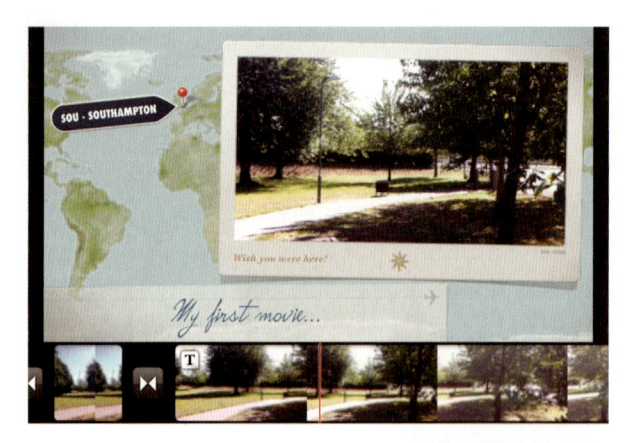

Add titles and transitions to improve your project
Discover how to edit your iMovie project like a pro on your iPhone

● Clarity
The timeline and transition boxes are very easy to use in iMovie – simply tap on any of the boxes to select and move them, or use a double tap to edit the way they behave

● Knowledge base
No transitions
It is also possible to remove transitions completely if you would rather spring from one scene to the next, or if you want to make two clips feel like they merge into one. Simply select None in the Transition Edit window and then bring the time value down as far as you can.

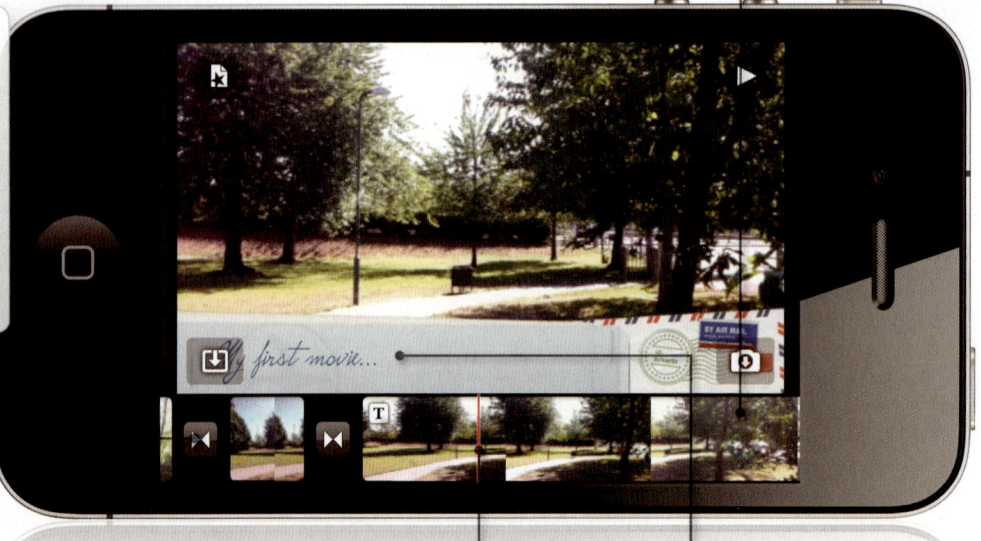

● Transition
In between each clip you add to the project, you will see the Transition button. The icon inside will change according to the transition you assign to it

● Use the playhead
Drag the project around and use the playhead to check that your title is appearing in the right part of the project to be effective

● Wonderful words
Titles allows you to set the scene of your video clip, introduce a person or just throw out facts about what's going on. Each theme has its own title style

Tips | Tricks | Hacks | Apps

Step-by-step | iMovie Add titles and transitions

1: Load it
Load your current project or the one you have just created. The project will start at the beginning and you can now begin to add the elements you want to make the project more professional.

2: Trim the clip
Use a single tap to select a clip in the timeline. When a clip is selected, two yellow pins appear at either end of the clip and you can trim the clip down if you need to before adding anything.

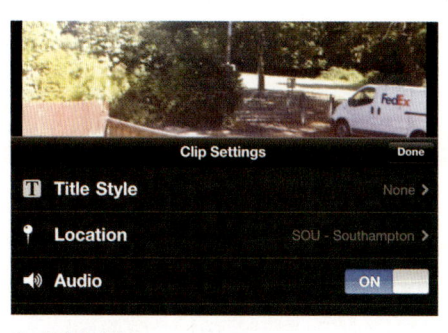

3: Add titles
Double-tap a clip to bring up the Clip Settings menu. It is here that you can add your titles. Tap the top option on the Clip Settings screen (Title Style) to add and edit your title.

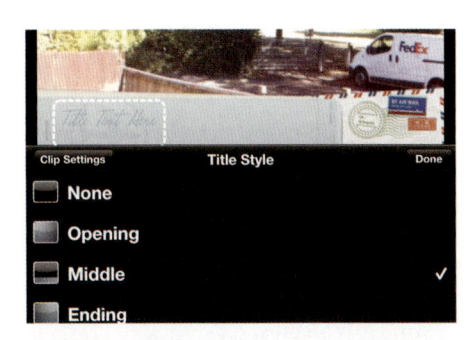

4: Title style
You now have the choice of where in your movie to add the title. Just tap on the one you wish to use (Opening, Middle or Ending). A tick will appear next to the selection you make.

5: Text it
Tap on the text at the top of the screen to edit the field. A keyboard will slide up from the bottom of the screen, and here you can type in what you want your movie title to be.

6: Edit
You can edit the title at any time by returning to this point. Remove the text using the cross button, and you can also activate cut, copy and paste in the same way as normal.

7: View it
Now you can drag the playhead to the start of the clip. Use the play button to watch your clip and view the newly added title. If you're still not happy with it, go back to step six.

8: Transition
When you add a second clip to your project, iMovie will automatically add a transition between this and your first clip. You can select which transition should be used by tapping it.

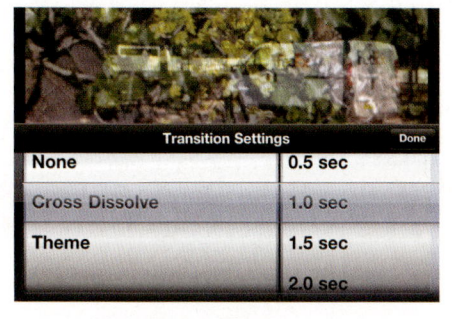

9: Double-tap to edit
Use a double-tap to bring up the Transition Settings to edit the transition. Flick through the available options and pick the one you would like. Return to the movie and play it back to make sure you're happy with it.

iPhone Tips, Tricks, Apps and Hacks **49**

Tips | Tricks | Hacks | Apps

Add a soundtrack to your iMovie project

A quality soundtrack adds professionalism to a film. Here's how to quickly add one to your iMovie creation

Task: How to add background sound to a movie
Difficulty: Intermediate
Time needed: 10 minutes

To most people's eyes, the fact that iMovie exists for the iPhone is something of a triumph in itself. After all, when you stop to think about it, the ability to not only record video on your iPhone but also to edit it on the same hardware – and even export it to YouTube – is incredible. But iMovie for iPhone isn't just an example of how far technology has come. When Apple set up creating an iPhone version of iMovie, it wanted to create a powerful video editor in its own right, not just a cut-down version of its big brother on the Mac. iMovie for iPhone is more powerful than you might think – it just takes a while to learn about its power.

Take audio, for example. You're not limited to the audio track you recorded when you filmed your masterpiece. Each iMovie theme comes with its own soundtrack, which you can optionally add to your movie, but you can also add audio from your iPod app (as long as it is non-DRM music). It also supports multiple audio tracks: as well as the movie's own audio track you can add a background music track and three foreground audio tracks.

Step-by-step | iMovie Adding a soundtrack to iMovie

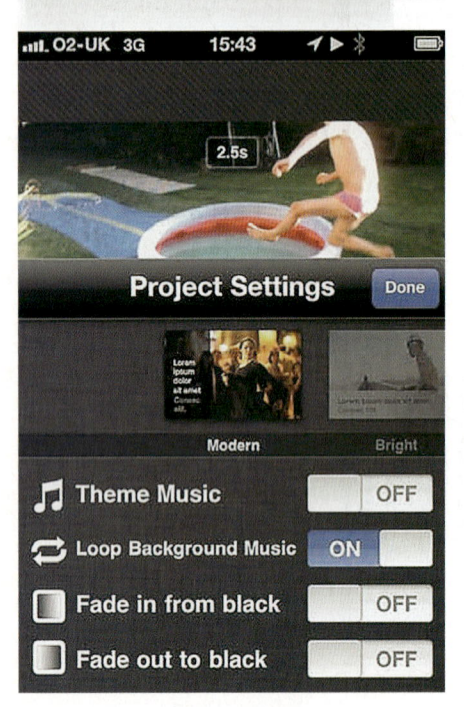

1: Use the built-in option
Tap on the Settings and choose a theme under the Select Theme heading. Set Theme Music to On to automatically add this soundtrack to your movie.

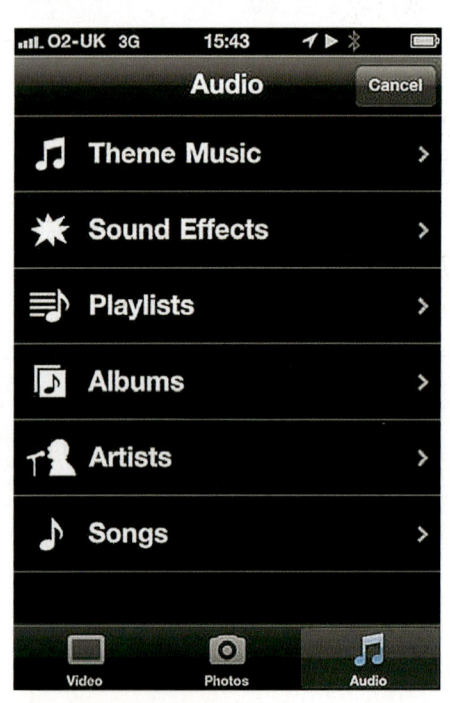

2: Add a sound effect
Tap the Media Library button, and then the Audio button. Tap Sound Effects to reveal a choice of pre-built effects. Tap one to add it to the soundtrack.

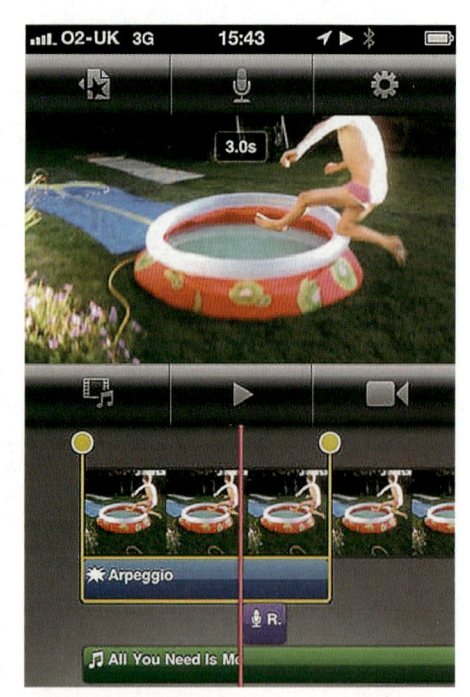

3: Adjusting audio
The effect appears as a blue bar. You can tweak it to fit your video. Tap the audio track and drag the yellow selection handles to adjust its length.

Tips | Tricks | Hacks | Apps

Adding tracks in iMovie

Here's how to add some atmosphere to your movie

● Knowledge base

iMovie's assumptions
How does iMovie distinguish between background and foreground audio? Simple: it treats imported files shorter than a minute as a foreground audio clip – a blue bar – and those longer than a minute as background music – a green bar.

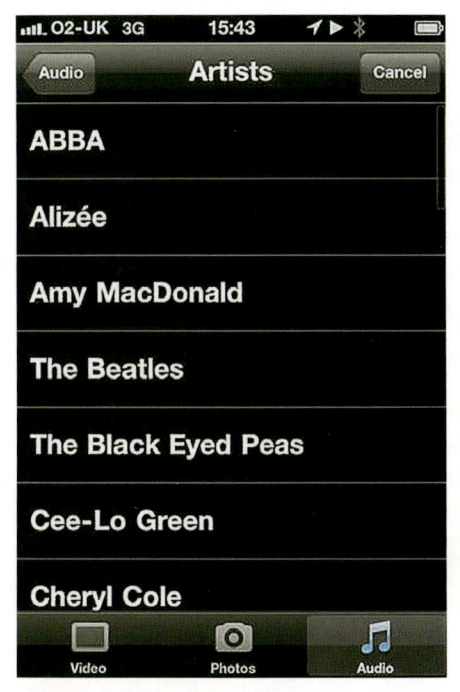

● Adding Theme music
You can add Theme music from the Project Settings window, although you can also add it from the Audio section of the Media Library

● Adding a voiceover
Want to add a voiceover? Tap the Microphone icon and record a track, and it will be added as a foreground audio effect in front of the background audio track

● Recognising audio tracks
Foreground audio clips appear as blue bars in the timeline; voiceovers are purple; and background audio appears as a green bar

● Background adjustments
The background music track has to start at the beginning of your project, and its volume is automatically adjusted when a video clip contains audio

4: Add your own soundtrack
Replace the audio with your choice of music. On the Audio menu tap Playlists, Albums, Artists or Songs to find a track. Tap the name of the clip to add it.

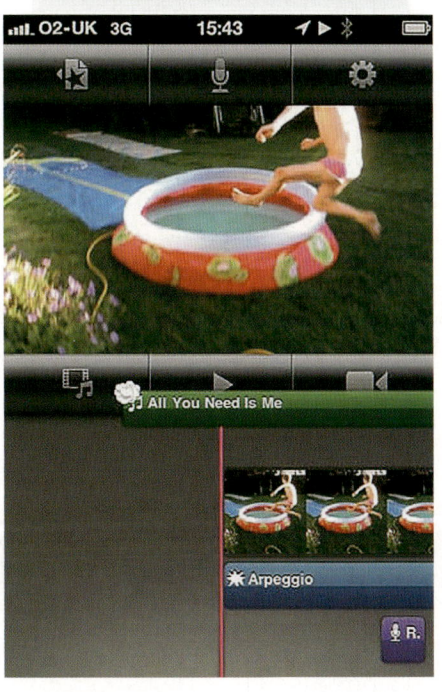

5: Delete audio
Change your mind? You can select another track to replace it, although a quick way to delete it entirely is to drag it away from the timeline.

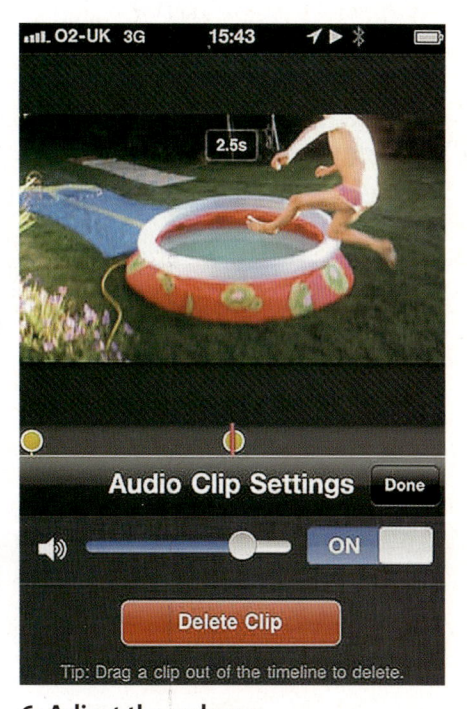

6: Adjust the volume
To adjust the background audio, double-tap the audio track to show a Settings menu. Here, you can adjust the clip's volume, or mute it.

Tips | Tricks | Hacks | Apps

Subscribe to videos you want to watch on YouTube

YouTube can be a jungle to navigate, but there are ways to tame the video giant by subscribing to content

Task: Subscribing to channels in YouTube
Difficulty: Intermediate
Time needed: 10 minutes

YouTube is one of the great successes of social media. It has launched careers, and educated and entertained millions, and the YouTube app on the iPhone is a great way to find and play content.

There's no doubt that you can often find great clips from literally millions of fellow YouTube users, but with gigabytes of content being uploaded every second, it's easy to lose your favourite videos and contacts, or miss the next big viral video. Of course, if you're a YouTube user it's possible to mark particular videos as favourites, so they're always accessible, but what if your favourite video producer creates another hit smash? Or how can you find out if a YouTube contact spots another unmissable video?

The answer is via subscriptions that allow you to follow channels on YouTube. Every member has a channel to house videos they have uploaded, and others that they have added as favourites. Once you're signed in to YouTube you can subscribe to other users' channels. So when a new video appears in that channel, it will appear in your subscription list. Subscriptions carry over between iPhone and desktop computer, so you'll always be close to your favourite videos.

Step-by-step | YouTube Adding subscriptions in YouTube

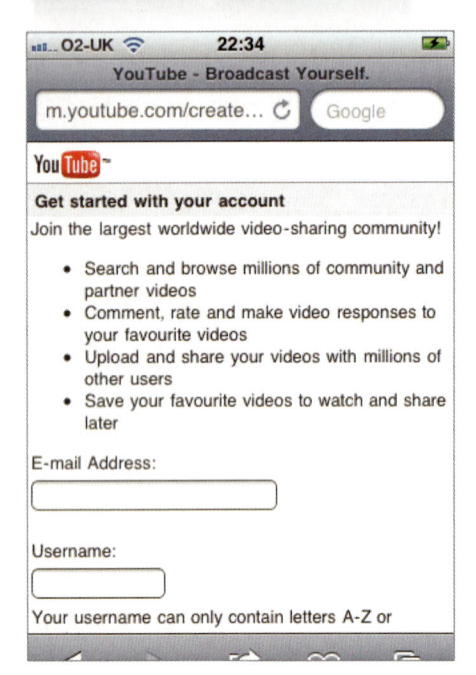

1: Signing up
In Mobile Safari, visit www.youtube.com. Scroll down the home page, tap 'Sign In' and select 'Create an Account Now'. Follow the instructions.

2: Signing in
Launch the YouTube app, tap the More button at the bottom, then tap the 'Sign In' button at the top and enter your user name and password.

3: Begin the search
Now return to the YouTube Home screen and click the 'Search' button at the bottom, where you can search for videos, or for particular users.

52 iPhone Tips, Tricks, Apps and Hacks

Tips | Tricks | Hacks | Apps

Sorting YouTube subscriptions
A look at the options of the YouTube app

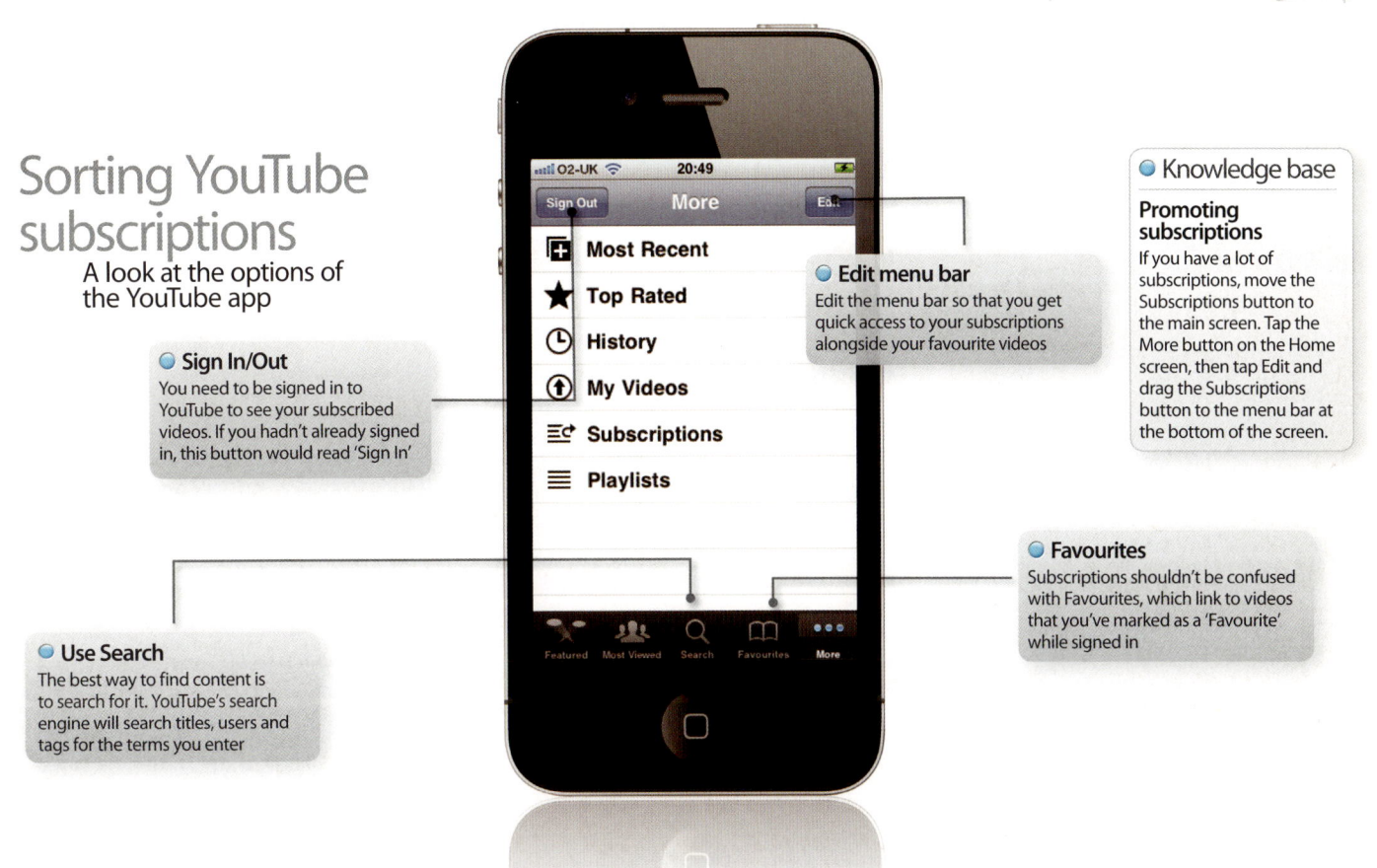

Sign In/Out
You need to be signed in to YouTube to see your subscribed videos. If you hadn't already signed in, this button would read 'Sign In'

Use Search
The best way to find content is to search for it. YouTube's search engine will search titles, users and tags for the terms you enter

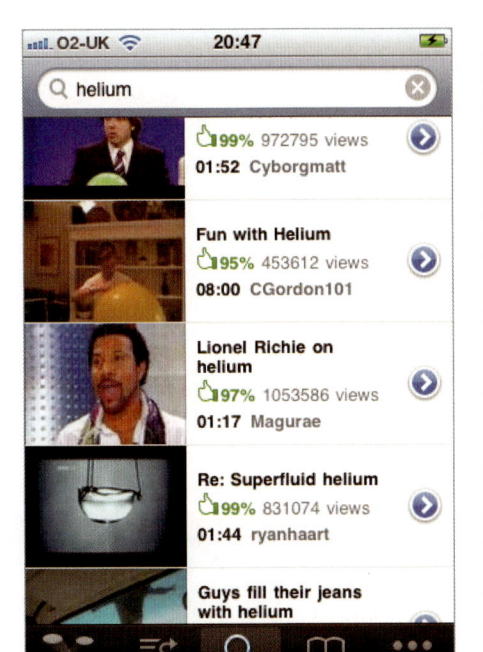

Edit menu bar
Edit the menu bar so that you get quick access to your subscriptions alongside your favourite videos

Knowledge base

Promoting subscriptions
If you have a lot of subscriptions, move the Subscriptions button to the main screen. Tap the More button on the Home screen, then tap Edit and drag the Subscriptions button to the menu bar at the bottom of the screen.

Favourites
Subscriptions shouldn't be confused with Favourites, which link to videos that you've marked as a 'Favourite' while signed in

4: Homing in
YouTube Search will return a list of videos. When you find the one you want to subscribe to tap the blue and white arrow button to the right of it.

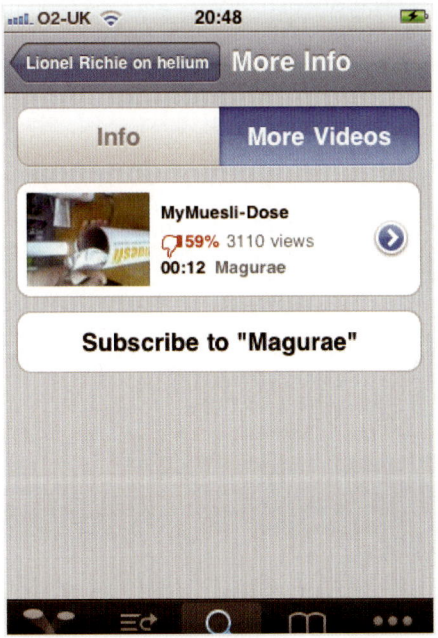

5: Getting subscribed
On the next screen tap the blue and white arrow and tap 'More Videos'. At the bottom of the screen there's an option to subscribe to the user's channel.

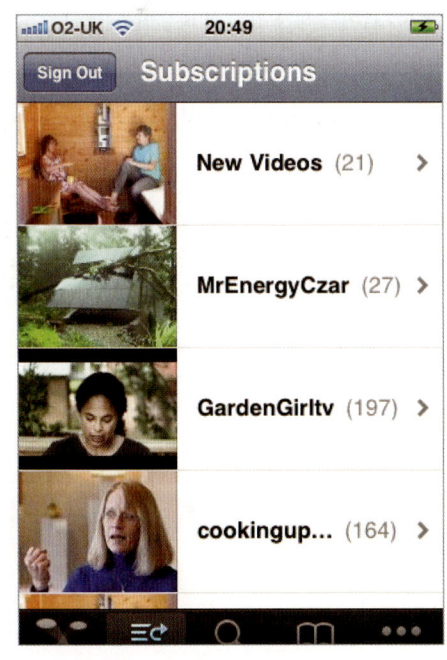

6: Check your subscriptions
Tap this button and that user's videos will be added to your list. Tap the Subscription button and you'll now see the videos that you're subscribed to.

iPhone Tips, Tricks, Apps and Hacks **53**

Tips | Tricks | Hacks | Apps

Broadcast footage of yourself live to the world

With the help of uStream you can now become a roving reporter, video podcaster or anything else you want to be. It's almost too easy

Task: Learn how to broadcast video
Difficulty: Beginner
Time needed: 10 minutes

The popularity of YouTube proves that millions of people want to get themselves seen on the internet, but the process of actually uploading newly created videos could be easier. uStream takes the idea further by allowing anyone to upload videos of themselves for others to view and even better, you can stream your videos live to the masses.

All you need is a wireless connection, a mobile device and you are good to go with a service that works extremely well no matter where you are. Videos can be scheduled so that your viewers will know when to start watching, which will help you gain more viewers over time if you make the description of your 'show' interesting enough.

Broadcasting live to many people is now extremely easy to do with an iPhone or iPad, but nothing beats the confidence of completing a few videos which will make your creations more watchable. With some free software and a mobile device, we have reached the point where everyone can report live on what is happening around them and it is a lot easier than you may think.

Step-by-step | uStream Broadcast from your phone

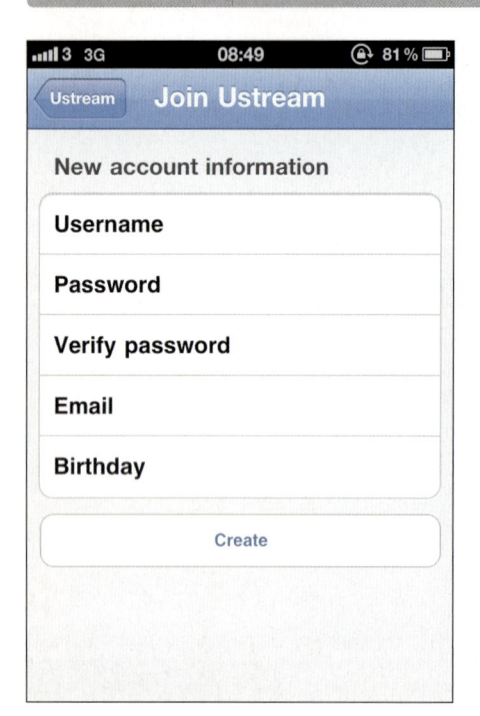

1: Get an account
Open the uStream app and tap the More icon. Slide the uStream slider to On and tap the 'Sign up' button. Fill in your personal details.

2: Check the settings
The default settings will work for most people, but it is worth checking to see if you would prefer to change some to suit your needs.

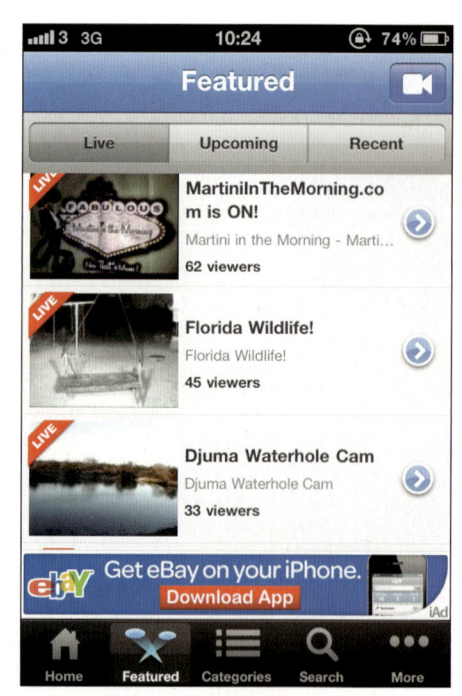

3: Familiarise yourself
Look at the current live streaming videos by going to Featured and pressing the Live tab. You can then gauge what people are currently watching.

54 | iPhone Tips, Tricks, Apps and Hacks

Tips | Tricks | Hacks | Apps

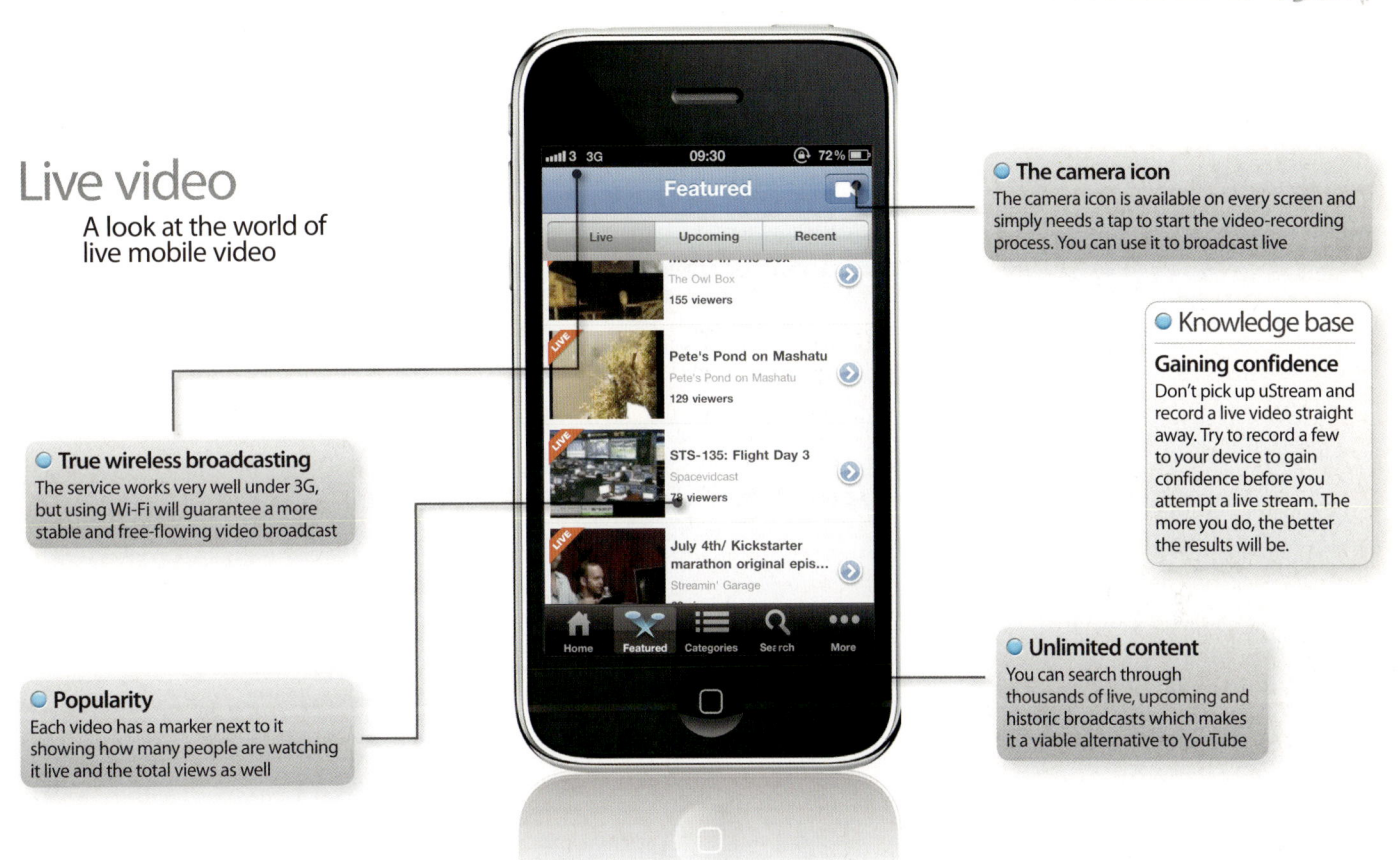

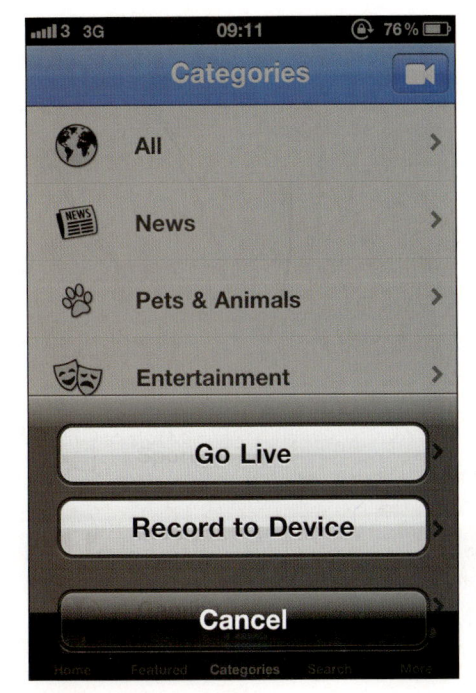

Live video
A look at the world of live mobile video

The camera icon
The camera icon is available on every screen and simply needs a tap to start the video-recording process. You can use it to broadcast live

Knowledge base

Gaining confidence
Don't pick up uStream and record a live video straight away. Try to record a few to your device to gain confidence before you attempt a live stream. The more you do, the better the results will be.

True wireless broadcasting
The service works very well under 3G, but using Wi-Fi will guarantee a more stable and free-flowing video broadcast

Unlimited content
You can search through thousands of live, upcoming and historic broadcasts which makes it a viable alternative to YouTube

Popularity
Each video has a marker next to it showing how many people are watching it live and the total views as well

4: The serious stuff
At the top of every screen is a camera icon. When you tap it you are given the option to Go Live or to record a video. Choose the record option first.

5: Start recording
Tap the red circle and start recording. When you have finished tap the icon again and you will be offered the opportunity to share it with one click.

6: Time to share
Once saved, go to More and tap My Broadcasts. You can now upload to uStream, delete or share the videos via Twitter and Facebook.

iPhone Tips, Tricks, Apps and Hacks **55**

Tips | Tricks | Hacks | Apps

Play and record guitar tracks through your iPhone

It is not always convenient to carry a recording studio with you, but now you can play and record guitar tracks through an iPhone

Task: Capture your guitar tracks on an iPhone
Difficulty: Intermediate
Time needed: 15 minutes

Serious, and not so serious, guitarists have to contend with a lot when it comes to creating new tracks or trying to perfect a song. Time can be a constraint, but an even bigger problem is the fact that it is incredibly difficult to capture what is being played on a guitar without sophisticated recording equipment. Thankfully, this can now all be achieved using the iPhone and a simple attachment which allows it to capture what is being played no matter where you are. AmpliTube is an app that works in conjunction with an accessory called the iRig. The iRig is attached to the iPhone via the headphone socket and the other end attaches to the output on a guitar. It is no larger than a standard cable and cheap at under £30, and will give you everything you need to record guitar tracks when the right moment arrives.

The number of features included within AmpliTube is almost bewildering and while professional guitarists will get the most from the app, it can also act as an aid to help you learn new songs and play them back. If you want to record guitar tracks on the move, this is the way to do it.

Step-by-step | AmpliTube Record guitar tracks on an iPhone

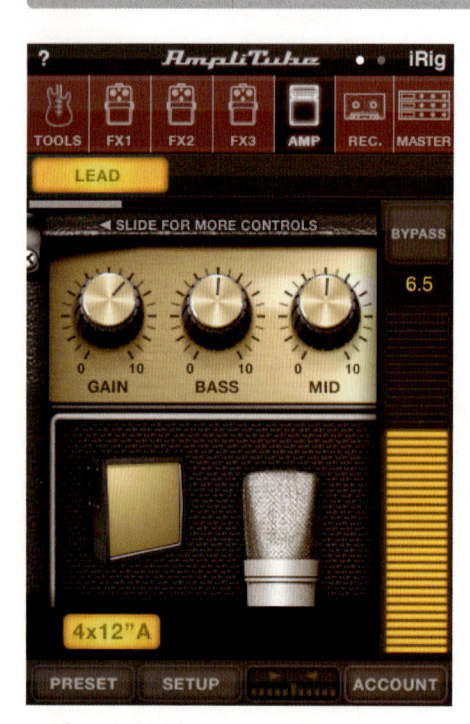

1: The controls
When you open the app, set the levels in the 'Amp' section. You may have to play around a little until everything sounds right to you.

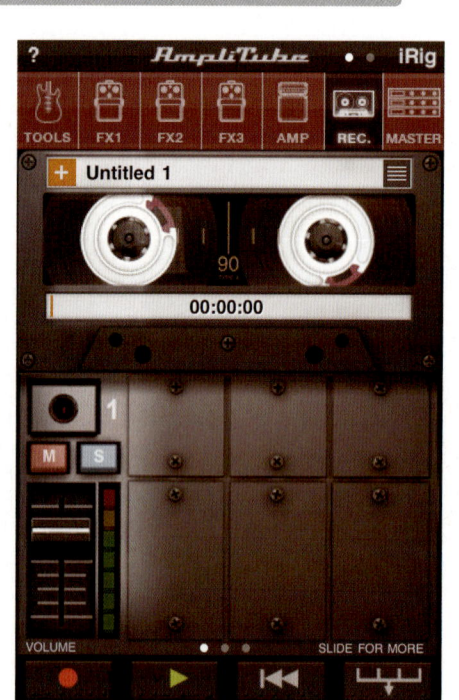

2: Capturing the moment
The 'Rec' function at the top lets you quickly record a track. You will see the tape spin and you can also play back your captured tracks from this section.

3: Clever effects
Set up and store multiple effects by choosing one of the 'FX' tabs at the top. Each song may require a different sound so this really speeds up the process.

Tips | Tricks | Hacks | Apps

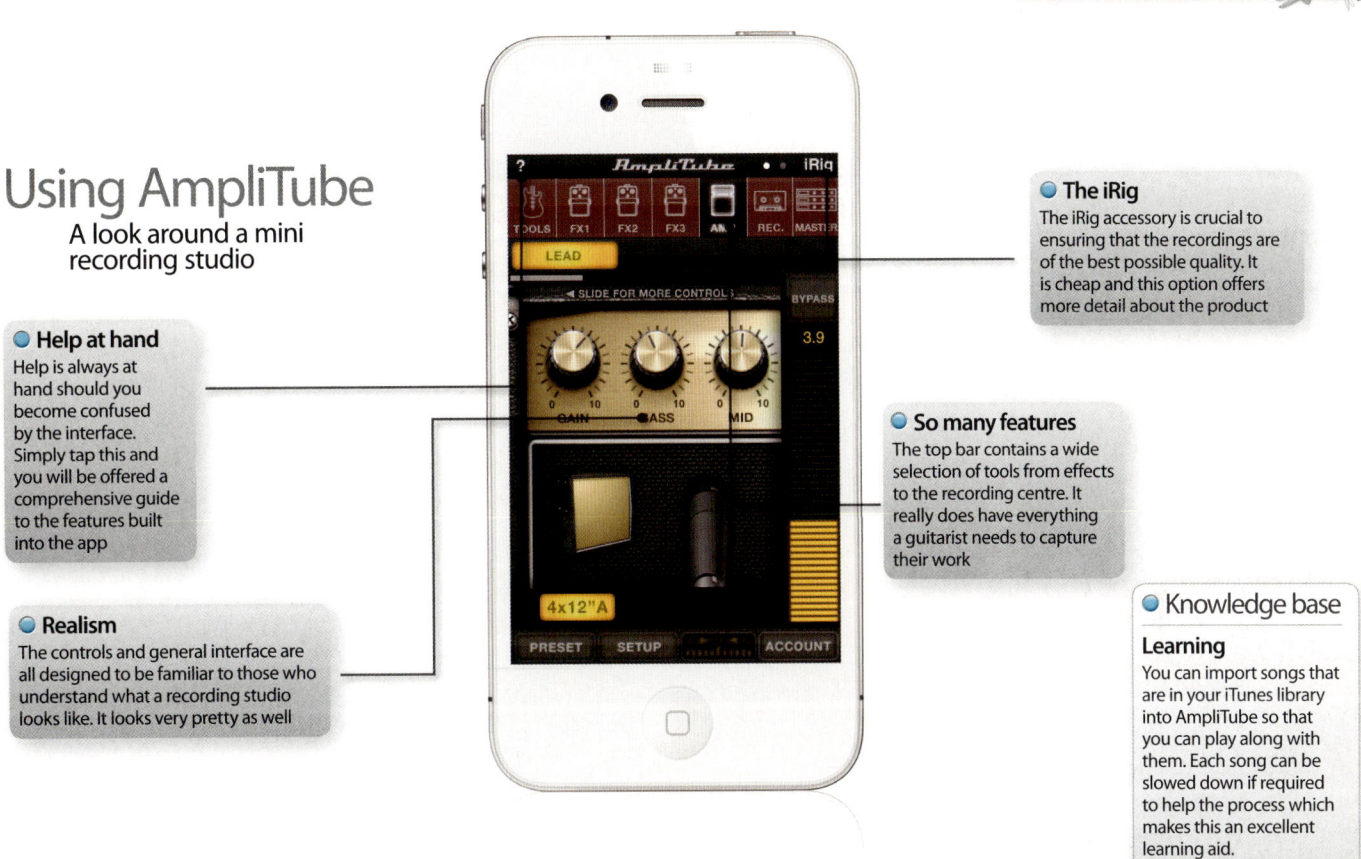

Using AmpliTube
A look around a mini recording studio

● Help at hand
Help is always at hand should you become confused by the interface. Simply tap this and you will be offered a comprehensive guide to the features built into the app

● Realism
The controls and general interface are all designed to be familiar to those who understand what a recording studio looks like. It looks very pretty as well

● The iRig
The iRig accessory is crucial to ensuring that the recordings are of the best possible quality. It is cheap and this option offers more detail about the product

● So many features
The top bar contains a wide selection of tools from effects to the recording centre. It really does have everything a guitarist needs to capture their work

● Knowledge base
Learning
You can import songs that are in your iTunes library into AmpliTube so that you can play along with them. Each song can be slowed down if required to help the process which makes this an excellent learning aid.

4: The master
Use 'Master' to tweak the sound to the point that the finished recordings could be usable outside of the confines of the iPhone.

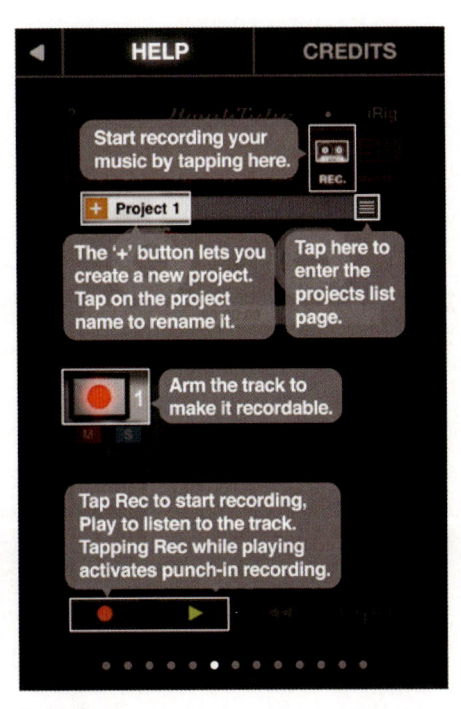

5: Help!
The interface is a little crowded, so simply tap the '?' in the top left-hand corner to view a selection of guides which will get you around the app quicker.

6: Taking it further
Selecting the 'Add Gear' option lets you purchase additional amp effects and even specialised virtual equipment to make the exact sound you want.

iPhone Tips, Tricks, Apps and Hacks **57**

Tips | Tricks | Hacks | Apps

Add and delete locations from Weather

The Weather app helps you choose whether to plan a barbeque or turn the central heating on. But you'll get best results by customising it

Task: How to edit locations in the Weather app
Difficulty: Beginner
Time needed: 5 minutes

The iPhone's Weather app is one of the more popular default apps. It provides an overview of the temperature highs and lows over the upcoming week, and its prognosis is generally accurate.

The only trouble is that the default Weather app settings – in particular the places that it covers – aren't much use to you; unless, of course you happen to live in Cupertino, California. It isn't difficult to add your home town though.

You can even see what the weather's like in your favourite holiday destination, while setting the app up to keep track of other towns and cities you're interested in, and can quickly switch between them to compare forecasts just by flicking your finger across the screen. However, there are a few things to watch for when editing your list of locations on Weather. For example, there are often several places around the world that share the same name, and it's very easy to select the wrong one.

Here's how to configure the Weather app so that it shows just the destinations you're interested in and no others.

Step-by-step | Weather Editing places in Weather

1: The default settings
The iPhone's Weather app comes with some default locations that you might not need, but it's easy to add your own.

2: Editing the list
Tap the small 'i' button at the bottom right-hand corner of the window screen to open the Settings panel where you can add and remove locations.

3: Adding locations
To add a location, tap the '+' button. Start entering the name of a town or city in the search field. Often it's even quicker to enter a postcode/zip code.

Tips | Tricks | Hacks | Apps

Editing places in Weather
A look at Weather's location settings

● **How many places?**
There's no limit to the number of cities or places that Weather can track, but performance is likely to be better with a smaller number

● **Borrowed services**
Weather information isn't supplied by Apple. Instead it comes courtesy of the internet giant Yahoo!. Weather connects to its servers each time you launch the app

● **Deleting**
Deleting an errant place name is easy: just tap the Delete button. If you change your mind you can easily add it again later

● **Fahrenheit or Celsius?**
Weather tracks temperatures by default in the Fahrenheit scale. If you're more comfortable with Celsius, switch to it by tapping the °C button

● **Knowledge base**
Not enough detail?
If you want a bit more detail in your weather reports, try tapping the Yahoo! icon on the main weather screen. This takes you to Yahoo!'s website, which provides information about humidity, wind and even sunset and sunrise.

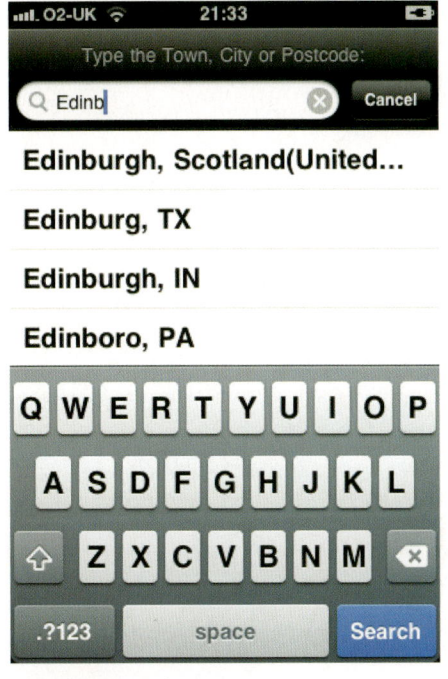

4: Validating locations
As you type the place name, the app will try to match locations, and begins displaying these as a list. Tap on the name of the location to add it.

5: Deleting locations
To delete a city, click on the small 'i' button. In the resulting list, tap the red box next to the place name and tap Delete to the right of the place name.

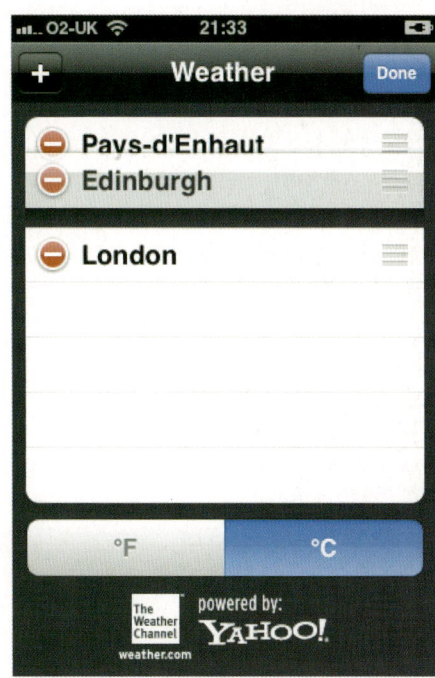

6: Re-ordering weather
Adjusting the order in which cities appear is simple. In the list of places tap and drag the icon on the right to reorganise the list.

iPhone Tips, Tricks, Apps and Hacks 59

Tips | Tricks | Hacks | Apps

Sync your iCal with your iPhone

It's a busy world, and you need to keep on top of your appointments. Here's how you can keep iCal and your iPhone in sync

Task: How to sync your iPhone with iCal
Difficulty: Beginner
Time needed: 10 minutes

The Mac's iCal application makes it easy to keep organised. It's powerful too, supporting multiple calendars, invitations and reminders. But its real value lies in its ability to sync with your iPhone to keep your whole life in sync wherever you are.

In fact, the iPhone's Calendar can sync with Outlook on the PC as well as iCal on the Mac, and whenever you connect your iPhone to your desktop computer using its USB cable events are synchronised between the two. But who wants to be tethered? If you schedule your life using a calendar service offered by Apple, you can synchronise your calendars between Mac and iPhone over the air – no need for a cable – so your diary will be up to date wherever you are.

There are various options available for 'over the air' syncing, and many of them are free. The choices include Apple's iCloud, which is replacing its venerable MobileMe service at the time of writing, as well as Yahoo! and Google. The advantage of these services is that they store the information you add to their calendars remotely. When you add an event on iCal it can be automatically uploaded to the cloud and synced with your iPhone's Calendar app.

Step-by-step | Calendar Sync your iPhone calendar

1: Sync with iTunes
Connect your iPhone to your Mac or PC. Launch iTunes, and under the Devices tab on the left of the iTunes window click your iPhone's icon.

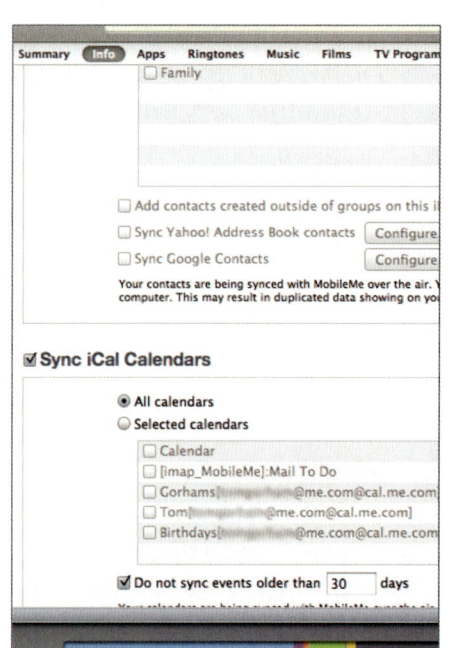

2: Sync your calendar
Under the Info tab, check the 'Sync iCal Calendars' box and click Apply. This will sync iCal between the desktop and your iPhone.

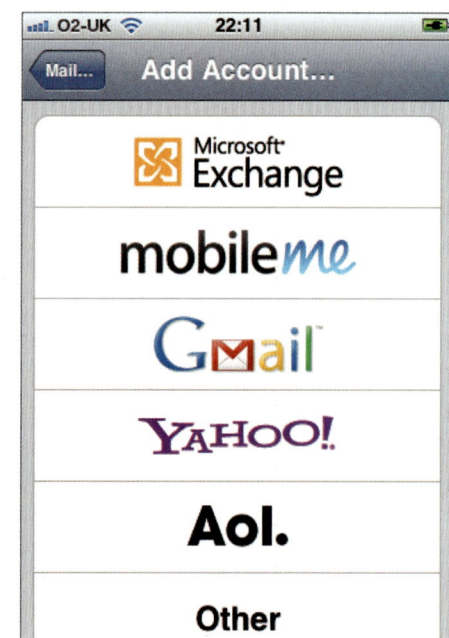

3: Sync over the air
Here, you'll need a service such as MobileMe. Open Settings>Mail Contacts>Calendars. To set up a new account, tap 'Add Account' and follow instructions.

60 iPhone Tips, Tricks, Apps and Hacks

Tips | Tricks | Hacks | Apps

Adding events in Calendar
How the iPhone's Calendar app works

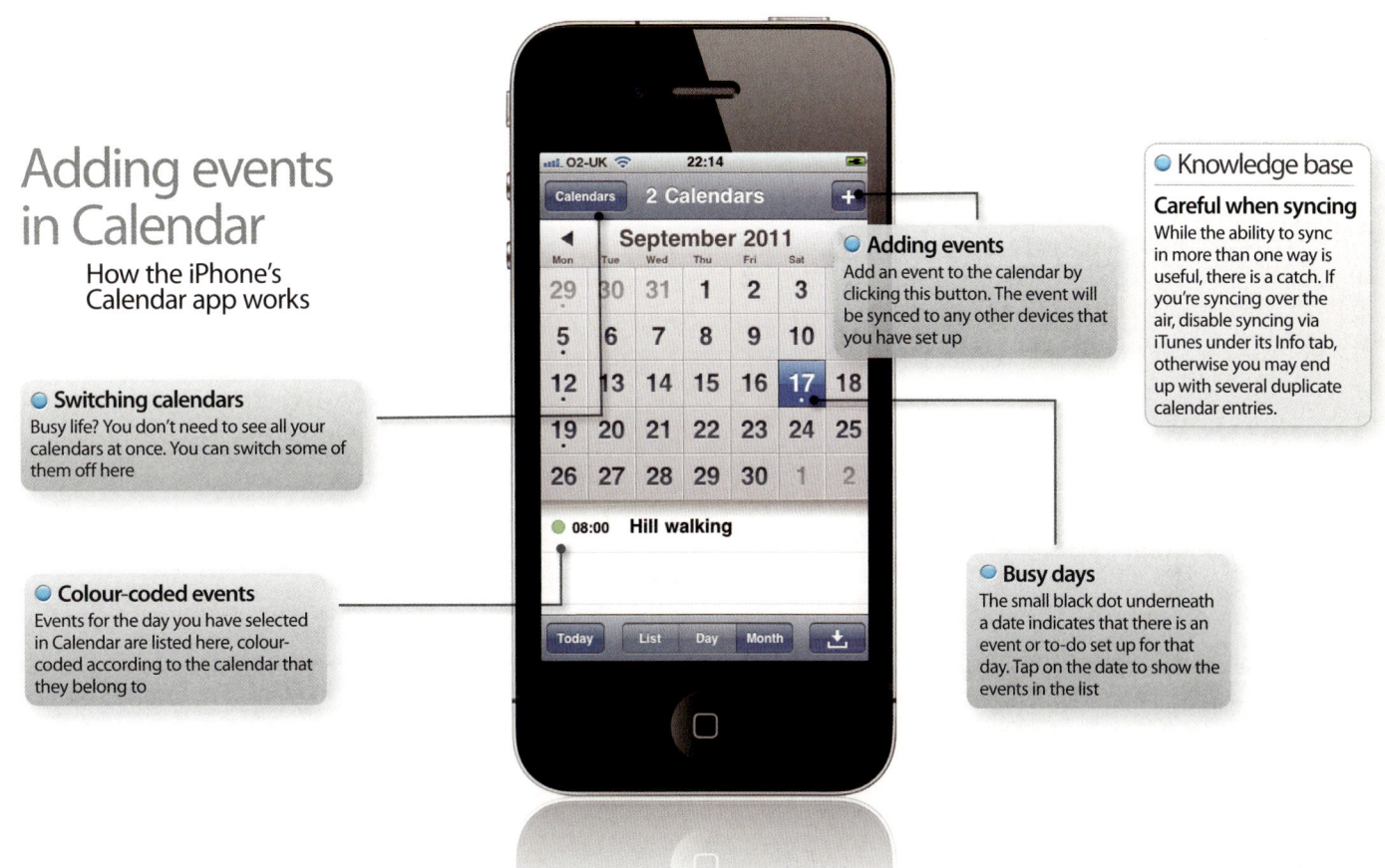

Switching calendars
Busy life? You don't need to see all your calendars at once. You can switch some of them off here

Colour-coded events
Events for the day you have selected in Calendar are listed here, colour-coded according to the calendar that they belong to

Adding events
Add an event to the calendar by clicking this button. The event will be synced to any other devices that you have set up

Knowledge base
Careful when syncing
While the ability to sync in more than one way is useful, there is a catch. If you're syncing over the air, disable syncing via iTunes under its Info tab, otherwise you may end up with several duplicate calendar entries.

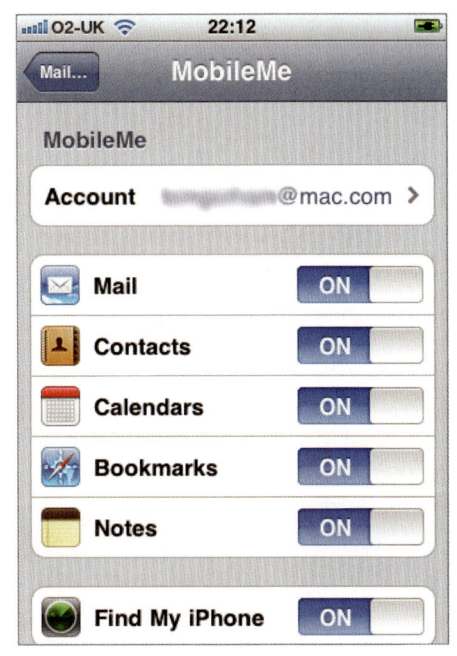

Busy days
The small black dot underneath a date indicates that there is an event or to-do set up for that day. Tap on the date to show the events in the list

4: Turning on calendars
If you have an account, select the one you'd like to sync to, and tap the Calendars option to turn it on. Events you add on your iPhone will now be synced.

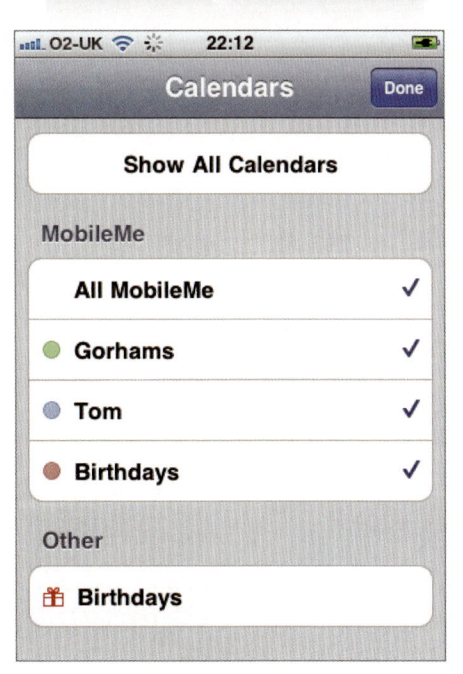

5: Limiting calendars
You subscribe to all calendars on the account, but you can limit which appear on your iPhone; tap Calendars and deselect any you don't want.

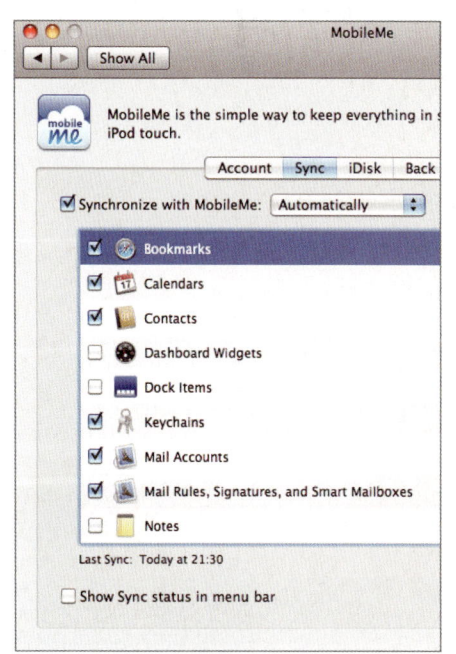

6: Syncing with Mac
If you're syncing using MobileMe on Mac, open the MobileMe System Preferences. Log in, click Sync and ensure that the Calendars box is checked.

iPhone Tips, Tricks, Apps and Hacks **61**

Tips | Tricks | Hacks | Apps

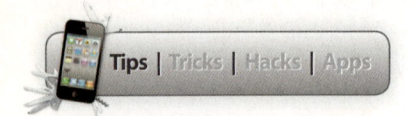

Improve your fitness using your iPhone

Nike+ GPS users can track and time a run, race against the clock or challenge online opponents via the Nike+ online community

Task: Get fit with your iPhone
Difficulty: Beginner
Time needed: 5 minutes

A GPS can track position, record distance travelled and even calculate speed of movement from A to B. All the essential information needed for a runner to keep a record of their goals and achievements. The Nike+ app teams up with GPS to track both indoor and outdoor workouts and runs. Users can run against the clock or set a specified distance. At the start of a run, users simply hit the start button and end when finished. The app then puts together a summary with distance travelled, pace achieved, time taken and calories burned.

Looking a little further, users can tag a run, recording how they felt, the type of weather and terrain, and store this all in History. Next time out users can challenge themselves to go faster, further and longer. To make each step just that little bit easier and inspire a runner to keep going, there is the option to add in a soundtrack and even a Powersong. The seriously competitive can sign up to Nikeplus.com to store runs and challenge the online community.

Step-by-step | Nike+ GPS Keep a record of runs with Nike+ GPS

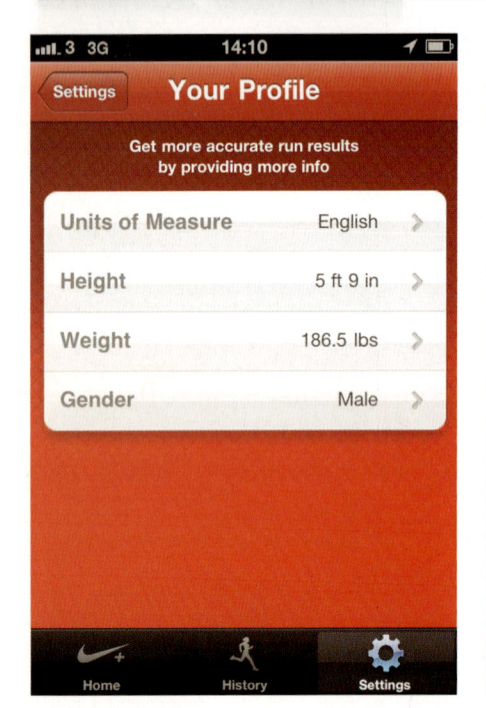

1: Your Profile
To set up Nike+, tap Settings>Your Profile and add stats and gender before setting the distance unit, adding a Powersong and setting voice feedback.

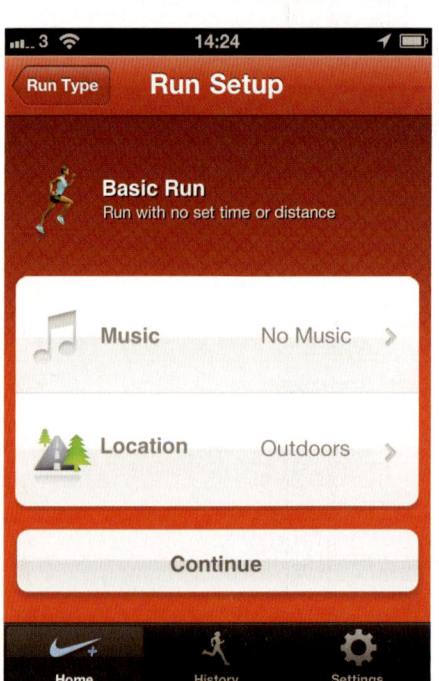

2: Start basic run
Tap Start a New Run, then Basic to view Basic Run options; tap Music to select a playlist; and Location to select Outdoors or Indoors. Tap Continue.

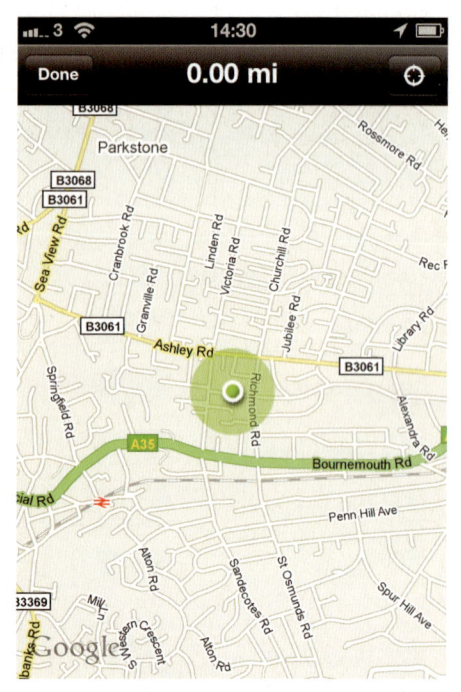

3: Start running
The GPS will find the current location. Tap the Basic Run button to start the clock and record speed and distance. Tap View Map to view current location.

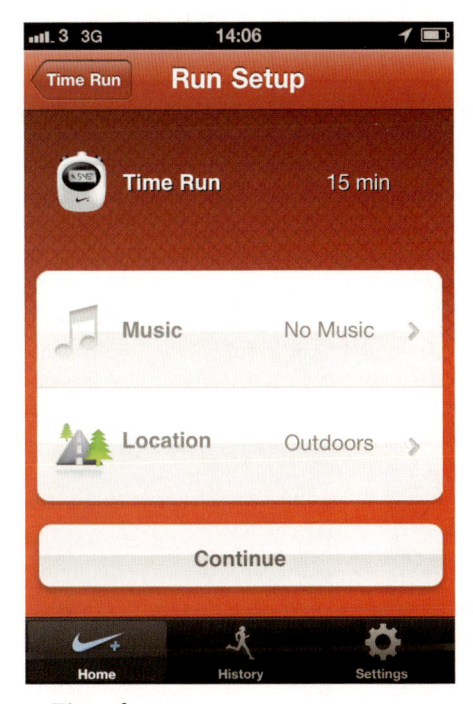

Tips | Tricks | Hacks | Apps

4: Timed run
To time a run select Time and choose one of the options. Alternatively, select Custom, set a time frame and tap Done. Tap Time Run to start.

5: Set run distance
To use a pre-defined distance select Distance and choose an option. Or tap Custom, select a mile marker and hit Done. Tap Distance Run to start.

6: Run summary
To end a run tap the End Workout button and a summary appears. This will give the distance travelled, pace, time, and calories burned.

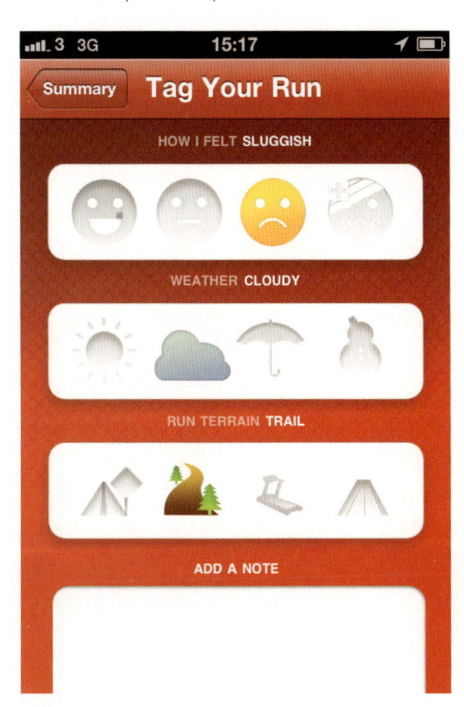

7: Tag a run
Tap How was your run? To view the Tag Your Run screen tap the icon for each category. If desired add a note to give a more detailed description.

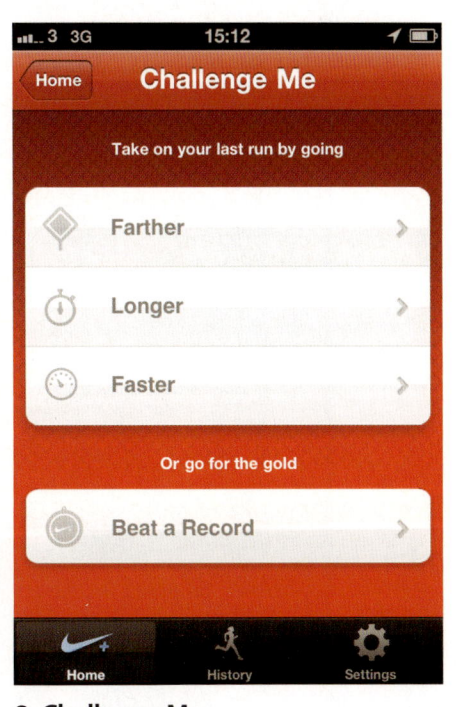

8: Challenge Me
After a single run Challenge Me appears – tap to view. Tap Farther, Longer and Faster or Beat a Record for more run suggestions.

9: History
A completed run is stored in History. Tap History to view runs and tap a run to view a summary. Tap Edit to remove runs from History.

iPhone Tips, Tricks, Apps and Hacks **63**

Tips | **Tricks** | Hacks | Apps

Tricks
Uncover the secrets of your iPhone and use it in ways you never expected

- **66** Wirelessly share photos, contacts and messages
- **68** Send photos from your camera to your iPhone
- **70** Transfer media directly to your iPad
- **72** Watch videos using Home Sharing
- **74** Stream audio and video
- **76** Turn your iPhone into a universal remote control
- **78** Share files wirelessy from your iPhone to your Mac
- **80** Use your iPhone as a mouse for your Mac
- **82** Turn your handwriting into text on an iPhone
- **84** Scan documents using your iPhone
- **86** Use your iPhone to scan barcodes
- **88** Translate text and understand foreign signs
- **90** Discover your geographical location
- **92** Identify and purchase a song in an instant
- **94** Test your eyesight with your iPhone
- **96** Measure your heart rate on the move

"Your iPhone can even test your eyesight"

88 Translate foreign text and signs

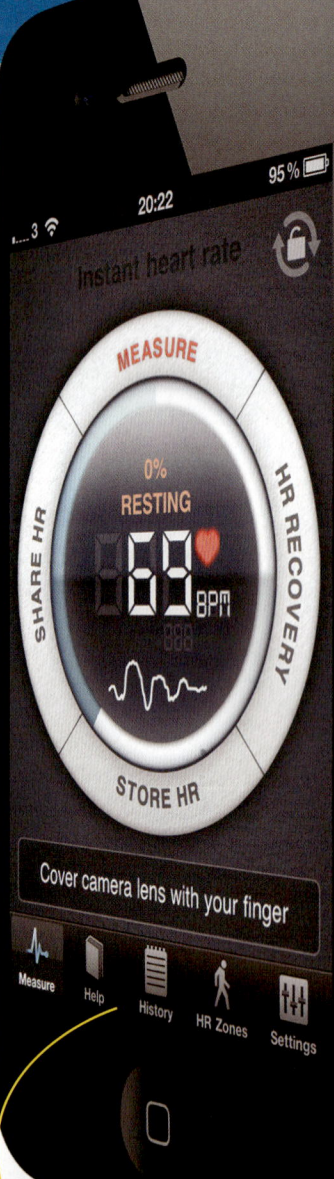

96 Measure your heart rate with your iPhone

64 iPhone Tips, Tricks, Apps and Hacks

Tips | **Tricks** | Hacks | Apps

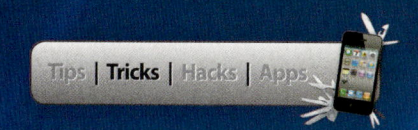

92 Identify a song and purchase it

HOT TRICKS
- ✔ Stream videos
- ✔ Control your TV
- ✔ Scan barcodes
- ✔ Test eyesight
- ✔ Transfer media

70 Transfer photos directly to your iPad

iPhone Tips, Tricks, Apps and Hacks **65**

Tips | **Tricks** | Hacks | Apps

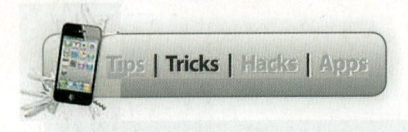

Wirelessly share photos, contacts and messages

You can now share all sorts of files and media by simply touching two devices together. It is easy to use and flawless in execution

Task: Share anything without wires
Difficulty: Beginner
Time needed: 5 minutes

There was a time in the early days of mobile computing that sharing files with other devices required fiddling with complicated settings and the use of infrared to share information. It was painfully slow and in time was replaced with mobile email and social networks. However, there is nothing quite like sharing information with friends when you are next to them, and this is where Bump comes in. It is a free app that lets you share files, photos, calendar entries, music and almost anything else by simply touching two devices together. This alone sounds impressive, but the speed at which it works takes sharing to a whole new level. Bump will quickly become your preferred method of sharing information when you are close to others.

You can search through your address book to find friends who use Bump, and this in turn lets you use the app as an instant messenger, which is a nice bonus. Sharing media with those around you is not an activity you will undertake all of the time, but Bump is incredibly handy when the time arrives, and it's likely to will stay on your device forever more thanks to its efficiency and ease of use.

Step-by-step | Bump Share files with anyone

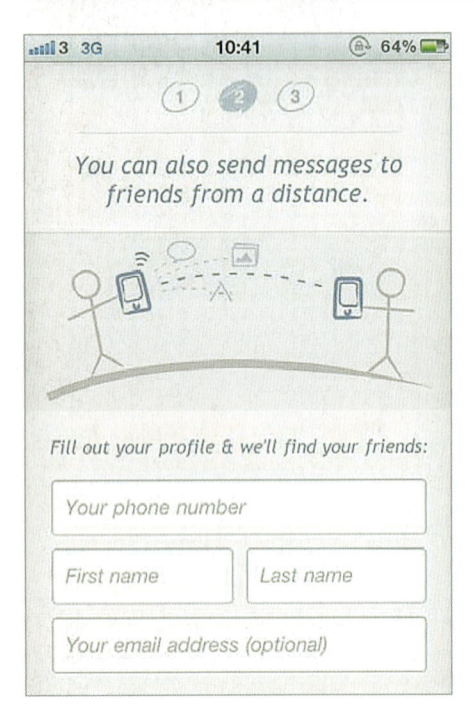

1: Setting up
First, fill out your profile so that friends who use Bump can find you. The email address is optional if you are concerned about spam.

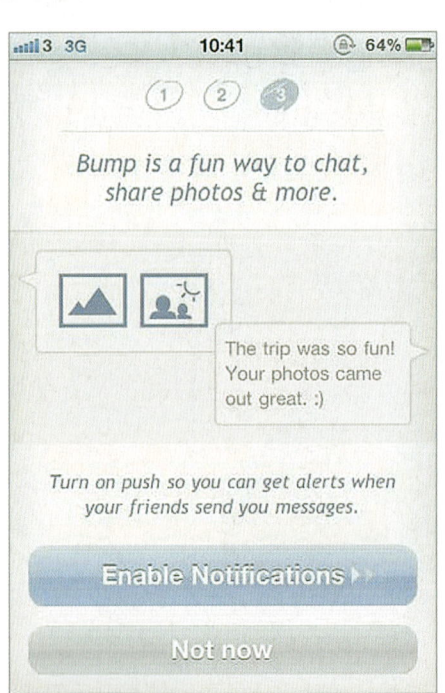

2: Notifications
Enable Notifications so that friends can instant message you. This could save you from having to use more than one messenger service.

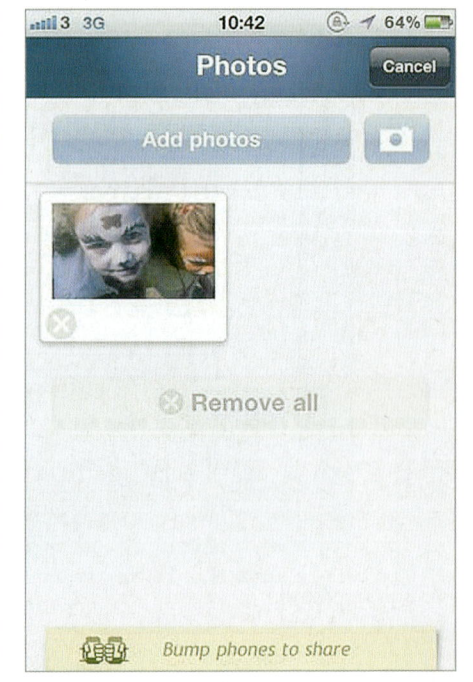

3: Sharing
When near someone using Bump, choose the media you want to share and add it to the pane. A notification appears at the bottom of the screen.

66 iPhone Tips, Tricks, Apps and Hacks

Tips | Tricks | Hacks | Apps

Sharing files with Bump
Getting the most out of the app's features

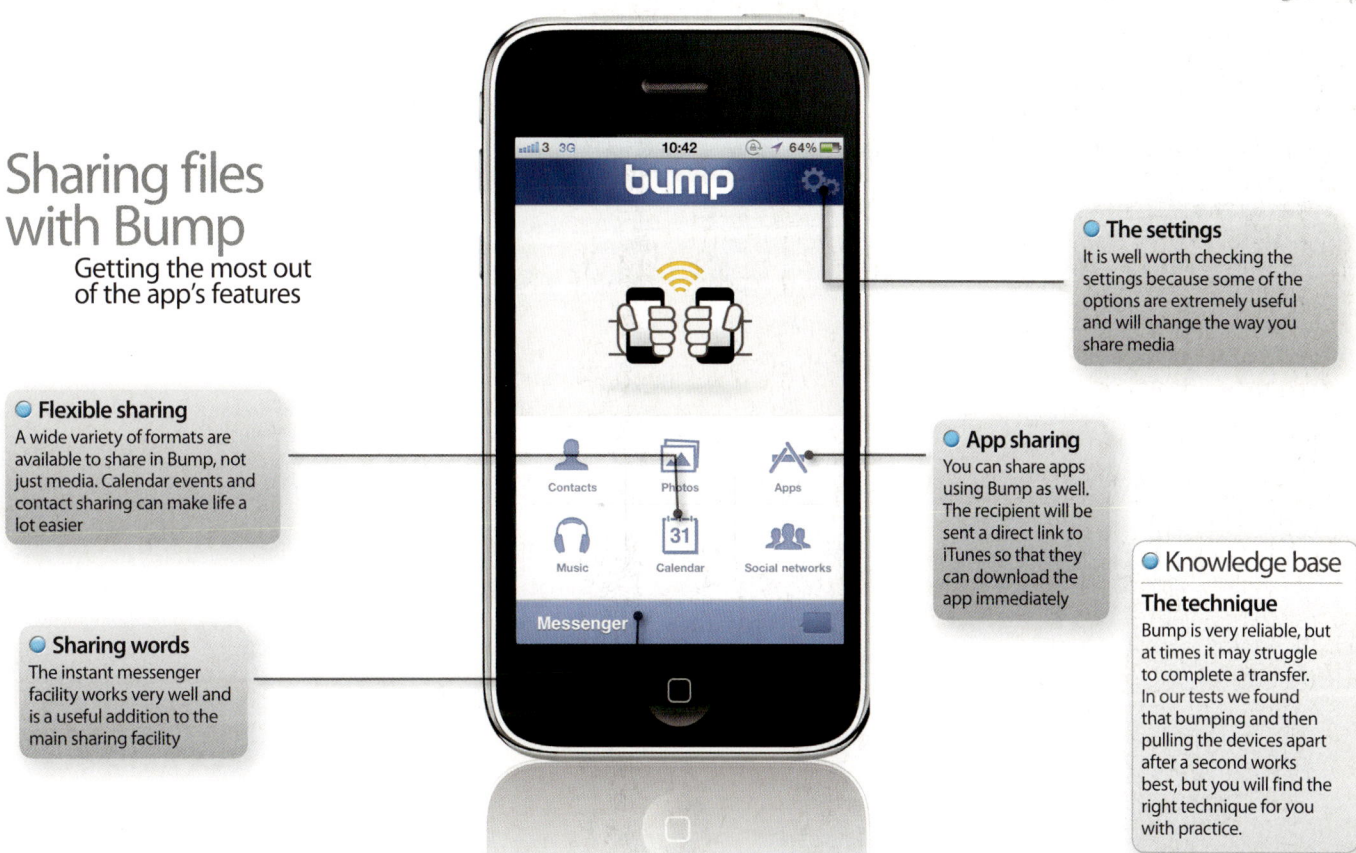

Flexible sharing
A wide variety of formats are available to share in Bump, not just media. Calendar events and contact sharing can make life a lot easier

Sharing words
The instant messenger facility works very well and is a useful addition to the main sharing facility

The settings
It is well worth checking the settings because some of the options are extremely useful and will change the way you share media

App sharing
You can share apps using Bump as well. The recipient will be sent a direct link to iTunes so that they can download the app immediately

Knowledge base

The technique
Bump is very reliable, but at times it may struggle to complete a transfer. In our tests we found that bumping and then pulling the devices apart after a second works best, but you will find the right technique for you with practice.

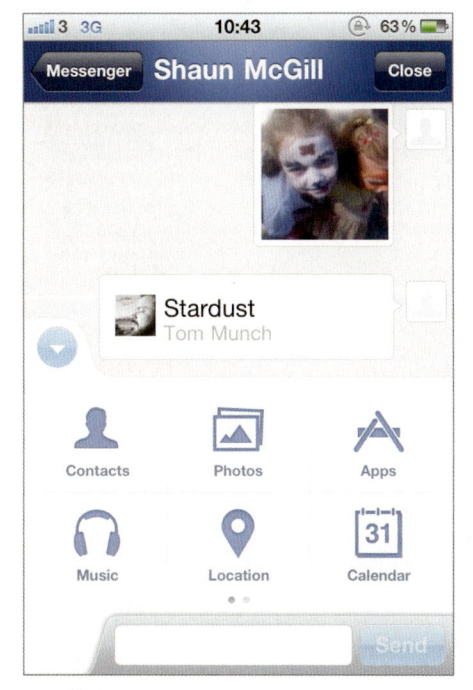

4: All done
You will see the sharing happen in real-time (and in many cases immediately). You can choose from a variety of options and can even share apps.

5: Bumping into others
Use Bump to search your address book and highlight others with Bump activated. This lets you see who is using it when in a crowd of people.

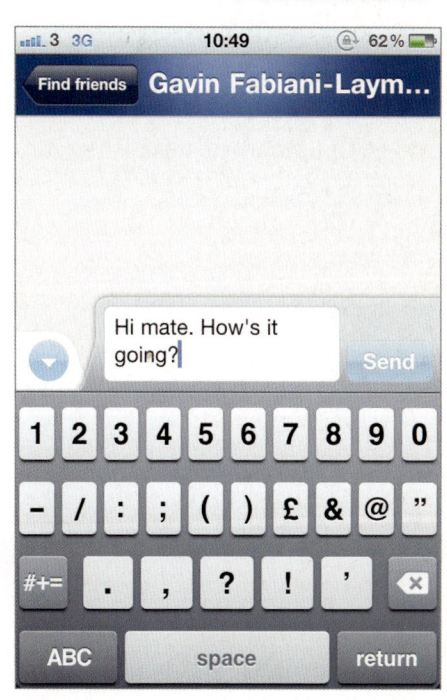

6: Speaking and sharing
Instant messaging works very well and lets you share speech as well as files with contacts. It sits perfectly next to the main physical sharing facility.

iPhone Tips, Tricks, Apps and Hacks **67**

Tips | **Tricks** | Hacks | Apps

Send photos from your camera to your iPhone

Using the incredibly cool Eye-Fi SD card, you can send hi-res pictures directly to your iPhone as soon as they're taken

Task: Send photos directly to your iPhone
Difficulty: Intermediate
Time needed: 20 minutes

Modern technology is a marvel – you've only to swipe to unlock your iPhone to learn that lesson – but that shouldn't stop you taking greater strides and investing in technology that can change the way you use everyday items, like your digital camera. When the digital camera was conceived, it got rid of the need for a dark room, speeding the viewing and storing process up by an unthinkable amount. The Eye-Fi SD card is the next great leap, making wires a thing of the past.

This orange SD card has its own Wi-Fi system that can send pictures directly to your iPhone (or computer) via a dedicated app. What's more, you don't even need to be on a Wi-Fi network as the card will generate its own when there isn't one around. The system takes a while to set up but, once it's done, you'll be blown away by the simplicity, ease and functionality of being able to use your camera and then having those deliciously crisp shots pop up on your iPhone in a few seconds. You will need to set the Eye-Fi card up on your home computer first of all, to register the product and set up an account.

Step-by-step | Eye-Fi Instantly share snaps

1: Download and open
Download the free Eye-Fi app from the App Store and then load it (you will have already set the card up on your computer). Log in using your details.

2: Time and Wi-Fi
The system will work over 3G when connecting to the server but is much faster using Wi-Fi, which will not cost you any of your mobile data plan.

3: Get pairing
Tap the button to commence card pairing with your iPhone. You can also do this with any other iOS device, although apps may differ.

Tips | **Tricks** | Hacks | Apps

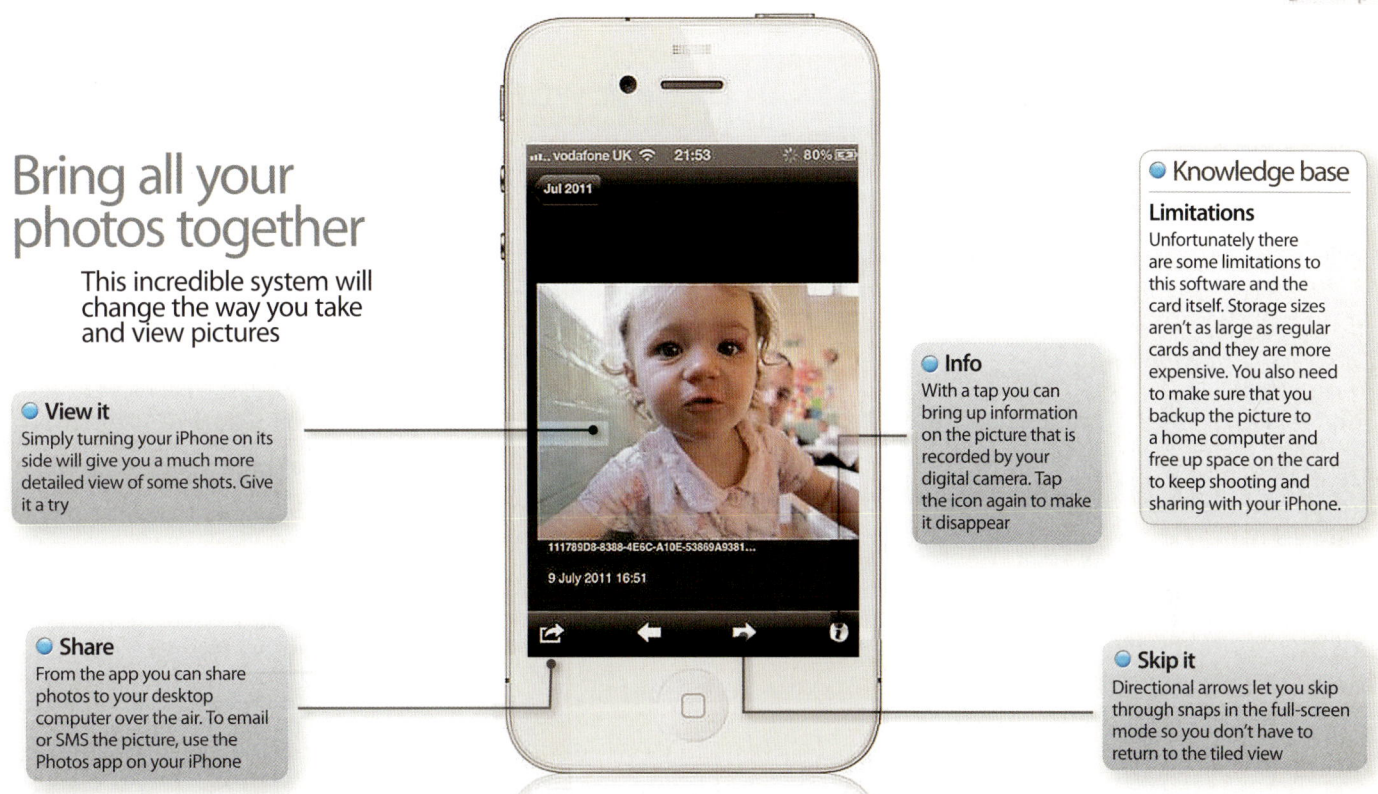

Bring all your photos together

This incredible system will change the way you take and view pictures

● View it
Simply turning your iPhone on its side will give you a much more detailed view of some shots. Give it a try

● Share
From the app you can share photos to your desktop computer over the air. To email or SMS the picture, use the Photos app on your iPhone

● Info
With a tap you can bring up information on the picture that is recorded by your digital camera. Tap the icon again to make it disappear

● Knowledge base
Limitations
Unfortunately there are some limitations to this software and the card itself. Storage sizes aren't as large as regular cards and they are more expensive. You also need to make sure that you backup the picture to a home computer and free up space on the card to keep shooting and sharing with your iPhone.

● Skip it
Directional arrows let you skip through snaps in the full-screen mode so you don't have to return to the tiled view

4: Be direct
This next page is for when Wi-Fi is unavailable. The card will generate its own signal and network and you can log into it here. Tap Done to continue.

5: Watch in wonder
As soon as the app is active and the camera is on, the transfer will begin. If you have a lot of snaps already on the card, this can take some time.

6: View it
You can now view all your pictures including those taken on your iPhone. They appear as a neat in-app mosaic as well as the Photos section of your iPhone.

iPhone Tips, Tricks, Apps and Hacks **69**

Tips | Tricks | Hacks | Apps

Transfer media directly to your iPad

Quicker than email, the Photo Transfer app enables you to transfer photos and video easily between devices

Task: Transfer media files between iOS devices
Difficulty: Beginner
Time needed: 5 minutes

Transferring large photographs and video files between devices can be a fiddly process that takes time and effort, especially if you're attaching the files to emails. There are apps available that strip out all of the hassle and make the process of wirelessly sending media files to another device quick and simple.

One such app is Photo Transfer. It is universal, meaning it works for both iPhone and iPad; once you have purchased and installed it on one device, you can download and install it free of charge on another. Once installed, data transfer is as easy as launching the app on both devices, selecting the files you wish to send and, provided both devices are connected by Wi-Fi or Bluetooth, tapping a button.

The process completes in no time at all, and the photos or video files will then be accessible from the Photos app. You can also transfer files between devices and computers by entering a unique URL provided by the app. You'll never have to twiddle your thumbs waiting for an email again.

Step-by-step | Photo Transfer Send photos and video wirelessly

1: Select device
When you launch the app you'll need to select the device that you are transferring to – in this case iPad, so select Device from the bottom bar.

2: Select media
After you have selected the device you wish to wirelessly send your media to, tap the 'Select Photos & Videos' button in the middle of the screen.

3: Choose assets
You will now be able to browse your Photos album for images to transfer. Tap on any you wish to transfer and a tick will appear on the selected items.

70 iPhone Tips, Tricks, Apps and Hacks

Tips | Tricks | Hacks | Apps

Transferring your files wirelessly
The interface for the Photo Transfer app is simple and uncluttered

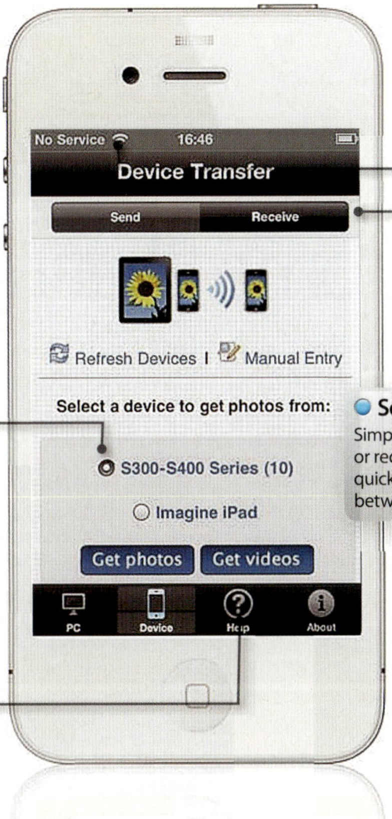

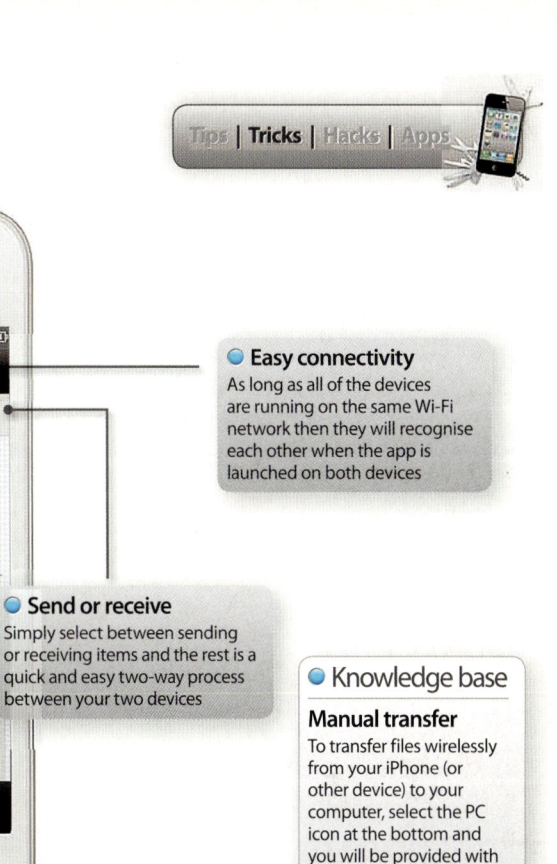

Select a device
You can transfer media between your iPhone, iPad or iPod touch and your computer, or between your devices

Help is at hand
If you need further assistance with using the app then tap on the Help icon at the bottom of the page and everything will be explained

Easy connectivity
As long as all of the devices are running on the same Wi-Fi network then they will recognise each other when the app is launched on both devices

Send or receive
Simply select between sending or receiving items and the rest is a quick and easy two-way process between your two devices

Knowledge base
Manual transfer
To transfer files wirelessly from your iPhone (or other device) to your computer, select the PC icon at the bottom and you will be provided with a Photo Transfer URL that is unique to your device. Input this into a browser on your Mac or PC and you'll be able to download your media from the site.

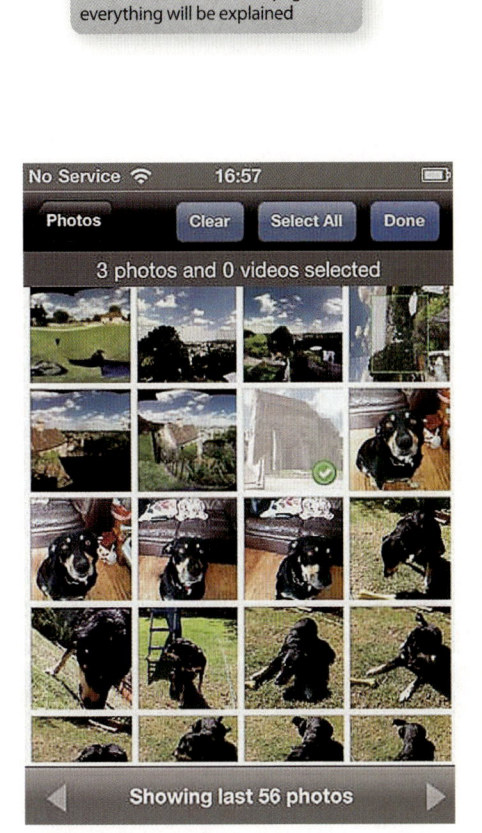

4: Moving items
Once you have selected all of the assets you wish to transfer (tap Clear to start again or Select All to transfer everything), tap Done.

5: Open the app on iPad
Open the Photo Transfer app on your iPad and then tap on the Devices tab at the bottom. Your iPhone should now be visible as the sending device.

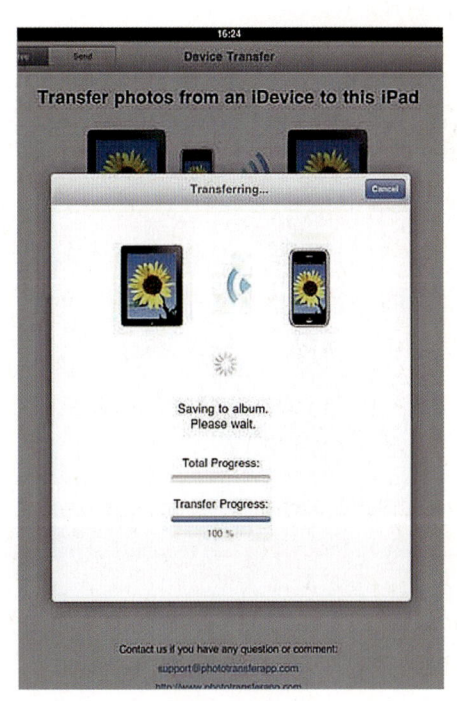

6: Confirm sending device
Tap to confirm and the files will begin transferring. This will take a few seconds, depending on size. A message will confirm when the job is done.

Tips | **Tricks** | Hacks | Apps

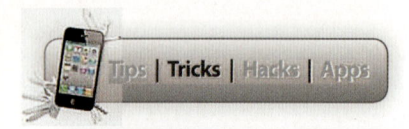

Watch videos using Home Sharing

With the most recent version of iTunes and iOS, you can now view movies and TV shows on your iPhone that you have purchased in iTunes on your PC or Mac

Task: Watch a video on your iPhone currently on your PC or Mac in iTunes
Difficulty: Beginner
Time needed: 5 minutes

Have you ever wanted to use your iPhone to view a movie you have on iTunes on your computer? With the recent iOS 4.3 update, your iOS device has the ability to use the iTunes Home Sharing feature, which allows you to connect your iPhone to your PC or Mac iTunes software. You can then view movies and TV shows that you have downloaded to your computer's iTunes on any iPhones in your local network.

Your iPhone can wirelessly connect to your computer's iTunes program, allowing you to browse videos currently downloaded to your computer. You don't need to download these movies or TV shows to your iPhone. Instead, when you view a video, your computer streams the movie to your device. Keep in mind that you can share your purchased movies and TV shows, but you cannot share movie rentals.

This tutorial takes you through turning on Home Sharing and connecting to your computer's iTunes with your iPhone.

Step-by-step | **Home Sharing** Share movies with your iPhone

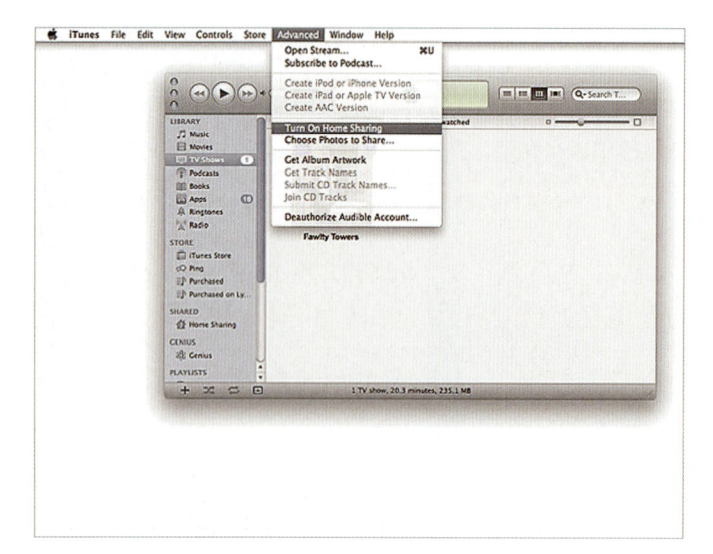

1: Activate Home Sharing
On the PC or Mac with the videos you wish to share, start the iTunes application. Choose Advanced>Turn on Home Sharing. Enter your Apple ID and Password and click Create Home Share. Leave iTunes running.

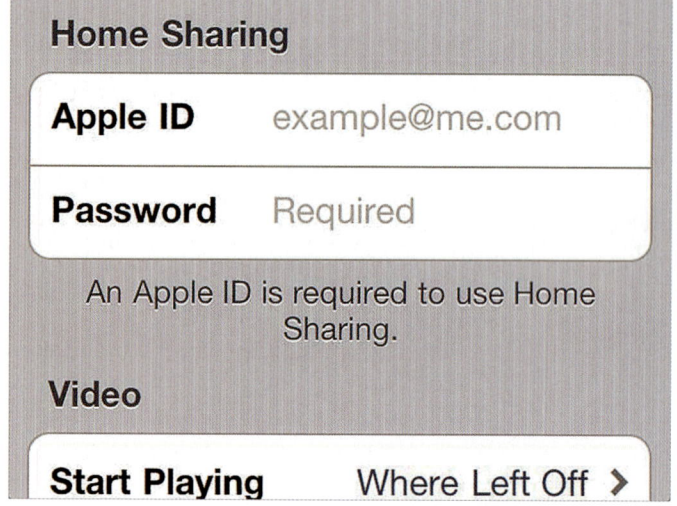

2: Change iPhone settings
Open Settings on your iPhone and tap the iPod icon in the list. Under Home Sharing, enter the same Apple ID and password that you entered in iTunes in the last step. This allows your iPhone to connect with your iTunes.

Tips | Tricks | Hacks | Apps

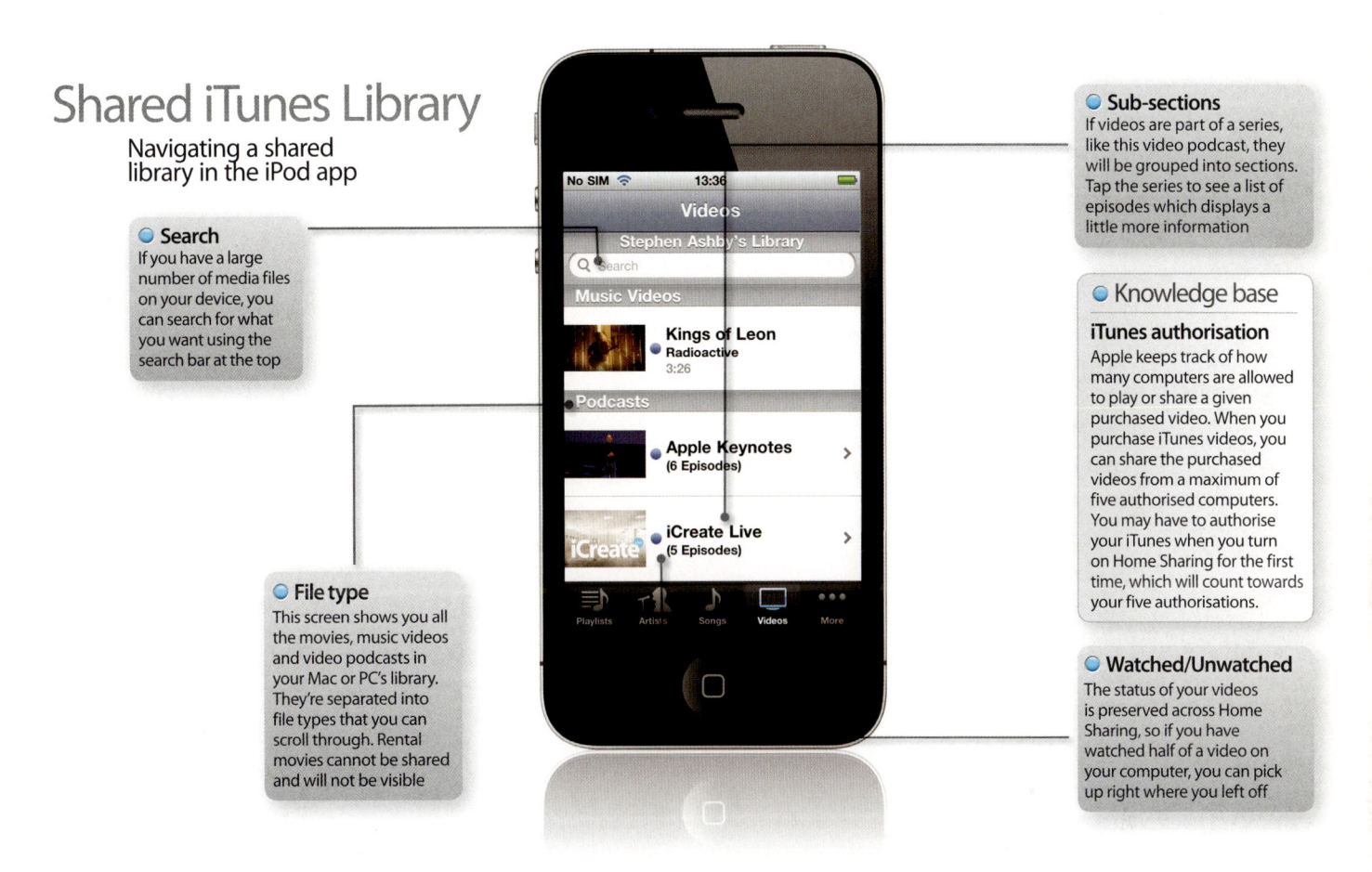

Shared iTunes Library
Navigating a shared library in the iPod app

Search
If you have a large number of media files on your device, you can search for what you want using the search bar at the top

File type
This screen shows you all the movies, music videos and video podcasts in your Mac or PC's library. They're separated into file types that you can scroll through. Rental movies cannot be shared and will not be visible

Sub-sections
If videos are part of a series, like this video podcast, they will be grouped into sections. Tap the series to see a list of episodes which displays a little more information

Knowledge base

iTunes authorisation
Apple keeps track of how many computers are allowed to play or share a given purchased video. When you purchase iTunes videos, you can share the purchased videos from a maximum of five authorised computers. You may have to authorise your iTunes when you turn on Home Sharing for the first time, which will count towards your five authorisations.

Watched/Unwatched
The status of your videos is preserved across Home Sharing, so if you have watched half of a video on your computer, you can pick up right where you left off

3: Access your media
Close the iPhone's Settings and tap on the iPod app. Tap on the More tab at the bottom of the screen and select Shared, which should be at the bottom of the list. Then, select the iTunes library you want to access.

4: Play a video
If you now tap the Videos tab, you'll see your computer's videos. If you have both movies and TV shows in your iTunes library, they will be separated in the list by dividers showing their type.

iPhone Tips, Tricks, Apps and Hacks **73**

Tips | **Tricks** | Hacks | Apps

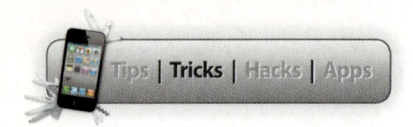

Stream audio and video

You can turn your iPhone into your home media hub by streaming audio and video to other devices in your house. Here's how…

Task: Stream media to your iPhone
Difficulty: Intermediate
Time needed: 15 minutes

While it's really great to be able to carry your favourite films, photos and music with you on your iPhone, let's be honest: the joy is a personal one, as the iPhone's speakers and screen are hardly built for sharing with a wider audience. Or at least it would be without the iPhone's killer feature: AirPlay. It allows you to stream your iPhone's music, video and images wirelessly across a local network.

The only extra you need to use AirPlay is a compatible device to stream your iPhone's content to. This could be an Apple TV, AirPlay-enabled stereo speakers – of which there are several available on the market – or an AirPort Express wireless base station, which comes with a socket that enables it to connect your iPhone to a home stereo system. You can even use a set of Bluetooth headphones if you invest in a new pair, with wireless personal audio as simple as tapping their name on the settings screen. A button tap is all it takes to free your audio and video and watch films on the big screen, or listen to your music collection on your best speakers. You don't need wires any more to enjoy your music and videos, which means you don't need to wander over to your stereo to change track or alter the volume – just pick up your phone and use it as you normally would when listening with headphones attached. We take you through how to get connected and streaming.

Step-by-step | AirPlay Set up your AirPlay connection

1: Check wireless settings
AirPlay works over a local Wi-Fi network, so check that your iPhone and the device you're streaming to are on the same one. On your iPhone, tap Settings and choose the Wi-Fi option. If your network is secured, enter its password.

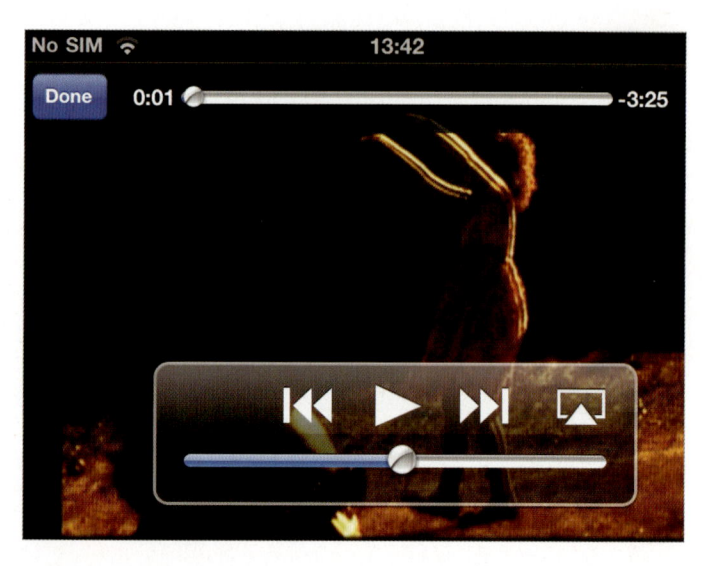

2: Open the media
When your devices are connected, start playing the media on the iPhone that you want to stream. Now tap the AirPlay icon (a hollow rectangle with a solid triangle) that appears on the media controller to activate AirPlay.

74 iPhone Tips, Tricks, Apps and Hacks

Tips | Tricks | Hacks | Apps

AirPlay on the iPhone in action

AirPlay is an impressive technology, but it's pretty simple to use

● Audio or video?
The TV icon indicates that audio and video will be streamed to the external device. If you see a speaker icon instead, only audio will be streamed over AirPlay

● More than video
It isn't just the media itself that can be sent over AirPlay. Song titles, artists, album names and artwork can all appear on AirPlay-enabled speakers that have graphical displays

● AirPlay's icon
The AirPlay icon itself is just a simple box with an arrow. The same icon appears on all iOS devices, and in iTunes on the Mac and PC too

● Knowledge base

AirPlay everywhere
AirPlay is a clever wireless technology, the usefulness of which isn't restricted to the iPhone. In fact, any iOS device with iOS 4.2 or later installed on it can use AirPlay – and so can the iTunes application on Mac OS X. AirPlay features are also present in Apple's free Remote iPad and iPhone app, which allows you to control an iTunes library from an iOS device. And thanks to the recent update to the iPhone's software, AirPlay works with third-party apps as well as Apple's own.

3: Choose your output
When you tap the AirPlay icon, a pop-up menu will appear, offering a choice of AirPlay-enabled devices. The currently selected output has a tick next to it, and it should be your iPhone. Tap the name of the device you want to stream to.

4: Streaming in action
Unfortunately, you're not able to watch the same video in two places at once. Once you have selected another output device from the list, the video or audio is sent there within a couple of seconds. The iPhone's screen will now go blank.

iPhone Tips, Tricks, Apps and Hacks **75**

Tips | **Tricks** | Hacks | Apps

Turn your iPhone into a universal remote control

Having more than one remote is so last century. This funky accessory will change your channel-changing life

Task: Control your TV with your iPhone
Difficulty: Beginner
Time needed: 10 minutes

It's a little irksome that the iPhone doesn't ship with any kind of infrared controller, as it would be great to use the device as a universal remote for our televisions, Blu-ray players and satellite receivers. Luckily, this missed opportunity by Apple has been seized upon by L5. It has created a tiny dongle and app that can do the job, turning your iPhone into an easy-to-use remote that can control anything with an infrared beam.

What's more, the set-up process is really straightforward, so you don't need to spend hours scanning through infrared wavelengths. Simply make sure that all the buttons you want are covered and then sit back and enjoy controlling your digital world. If you have a mischievous side, you could neglect to inform a partner that you have enabled your iPhone as a remote control and torture them by constantly changing channel during their favourite show, though we take no responsibility for such behaviour! In this step by step, we'll teach you how to set up the remote once you've bought the dongle and plugged it into the connector at the bottom of your iPhone.

Step-by-step | L5 Remote Combine every remote you'll ever need into one app

1: Quick or not
Here you can decide whether to use a template for your remote or custom build one. We suggest opting for a Quick remote if you are new to the app.

2: Button up
Follow the prompt and tap on the first button you want to assign. Volume is a good starting point. Have your TV remote ready to go.

3: Press 'em
Press on the volume up button on your remote and the L5 will detect the signal and then copy it so that it can use it on your own TV. Clever stuff, eh?

Tips | Tricks | Hacks | Apps

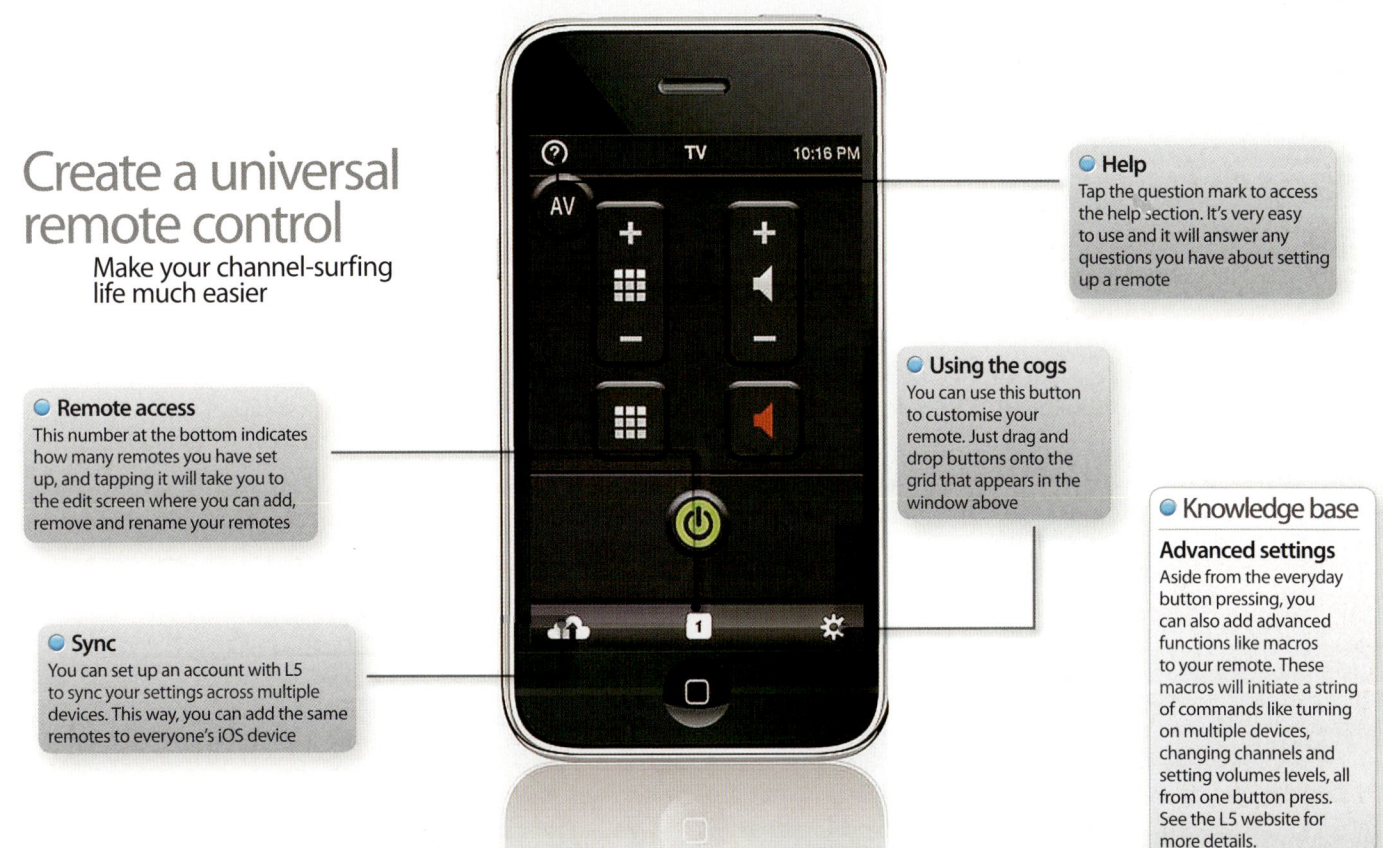

Create a universal remote control
Make your channel-surfing life much easier

● Remote access
This number at the bottom indicates how many remotes you have set up, and tapping it will take you to the edit screen where you can add, remove and rename your remotes

● Sync
You can set up an account with L5 to sync your settings across multiple devices. This way, you can add the same remotes to everyone's iOS device

● Help
Tap the question mark to access the help section. It's very easy to use and it will answer any questions you have about setting up a remote

● Using the cogs
You can use this button to customise your remote. Just drag and drop buttons onto the grid that appears in the window above

● Knowledge base
Advanced settings
Aside from the everyday button pressing, you can also add advanced functions like macros to your remote. These macros will initiate a string of commands like turning on multiple devices, changing channels and setting volumes levels, all from one button press. See the L5 website for more details.

4: Status
As you add each button to the remote you'll see status bars, which let you know that the app is working and the hardware is too.

5: Name it
As you can add multiple remotes, you now need to name the one you've created. Tap the number 1 at the bottom of the screen and then the Edit button.

6: Make it easy
Give your remote the easiest name possible so you'll never get confused. You can now add as many as you like and name them all differently.

iPhone Tips, Tricks, Apps and Hacks **77**

Tips | **Tricks** | Hacks | Apps

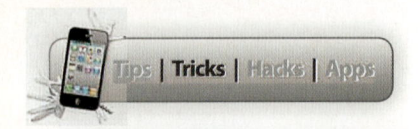

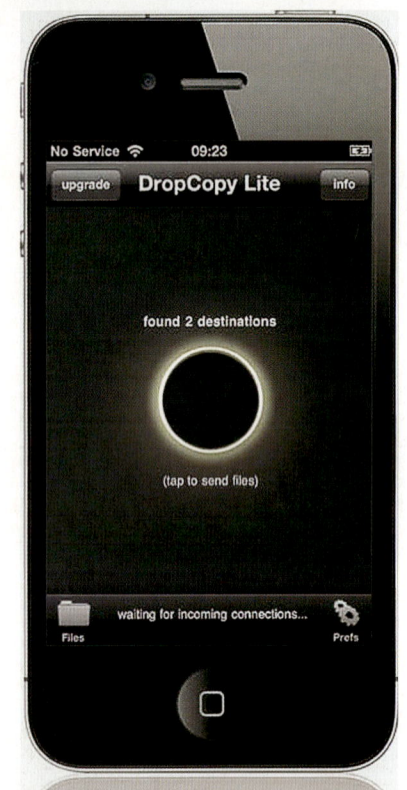

Share files wirelessly from your iPhone to your Mac

The are many apps available which enable you to transfer files wirelessly between devices. We examine one of the simplest

Task: Transfer docs, images and A/V content in seconds
Difficulty: Beginner
Time needed: 5 minutes

Even a few years ago, transferring files between devices without wires, dongles and discs would have been considered witchcraft. But nowadays there are thousands of apps available to perform this task. Apps such as Dropbox and Documents To Go are considered the market leaders, but even they require a fiddly set-up process that can take several minutes to set up before you can start moving files between systems.

In DropCopy you get a transferral system that ranks as by far the simplest we have encountered. To make it work you simply download the app for your iPhone and Mac, and – provided both devices are on the same Wi-Fi network and can 'see' each other – simply drag files into the portal on your desktop or choose the destination from your iPhone. Documents, PDFs, images, music and video can be swapped between devices in seconds.

The simplicity of the process is staggering and, while it is currently only available to Mac users, a PC version is on the way. You can also install the app on your iPad and iPod touch, and link up all four devices for easy file transferral.

Step-by-step | DropCopy Transfer files wirelessly

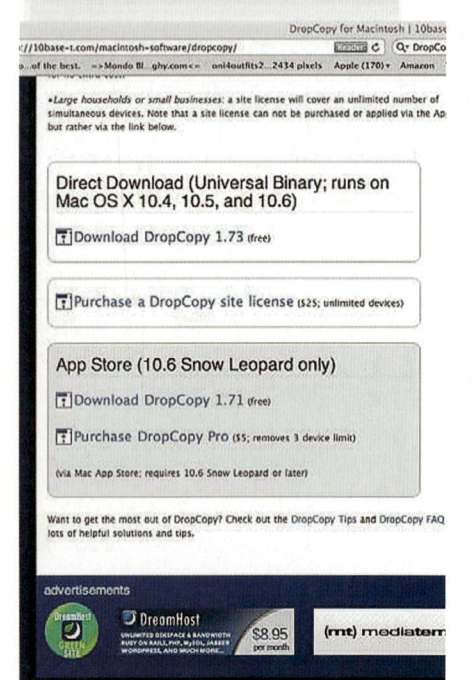

1: Download the apps
Go to http://10base-t.com/macintosh-software/dropcopy to download the DropCopy app for your iPhone and your Mac.

2: Launch the apps
Next, open up the apps on both machines. The iPhone version should say 'found 1 destination' when a connection has been established.

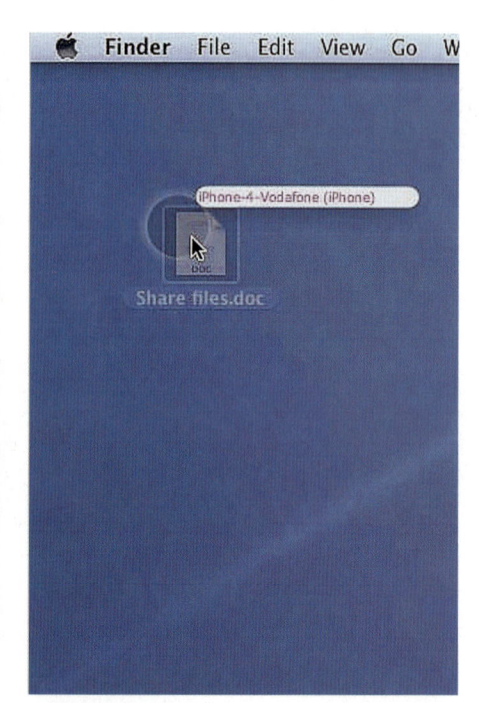

3: Transfer files
When DropCopy launches, you will notice a circle on your desktop – drag files into this circle and they will copy across in seconds.

78 iPhone Tips, Tricks, Apps and Hacks

Tips | Tricks | Hacks | Apps

Your personal file transfer portal
A simple app for a simple process

● Info
The Info panel provides a full tutorial for using the app, troubleshooting tips and the option to see what additional features the paid-for app provides

● Knowledge base
Wireless vs email
The most universal method of transferring files wirelessly is still emailing them as attachments, and the advantage of using specific apps to carry out this task is mainly speed-related. Attaching large files to emails can often mean they take several minutes to send, but by using apps such as DropCopy the process can be done in seconds.

● Destination
With the app running simultaneously on your iPhone and your computer, the circle in the middle of the screen shows that a connection is established

● Files
This is where all of your transferred files are stored and sorted into categories depending on the file type – docs, PDFs, images and audio/visual

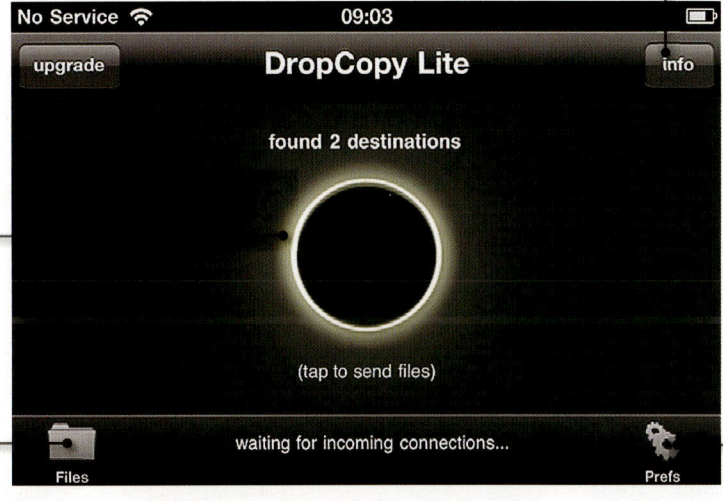

● Preferences
By accessing the Preferences panel you can apply additional layers of security to approve incoming file transfers and obtain assistance

4: Transfer complete
The files will be transferred into the iPhone app. Check the relevant folder that corresponds with the transferred file type to check it is there.

5: Transferring from iPhone
To transfer files back, tap on the file you wish to transfer and then choose a destination. The link to your computer should be present.

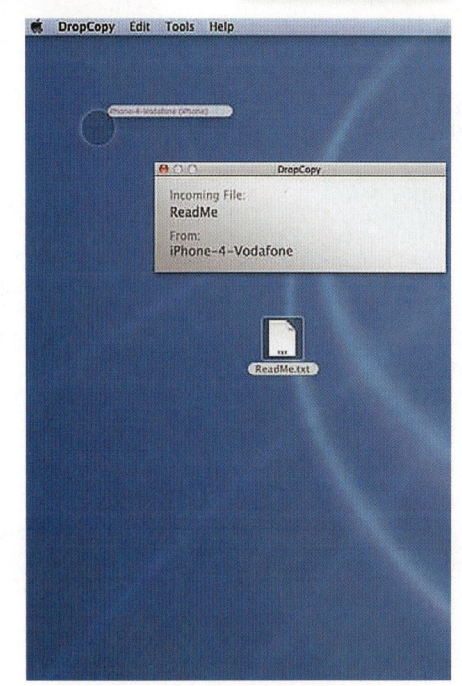

6: Message of confirmation
As the file copies across, you will receive a message on your computer that a file is incoming. Before long it will appear on your desktop.

Tips | Tricks | Hacks | Apps

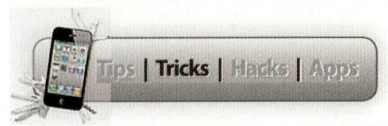

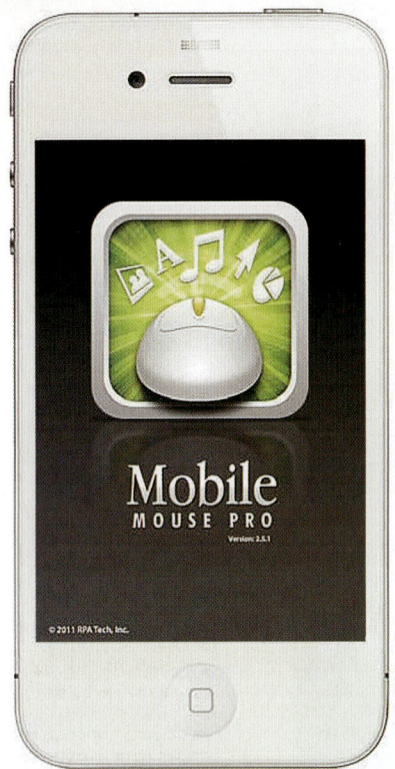

Use your iPhone as a mouse for your Mac

Some say the days of the humble computer mouse are numbered. If that is true, then the iPhone could be the ideal replacement

Task: Turn your iPhone into a wireless mouse
Difficulty: Beginner
Time needed: 5 minutes

Anyone who has used a computer has used a mouse, but as computers take on more diverse roles in the home things need to change. The mouse is the one object that ties the user to a computer, so it makes sense to look for a wireless solution. If you consider media streaming and the fact that many computers now reside in the living room, the need for remote control becomes apparent.

This need can be transferred to those who need to do presentations from a laptop, and in all sorts of other circumstances where wireless control would be highly useful. Mobile Mouse Pro is the perfect tool to enable wireless control because it works using Wi-Fi, so line of sight is not needed. It also comes with features that enable it to act like a mini computer thanks to shortcuts that are built into the app. It feels like a novelty when you first use it, but this novelty quickly grows into a whole new way of working, and one that feels more natural than a conventional mouse for many tasks. Here, we will show you how to get started with wireless control using just your iPhone and Mobile Mouse Pro.

Step-by-step | Mobile Mouse Pro | Use your iPhone as a mouse

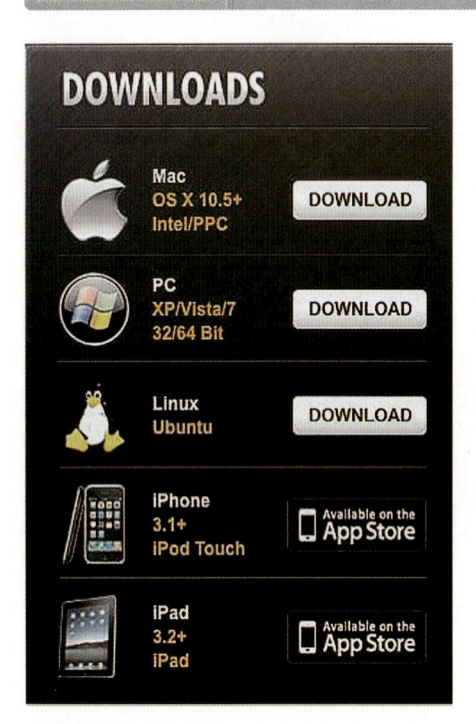

1: Set up your PC
Go to www.mobilemouse.com and download the desktop software compatible with your operating system. The installation process is quick and simple.

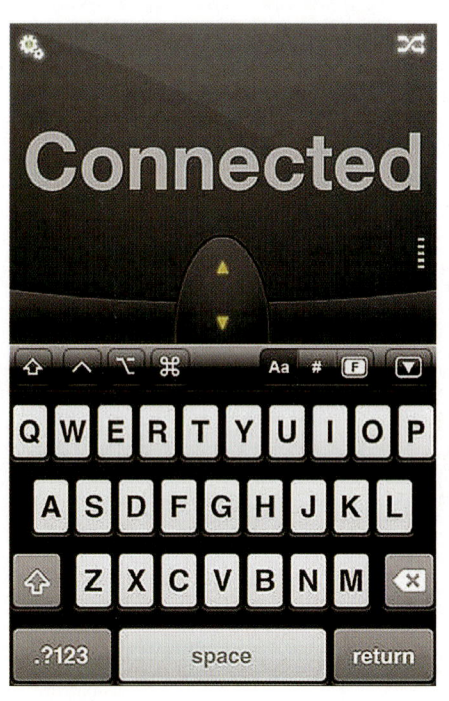

2: Starting up
Start the app up and wait. You should see the word 'Connected' automatically pop up on the main screen, which means you are ready to start.

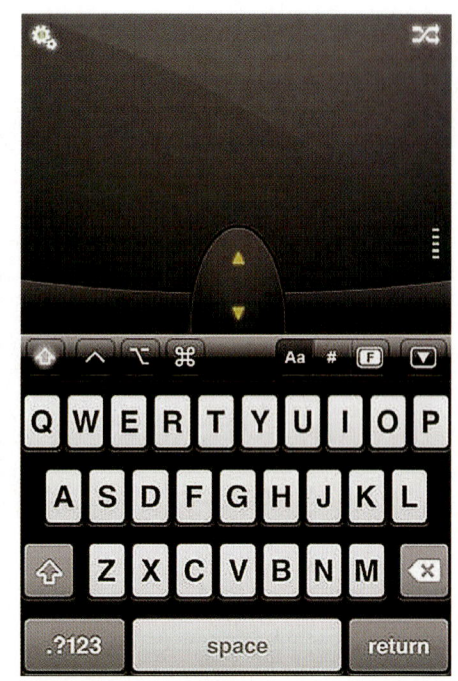

3: Check the interface
You will see the standard Mac command keys above the keyboard. You can use them via multi-touch on the iPhone as you would on a normal keyboard.

80 iPhone Tips, Tricks, Apps and Hacks

Tips | **Tricks** | Hacks | Apps

True wireless control for Mac
A multi-functional virtual mouse

Settings
The settings are worth playing with to make the experience as personal as possible. Every scenario has been covered

Mac functions
The main Mac keys are included in the interface to make using the virtual mouse as familiar as possible. The multi-touch iPhone screen helps here

Mouse pointers
The familiar mouse pointers are included alongside a generously sized mouse area for navigation. It works very efficiently

Modes
Various modes are built in, such as remote control, quick app access and a large number pad. This can be quicker to use than a real keyboard

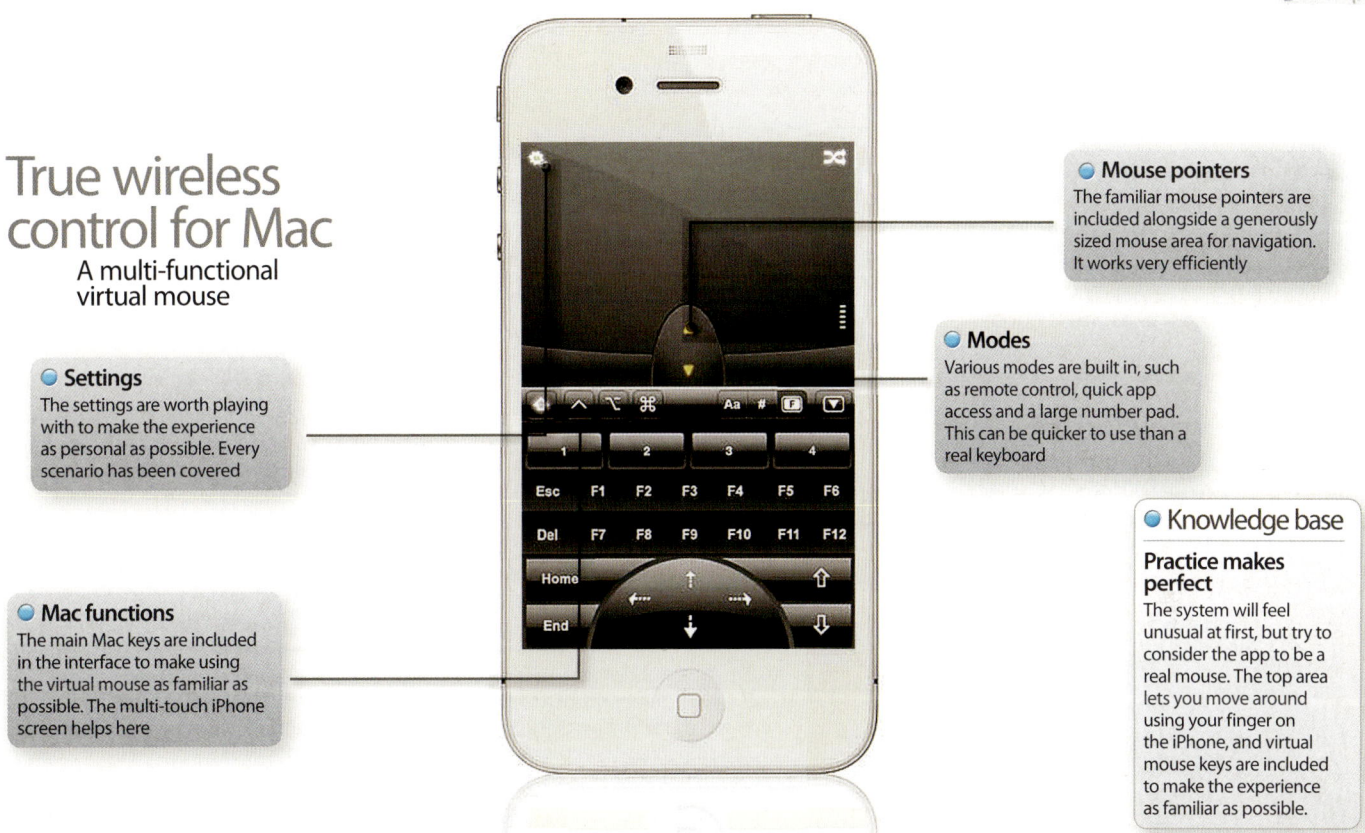

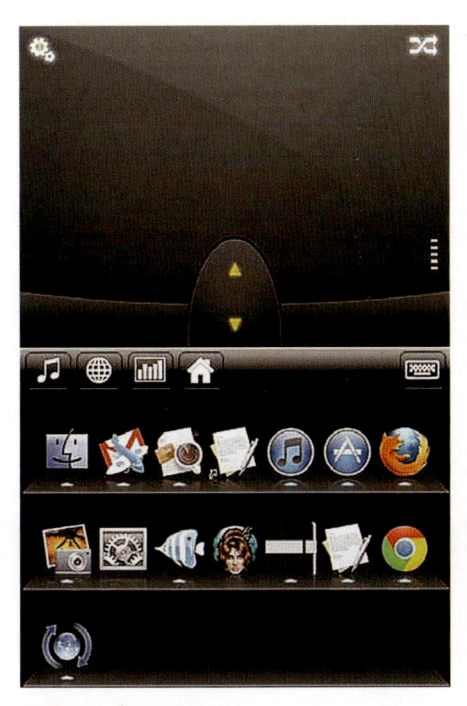

Knowledge base
Practice makes perfect
The system will feel unusual at first, but try to consider the app to be a real mouse. The top area lets you move around using your finger on the iPhone, and virtual mouse keys are included to make the experience as familiar as possible.

4: Extra functions
Tap the far right arrow above the keyboard to pop up all of the apps that currently reside in the Mac dock. Tap an icon to start the program.

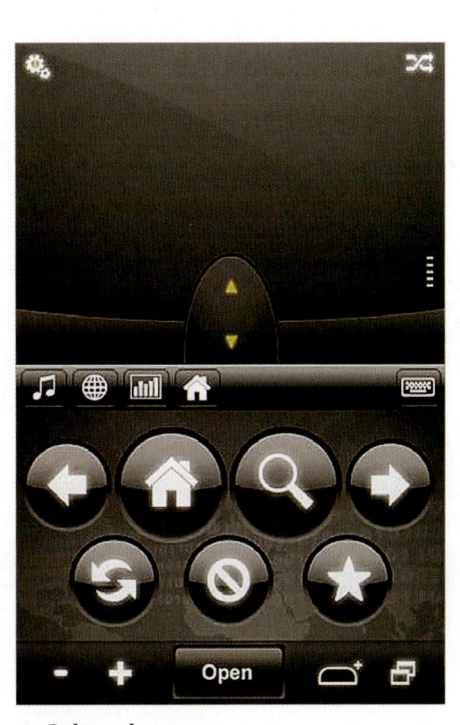

5: Other shortcuts
Notice the icons to the left. These are shortcuts to the web, music and a special presentation module, and are potentially the most beneficial features.

6: Even more
A number pad is accessible via the '#' icon, and all of the main function keys via the 'F' icon. Every single part of the system is covered in abundance.

iPhone Tips, Tricks, Apps and Hacks **81**

Tips | **Tricks** | Hacks | Apps

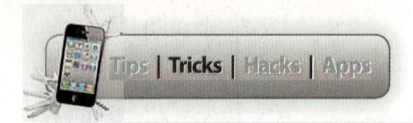

Turn your handwriting into text on an iPhone

Keyboards are great for the digital era, but nothing comes close to your own handwriting. We show you how to write on an iPhone

Task: Learn how to write on an iPhone
Difficulty: Beginner
Time needed: 10 minutes

Keyboards are the default method of data input for most people, and whether they are desk-based or the touch screen type on smartphones, we are all familiar with them. The problem is that they can be slow to use, particularly on phones, and they do not offer the sensation of writing. There is another way, however, and FastFinga is one app among many that enables you use your own handwriting in emails, notes and even tweets.

Despite the small screen size of the iPhone, the app makes use of software trickery to ensure that the resulting notes are easy to read and include as much text as possible on one page. You can use your finger or a stylus, the latter of which produces a cleaner result. However, no matter what method you use, handwritten notes on an iPhone are possible, and in many cases preferable because they add more personality to the finished article. For many years there has been a quiet push towards making digital products work naturally with people who want to write notes, and we are quickly reaching the stage where the technology makes the experience feel the same as writing on real paper.

Step-by-step | FastFinga Hand-write on your iPhone

1: Getting started
Upon opening the app you will see a blank page with a '+' button at the bottom. Tap this and a new window will open up. You are ready to start writing.

2: Start writing
Use your finger to write some words. For obvious reasons you will not be able to write much along the screen, but at least try to complete a word.

3: Use the thumb
Press the thumb at the bottom of the screen and the text is made a lot smaller and will appear in the note as normal-sized writing.

Tips | Tricks | Hacks | Apps

Using your handwriting
How does FastFinga do its magic?

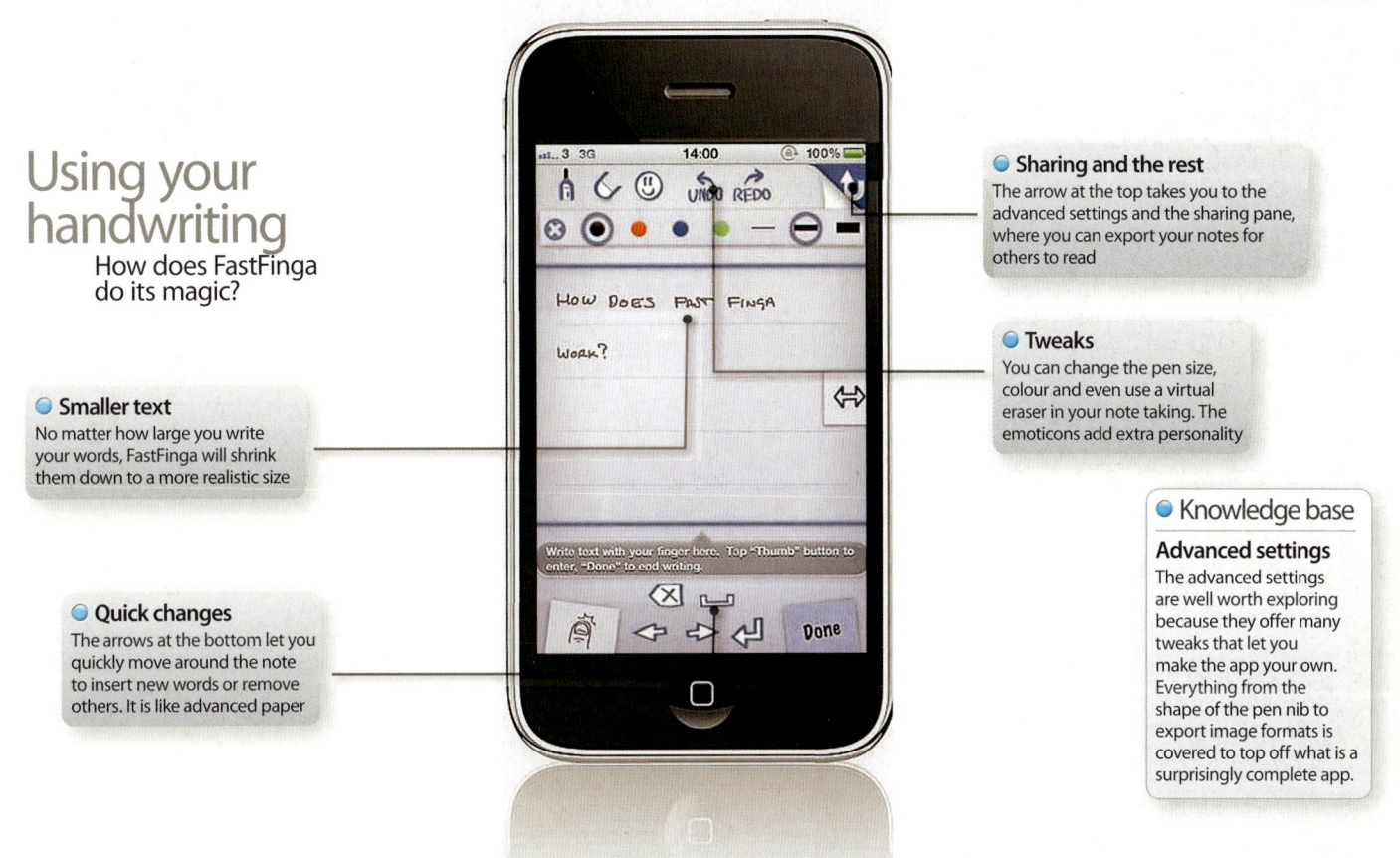

- **Smaller text**
No matter how large you write your words, FastFinga will shrink them down to a more realistic size

- **Quick changes**
The arrows at the bottom let you quickly move around the note to insert new words or remove others. It is like advanced paper

- **Sharing and the rest**
The arrow at the top takes you to the advanced settings and the sharing pane, where you can export your notes for others to read

- **Tweaks**
You can change the pen size, colour and even use a virtual eraser in your note taking. The emoticons add extra personality

- **Knowledge base**

Advanced settings
The advanced settings are well worth exploring because they offer many tweaks that let you make the app your own. Everything from the shape of the pen nib to export image formats is covered to top off what is a surprisingly complete app.

4: Change the pen
At the top you can change the pen size and colour, undo your latest writing or use the eraser to scrub out words that you no longer want to include.

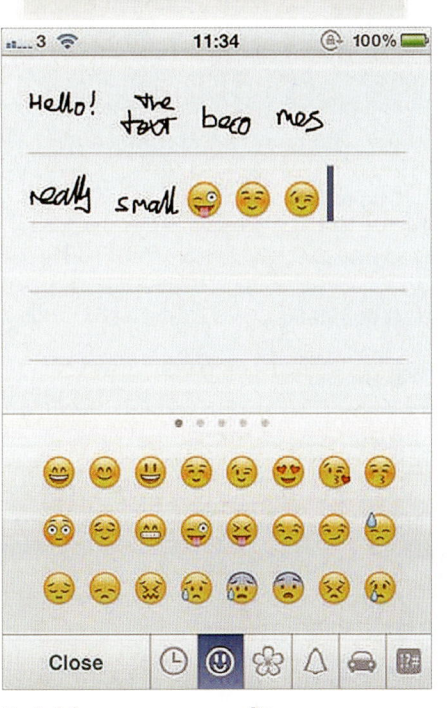

5: Add some personality
There is a large selection of emoticons that can add personality to each note. Simply select the one you want to use and it will appear in the note.

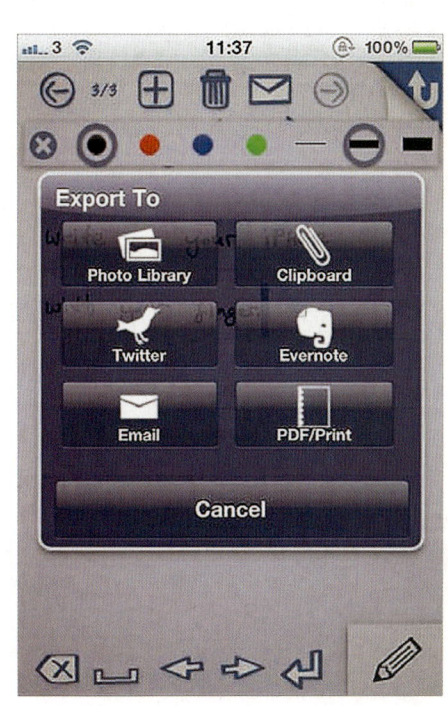

6: Sharing
Once complete, you can share the note via email, Twitter and Evernote, or save it to your photo album – you can use your notes for almost any purpose.

iPhone Tips, Tricks, Apps and Hacks **83**

Tips | Tricks | Hacks | Apps

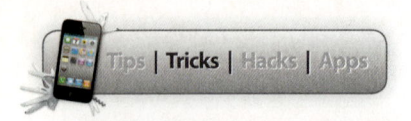

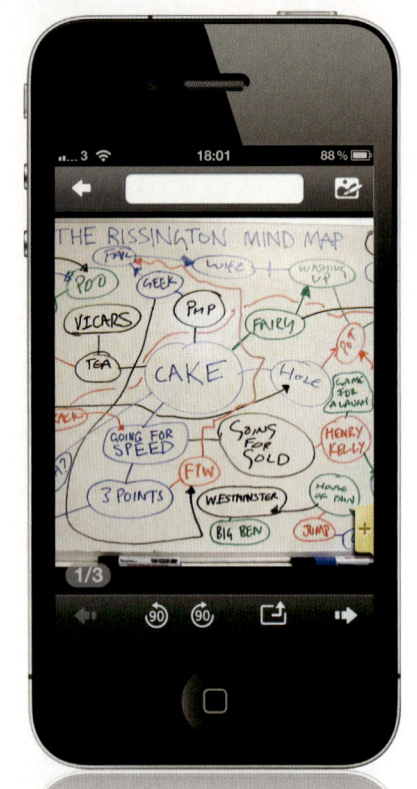

Scan documents using your iPhone

You can now digitise all of your paper documents and keep them safely stored in your iPhone to carry with you

Task: Scan documents using CamScanner+
Difficulty: Beginner
Time needed: 5 minutes

It would be easy to think that simply taking a photo of an important document is enough to keep it in a digital format, but there are so many reasons why using an app designed specifically for this task is advantageous. Not only will you increase the security of the documents you scan, but the quality and accuracy of each document will be improved as well. On top of this, the organisational side is also covered, which makes searching through your documents and sharing them with online services much easier.

Once you get started with scanning documents, you may find that it becomes completely natural to scan bills, letters and other paper-based data. The ability to export to the PDF format is an advantage, and even more vital is being able to password-protect scanned docs. This is particularly important if you want to share your sensitive files with online services or specific people. You can also synchronise scans with a desktop PC for added security, and choose set sizes such as A4 or Letter to make them look more like the original paper documents.

Step-by-step | CamScanner+ Turn your paper into a digital version

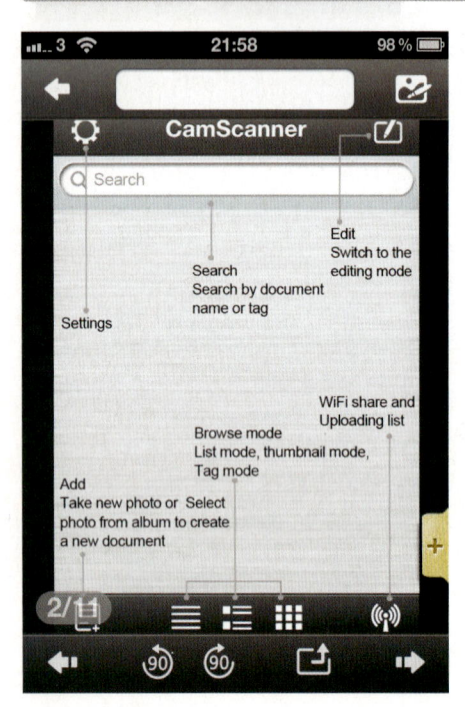

1: Get some help
When you fire up the app, tap the tutorial category to read instructions. These will offer some quick guides to get you up and scanning in no time at all.

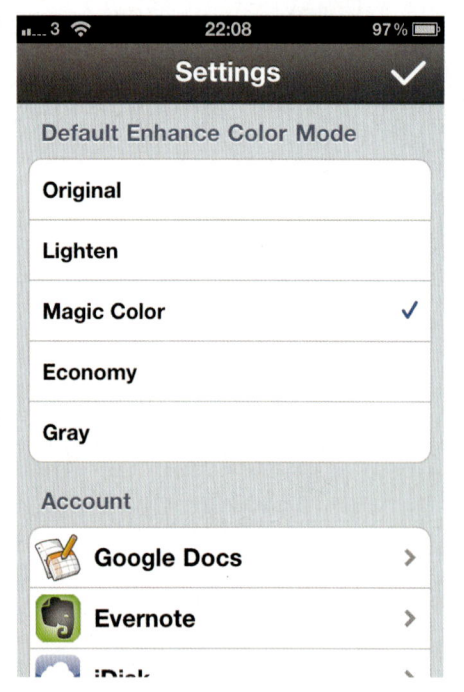

2: Enhancements
Tap the cog in the top left-hand corner. Scroll down and choose the colour mode you want. We would suggest sticking to the 'Magic Color' option at first.

3: Exporting
Scroll down and tap on the account to export your documents. 'AutoSave' will automatically add the scanned docs to the account you choose.

Tips | Tricks | Hacks | Apps

The main features
A look at the simple CamScanner+ interface

● The settings
The settings can make a great deal of difference to how you use the app if you take the time to set them up correctly

● Taking a scan
Creating a scan is as easy as tapping an icon, choosing an option and snapping the picture. It is basically the same as taking a photo

● Smart and clean
Your scans can be displayed in a list with or without extra detail, or via attractive thumbnails that make organisation as easy as can be

● Wireless sharing
You can share your scans with a PC or Mac by tapping this icon. All you have to do is enter a URL to access them

● Knowledge base
Smarter images
CamScanner+ uses smart image processing to detect the edges of objects and to automatically enhance images. Try taking a normal photo of a document and then using CamScanner+. The difference in quality is immediately obvious.

4: Your first scan
Tap the bottom left-hand icon, and choose the 'Take Photo' option to start creating your first scan. You can also choose a photo from the iPhone library.

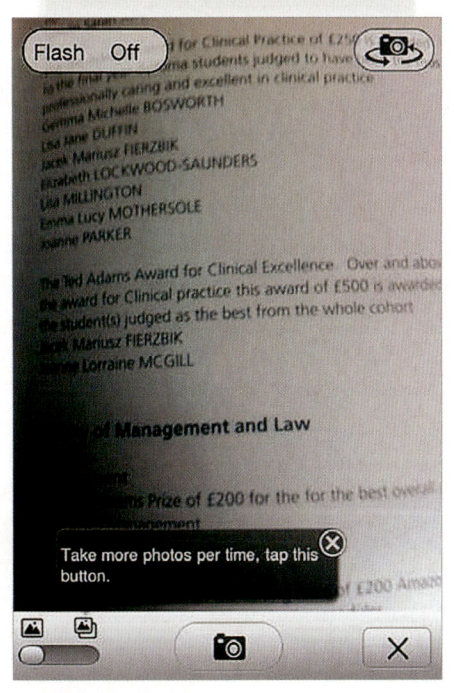

5: Time to click
Hold the phone steady and try to ensure that the text on the object is straight. Now tap the capture button just as you would when taking a photo.

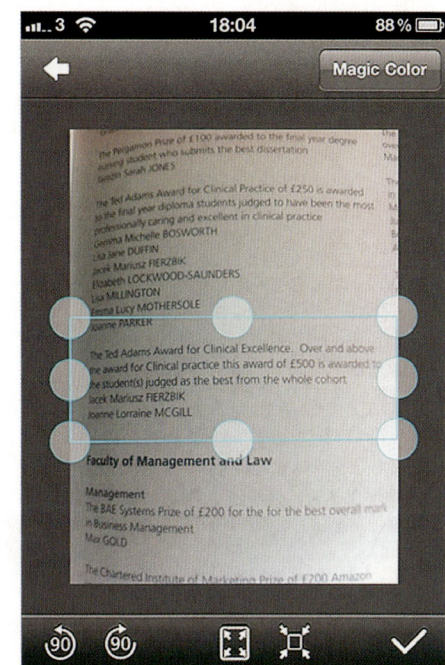

6: Adjustments
You can now crop the photo to make sure you have captured the text you require. Even a bad photo can be adjusted to create a decent scan.

iPhone Tips, Tricks, Apps and Hacks **85**

Tips | **Tricks** | Hacks | Apps

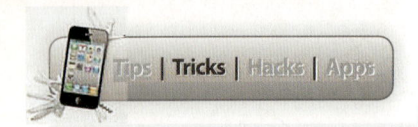

Use your iPhone to scan barcodes

Barcodes aren't just for shops and supermarkets any more. Now you can scan them on your iPhone for fun and to find a bargain

Task: Scan barcodes using RedLaser
Difficulty: Beginner
Time needed: 10 minutes

Until recently, the barcodes on the backs of books and other products didn't mean much to the average consumer. But the arrival of apps such as RedLaser have changed all that. RedLaser scans product barcodes impressively accurately and uses this information to identify the product. It's such a lot of fun to finally unlock the key of the barcodes that for the first few hours after installing it you'll probably be wandering around the house hunting down any old code to scan.

But there is a serious purpose to this technological wonder. RedLaser uses the product information to search online for that item, comparing prices from a number of search engines including Google Product Search, an online database of available products and auction site eBay (eBay now owns RedLaser).

The result is that you can often find the product you're scanning cheaper and, in a couple of clicks, order it. Given the sometimes lengthy list of returned results, you'll be relieved that RedLaser keeps track of your scans and searches. You can even email yourself the list if you want to do more research down the line.

Step-by-step | RedLaser How to scan a barcode

1: Opening screen
When you launch the app you're presented with an empty scanned items list. To add your first item, tap the Lightning icon at the bottom of the window.

2: Scan a code
The viewing window appears. Scan a barcode by moving it into position. When the barcode is recognised it will be added to the product list.

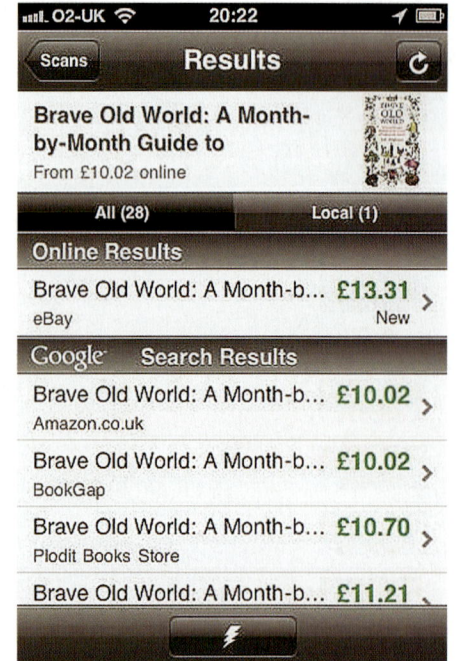

3: Find matching products
The app searches for matching products, online or locally depending on your preferences. Tap the link next to each result to see more details.

86 iPhone Tips, Tricks, Apps and Hacks

Tips | Tricks | Hacks | Apps

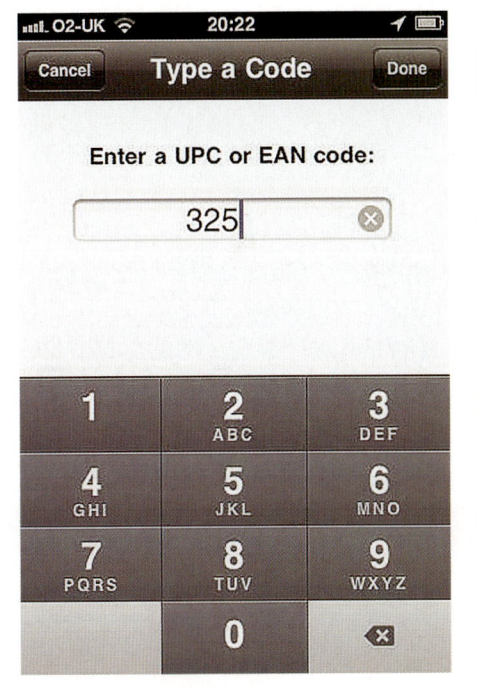

Scanning for profit
A barcode reader can save you time and money. Here's how

- **Hold steady**
For best results to keep the barcode straight between the arrows, and hold the iPhone steady during the split-second recognition process

- **Batch scanning**
You can scan items in a batch by sliding the Multiple option to On. This saves the app from looking up every item after you scan it

- **Types of code**
RedLaser recognises UPC and EAN barcodes, used on most products, as well as QR barcodes that are growing in popularity on signs and websites

- **Quick scanning**
There's no delay when RedLaser scans. It's very fast as the barcode is automatically recognised without you having to do anything

- **Knowledge base**

    Developing scanning technology
    RedLaser's impressive scanning technology could be useful in all sorts of situations. Its developer offers a software development kit that gives third parties access to its barcode scanning technology. So chances are someone else is already extending its potential uses.

4: Add manually
If the app has trouble scanning the barcode you can manually enter a UPC or EAN code. Tap the Edit icon at the top of the list and type in the code.

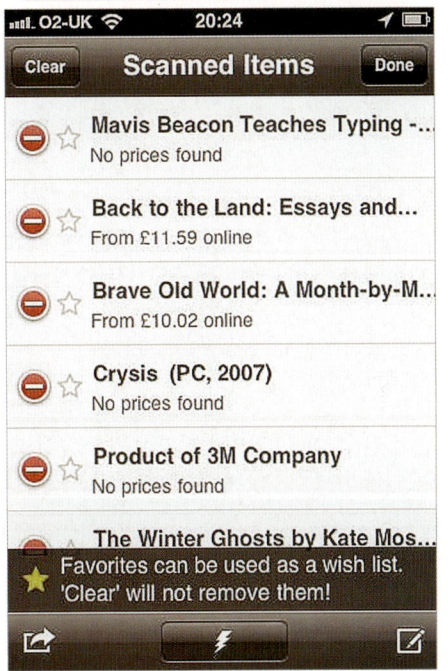

5: Edit the list
Delete a product from the list by tapping Edit and pressing the red button next to the item. You can keep an item by tapping the star next to its name.

6: List by email
Keep a permanent record of the current product list by tapping Email at the bottom left of the screen. This copies a text version of the list to Mail app.

iPhone Tips, Tricks, Apps and Hacks **87**

Tips | **Tricks** | Hacks | Apps

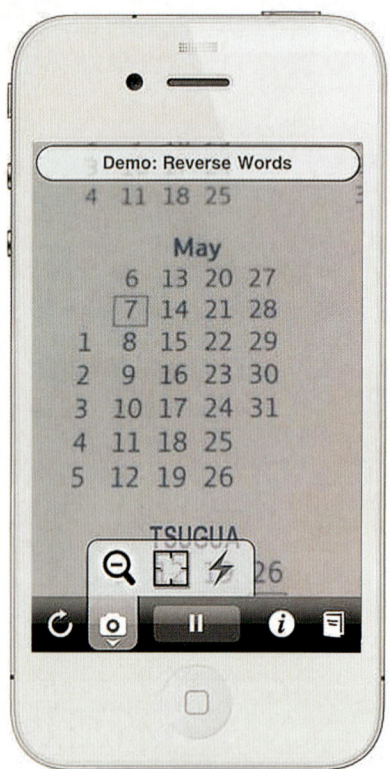

Translate text and understand foreign signs

Translating foreign languages has just become easier than ever before and this development could change many aspects of your life

Task: Learn to translate words with Word Lens
Difficulty: Beginner
Time needed: 5 minutes

Learning a new language is never easy and can take months or years of studying. Phrase books have long been a staple accessory of people travelling abroad, but now there is a new way. Word Lens is an ingenious app that can translate foreign language words by simply holding up an iPhone camera to the text. It replaces the words you are viewing on the screen with a literal translation and the characters are readable and really do look like they are in the correct language.

This technology can be used in many circumstances such as reading road signs abroad, understanding menus and anywhere that requires translation. In theory you could even read a foreign language book using Word Lens, but at the time of writing only translations between English and Spanish are available. In total, you will pay £14 for the translation so it depends on how often you need to translate. Hopefully further languages will be available in the future which will increase the flexibility. The potential is great and the implementation clever, making sifting through various phrase books a thing of the past.

Step-by-step | Word Lens Translate with your camera

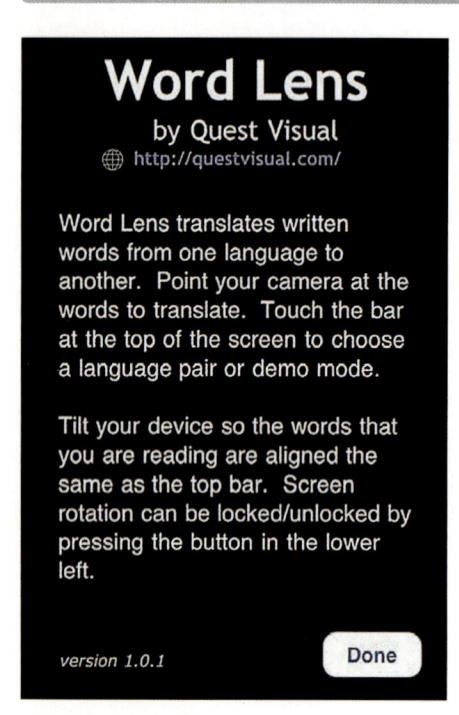

1: Getting started
When you first open the app you should tap the 'i' at the bottom of the screen which offers a guide. The app is exceptionally easy to use.

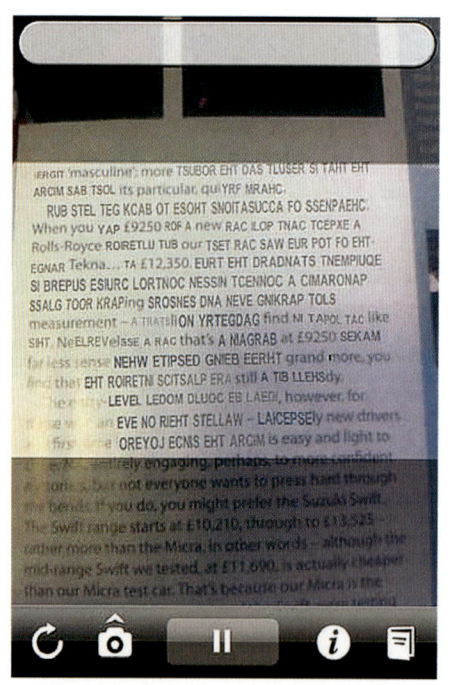

2: Translate
Hold up your camera to a piece of foreign text. It can be a road sign, magazine or anything typed. Handwritten text is difficult to translate visually.

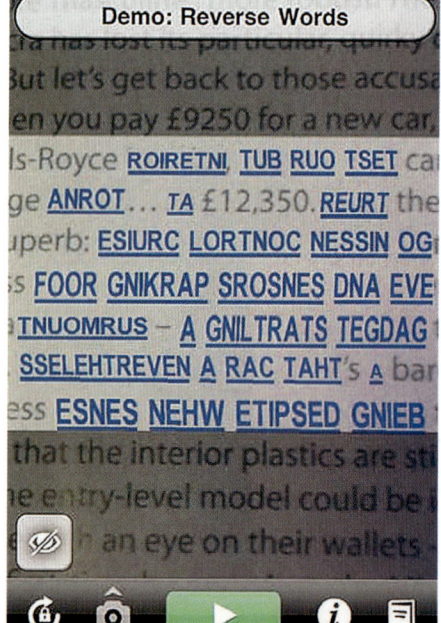

3: The results
Translated words are highlighted in blue when you press pause, showing words that the app doesn't recognise. The success rate is high, though.

Tips | **Tricks** | Hacks | Apps

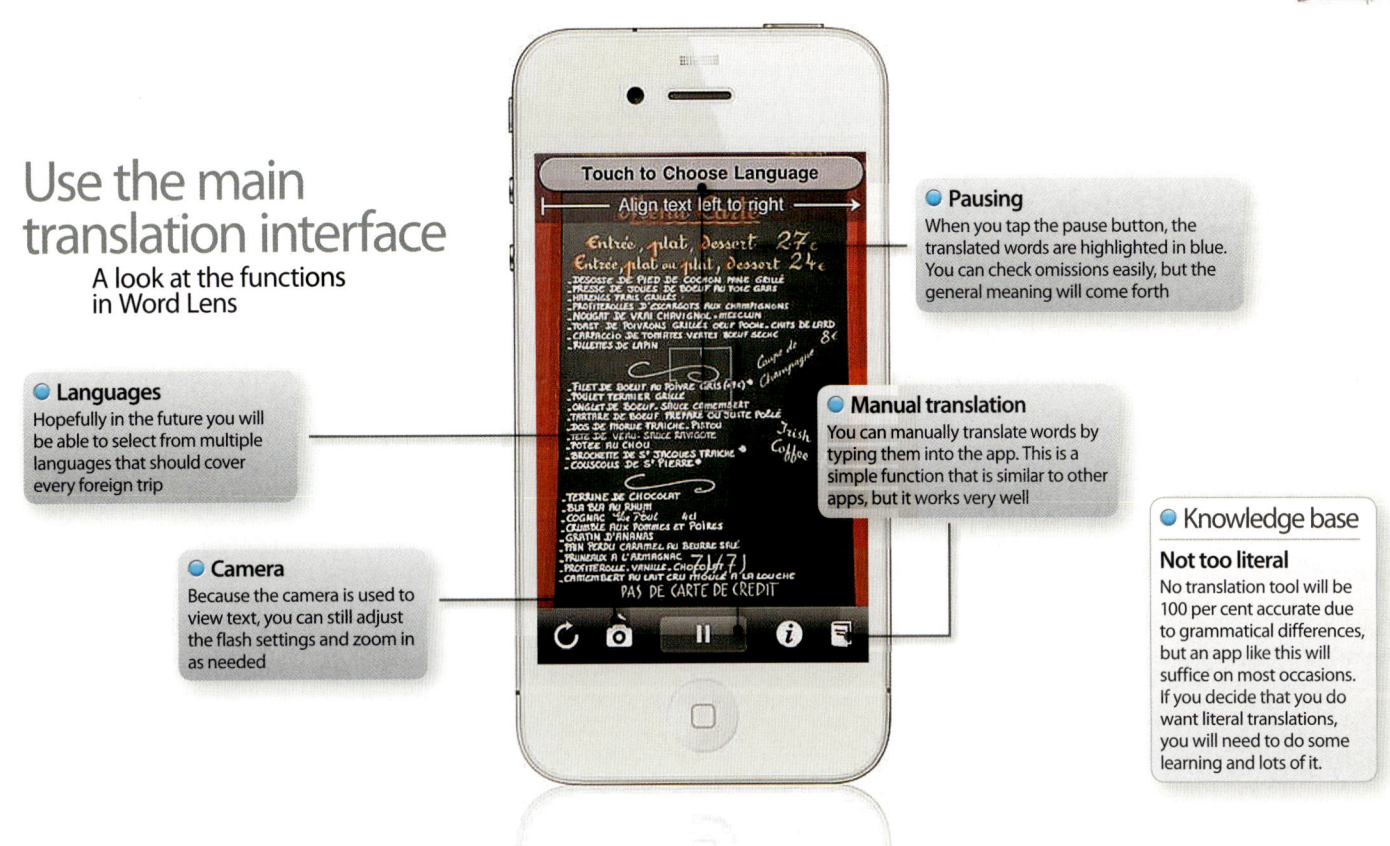

Use the main translation interface
A look at the functions in Word Lens

● Languages
Hopefully in the future you will be able to select from multiple languages that should cover every foreign trip

● Camera
Because the camera is used to view text, you can still adjust the flash settings and zoom in as needed

● Pausing
When you tap the pause button, the translated words are highlighted in blue. You can check omissions easily, but the general meaning will come forth

● Manual translation
You can manually translate words by typing them into the app. This is a simple function that is similar to other apps, but it works very well

● Knowledge base

Not too literal
No translation tool will be 100 per cent accurate due to grammatical differences, but an app like this will suffice on most occasions. If you decide that you do want literal translations, you will need to do some learning and lots of it.

4: Tweaks
You can tweak the app by tapping the camera button at the bottom. This lets you select portions of the screen with autofocus, use the flash or zoom.

5: Manual translation
You can type in words to get their true meaning by tapping the icon at the bottom. This is a feature that comes in handy time and time again.

6: Make it work
Tapping the bar at the top gives you the option to purchase two-way translations and restore purchases if you have had to reset your device.

iPhone Tips, Tricks, Apps and Hacks **89**

Tips | Tricks | Hacks | Apps

Discover your geographical location

We all presume that we know exactly where we are at any given time, but do we really? You can get precise location information with just an iPhone

Task: Find your location using Theodolite
Difficulty: Beginner
Time needed: 10 minutes

GPS is, of course, built in to the iPhone and is ideal for satellite navigation and other location-aware activities. It is, however, just one method among many and there is an app that can offer tracking previously reserved for specialist equipment. Theodolite has its roots in professional communities who need specific data, but it is a useful tool for anyone who wants to know their position. It looks complicated, but there is a good reason for that. It has to display a large amount of information and once you are used to the way it works, you will understand all of the data presented.

The app can work as a compass, GPS, two-way inclinometer and offers a variety of information. In this tutorial we will explain the benefits of the app and how to make the most of the various components and information included.

Features of Theodolite
What do all of the icons mean?

● **Targeting**
To get the level just right you need to move the iPhone until the box turns green; a simple indicator that means a lot

● **Maps**
The map functions are incredibly useful and help in a variety of ways. Think of it as an advanced Google Maps

● **Knowledge base**
Just the data
If you do not need images, but are more concerned with the data produced, you can use the Copy function in the HD or Pro version to select the position, altitude and other results in simple text form. This makes it much easier to share the data with others.

● **Accuracy**
The data displayed on-screen is incredibly accurate and enables you to make fine adjustments without touching the screen at all

● **Camera functions**
The camera is the heart of the program for collecting data and is essential for displaying and sharing everything you capture with the app

Tips | Tricks | Hacks | Apps

Step-by-step | Theodolite Find your geographical location

1: Start the right way
When the app starts, make sure you click OK when it asks if it can use your current location. If you click Don't Allow it won't work as it should do and many of the features will be unable to function.

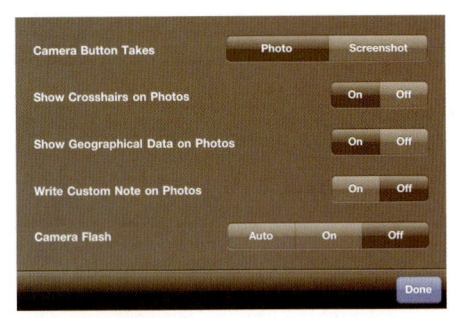

2: The settings
It is worth tapping the Pref icon at the top left early on so that you can choose how you want the camera to work and the units you would like to use. You can also access the help documentation here.

3: Calibration
Tap the CAL icon on the main screen to calibrate the iPhone. This is incredibly important and enables the various measurements to be taken accurately. Remember that we are getting very precise.

4: Positioning
You will see a red square in the middle of the screen. Move the iPhone around until it lines up with the white cross. When it turns green you can be sure that you have the iPhone held level, vertically and horizontally.

5: Mapping
Press the MAP icon on the main screen to use the mapping feature. Here you can choose to show the map in satellite, hybrid or as a Google Map and it will always show exactly what direction you are facing.

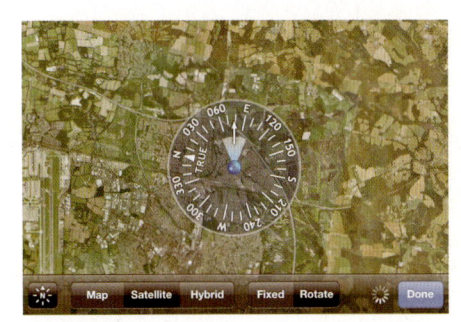

6: Clever mapping
When in the map function you can also choose the Rotate option which will keep you facing in one direction and rotate the map as you move. This could be useful if you need to follow a specific track.

7: Notes
In Preferences you can select an option that will let you write notes against each photo. This is useful if you are taking multiple photos in one location and need to differentiate between them.

8: Taking things further
Once you are used to the system, you may want to take things further by investing in the HD or Pro version which offers facilities such as Optical Rangefinder and the ability to judge distances.

9: Low light
In the HD or Pro version you can use the Lens feature to toggle coloured filters which will help preserve the images in low light conditions or even at night using night vision.

iPhone Tips, Tricks, Apps and Hacks 91

Tips | **Tricks** | Hacks | Apps

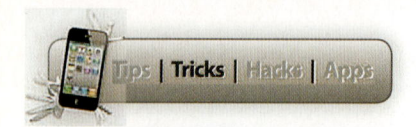

Identify and purchase a song in an instant

Music recognition services save frustration by making it simple to accurately identify songs just by listening to them

Task: Identify music using Shazam
Difficulty: Beginner
Time needed: 5 minutes

Remember that frustration you felt when you heard a snippet of a track on the radio, but the disc jockey didn't even tell you what it was? Invariably you end up spending the rest of the day humiliating yourself by humming what you can remember of the track to friends and family in the hope that they can help identify the song.

Thankfully, a free music recognition app like Shazam for the iPhone brings that sort of frustration to an end. It does something that we are able to do far too infrequently; it recognises music by listening to it. With a few seconds' worth of analysis, it will tag the track, identifying its title and artist. That's a boon in itself, but it goes further, with one-click access to song lyrics, so you can sing along to your new discovery, and even buy and download the song through a link to the iTunes Store.

The free version of Shazam lets you tag up to five songs every month. That should be enough for most occasional listeners, but a paid-for version offers unlimited tagging and other features including recommendations.

Step-by-step | Shazam | How to recognise a song with Shazam

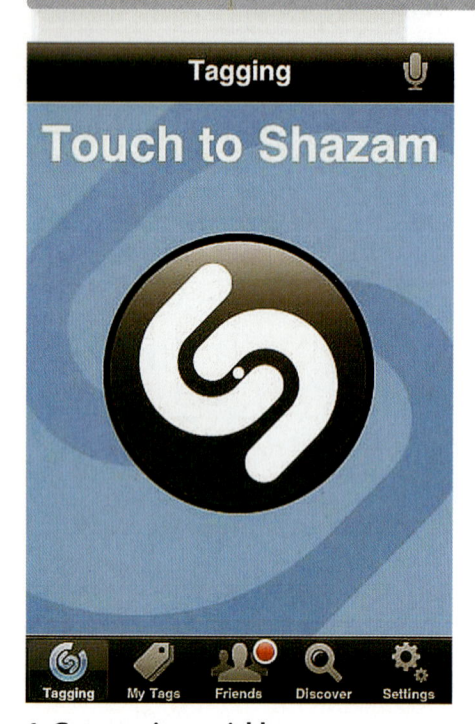

1: Get tagging quickly
Shazam is built for speed so is a basic affair. Hold the iPhone's microphone close to the source of music and touch the large icon to begin.

2: Analysis stage
The sound you've just recorded is sent to the Shazam servers and analysed. It should only take a few seconds for Shazam to return a result.

3: Showing the details
If it's successful in its recognition attempt, Shazam will display the song's title, artist and often a thumbnail image of the album artwork.

Tips | Tricks | Hacks | Apps

Organising music
Keeping on top of your tracks in Shazam

- **Shared music**
  What are your friends listening to? Set up an account – you can do it through Facebook – to share the music you are listening to and tagging

- **Quick tagging**
  You're never far away from instant recognition. Tap the Tagging button here to start listening to any music

- **Sign up for unlimited tagging**
  The free version of Shazam is limited by the number of songs it can tag during a month. The commercial version is free from such restrictions

- **Changing settings**
  Customise Shazam to enable tagging when the app launches. This saves vital seconds if you need to identify a song quickly

- **Knowledge base**
  Organisation is key
  If you have amassed a lot of tags things can get a bit cluttered on the tags page. But you can organise your finds. Tap the information button at the top of the screen to organise your tags by date or artist.

4: Read the lyrics
But you'll find more related information on the same page. For example, tap the Lyrics button to follow the lyrics to the song.

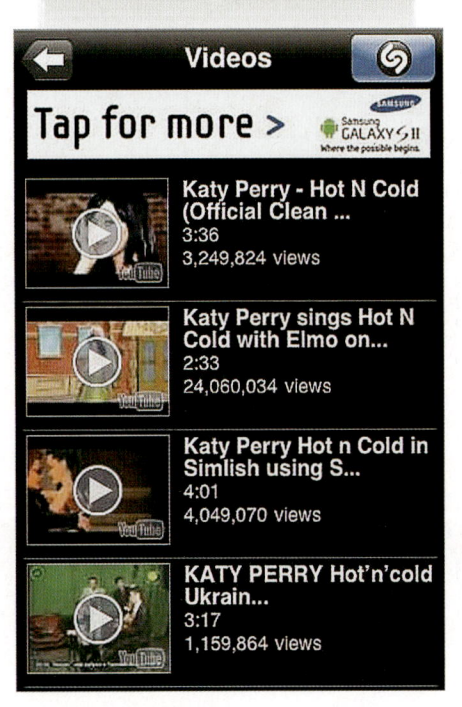

5: Watch the video
Shazam also links to videos. Tap the Videos button for a list of YouTube videos of that song (where available). Just tap the thumbnail to play.

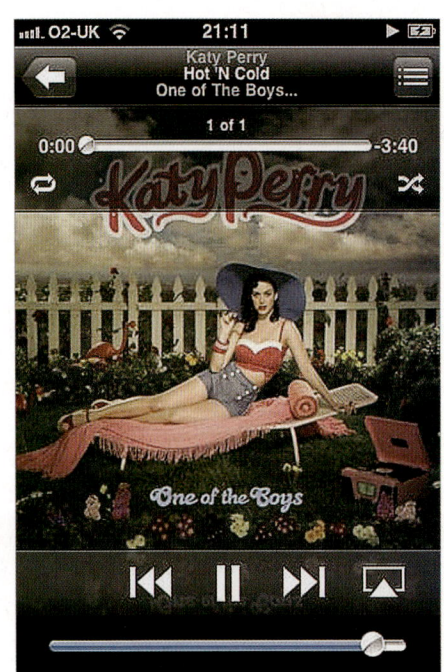

6: Buy the track
Tap the iTunes button to download the track. Within seconds of hearing it, it's now in your iTunes library and yours to play and keep.

Tips | **Tricks** | Hacks | Apps

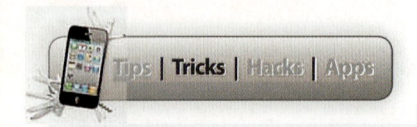

Test your eyesight with your iPhone

Is your eyesight as sharp as you think it is? A fun test can show you how well you can see

Task: Test how well you can see
Difficulty: Beginner
Time needed: 10 minutes

Of all the purposes to which an iPhone could be put, it's unlikely that many could have foreseen a tool to test eyesight. But thanks to apps like Vision Test, an iPhone can even check for eye problems, although it isn't designed to replace a visit to an optician (there are all sorts of eye problems, including eye disease, that can't be identified using an iPhone application). In fact, the app makes it clear that the tests it runs do not replace a professional examination, and only after acknowledging this can you access the tests.

Vision Test's programme involves checking your eyesight while holding the iPhone at a set distance. The selection of tests mimic those that an optician would run. The app's Visual Acuity checks how well you can see objects in the distance, while another checks for signs of astigmatism – which can cause an eye to be unable to focus. A 'duochrome' test mimics those red and green optician tests to check for aberration in focus, while another test checks for colour blindness. A short question and answer test asks basic questions to identify future risks to your eye health. You end up with a short eyesight report.

Step-by-step | Vision Test Check your iPhone eyesight

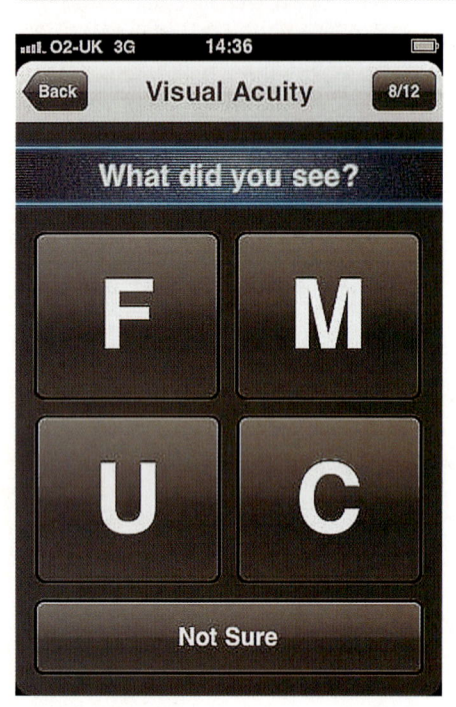

1: Visual Acuity
Hold your iPhone at arm's length and cover each eye. A dozen letters are displayed one-by-one at decreasing sizes. Try to correctly identify them.

2: Checking for astigmatism
Cover an eye at a time. The astigmatism test shows a pattern of lines, and you must identify whether any lines appear darker than others.

3: Duochrome test
The Duochrome test shows an image on red and green backgrounds. You simply have to answer whether any of the lines appear darker.

Tips | Tricks | Hacks | Apps

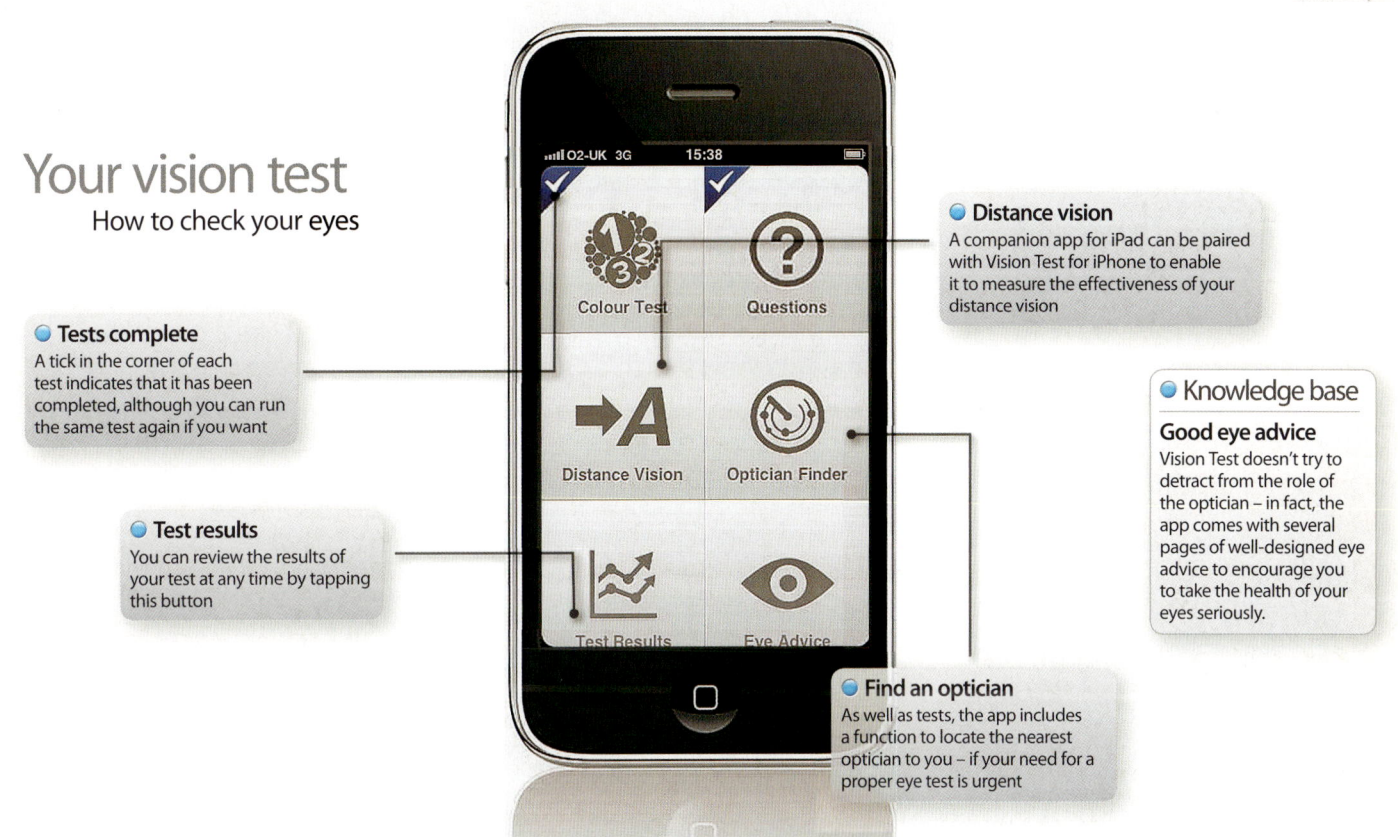

Your vision test
How to check your eyes

Tests complete
A tick in the corner of each test indicates that it has been completed, although you can run the same test again if you want

Test results
You can review the results of your test at any time by tapping this button

Distance vision
A companion app for iPad can be paired with Vision Test for iPhone to enable it to measure the effectiveness of your distance vision

Knowledge base
Good eye advice
Vision Test doesn't try to detract from the role of the optician – in fact, the app comes with several pages of well-designed eye advice to encourage you to take the health of your eyes seriously.

Find an optician
As well as tests, the app includes a function to locate the nearest optician to you – if your need for a proper eye test is urgent

4: Testing colour blindness
This test displays four coloured patterns made up of circular dots. You're tested on your ability to identify the different-coloured number displayed in each.

5: Final test
The final test comprises three questions covering other issues that might affect your eyes. You need to answer the questions as truthfully as you can.

6: Test results
A summary of how well you did appears. Test Vision stores results for future reference, and if the results indicate problems, suggests visiting an optician.

iPhone Tips, Tricks, Apps and Hacks **95**

Tips | Tricks | Hacks | Apps

Measure your heart rate on the move

Being able to monitor your heart rate may sound like a gimmick, but it has benefits such as showing whether you are healthy

Task: Measure your heart rate with Instant Heart Rate
Difficulty: Beginner
Time needed: 2 minutes

It sounds like the stuff of science fiction, but you can measure your heart rate with an iPhone. Instant Heart Rate enables you to monitor your heart rate in just a few seconds and will store your results over time so that you can keep a close eye on your general health. Your heart rate can indicate how generally healthy you are, and this is a quick way to see if it is, on average, too high. You can take readings in moments of stress or after exercise to see how quickly your heart rate decreases, which is a useful indicator of your fitness, and the whole process is completed using camera and your finger.

Some handy information is included in the app to give you an idea of where your heart rate should be, and you can also email your results to others, should they want a record of your heart rate over time. It is a simple app that takes a little time to get used to, but once you are conversant with the exact technique needed to take accurate readings it is worthwhile continuing to take readings every day. The more you use it, the more accurate the results will be over time and – you never know – it could save your life.

Step-by-step | Instant Heart Rate Measure your heart rate

1: Your first test
Open the app and tap the 'Measure' icon at the top. Now hold your finger over the camera lens as flat as you can.

2: Perfect your technique
Try it a few times and make sure you completely cover the lens. Don't push too hard and try to relax; watch the blue circle to see it is tracking a heartbeat.

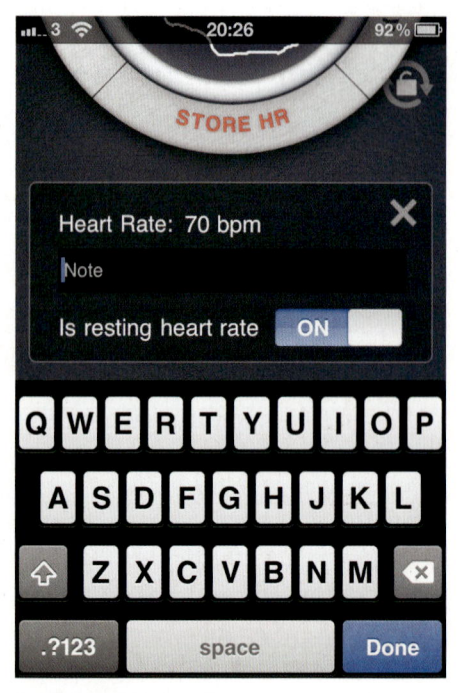

3: Store the result
Tap the 'Store HR' button to keep the result forever. It will be stored alongside the date and time and kept in a list with all of your other saved readings.

Tips | **Tricks** | Hacks | Apps

The heart of the app
A look at the very simple interface

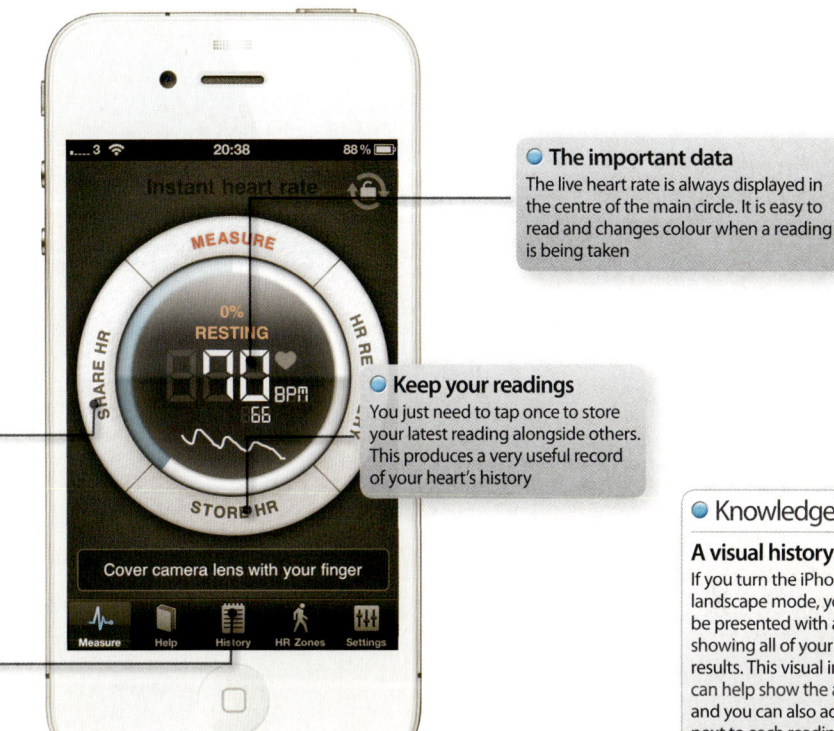

○ Time to share
You can share your heart rate history with your doctor or family, or just keep it as a record to see if extra exercise improves your future readings

○ The history
The history shows the date and exact time of each reading, and is available directly from the main screen. The time readings are useful indicators to help you manage your health

○ The important data
The live heart rate is always displayed in the centre of the main circle. It is easy to read and changes colour when a reading is being taken

○ Keep your readings
You just need to tap once to store your latest reading alongside others. This produces a very useful record of your heart's history

○ Knowledge base

A visual history
If you turn the iPhone into landscape mode, you will be presented with a chart showing all of your past results. This visual indicator can help show the average and you can also add notes next to each reading.

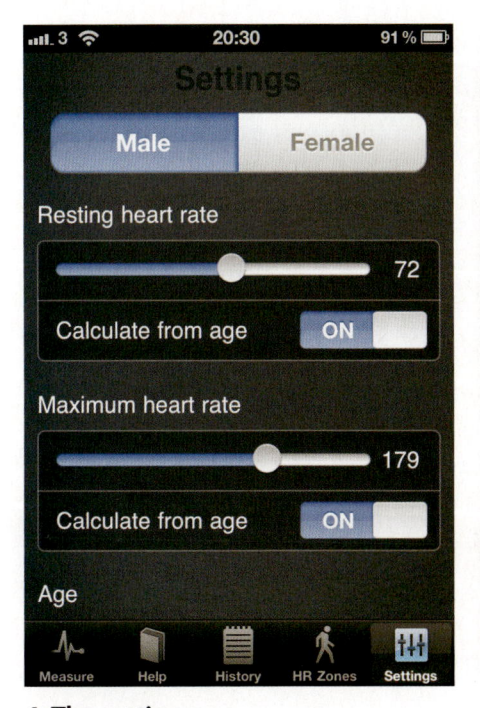

4: The settings
Make sure that the settings are correct. You can choose your gender, age and set your exact preferences to help you get the most from the app.

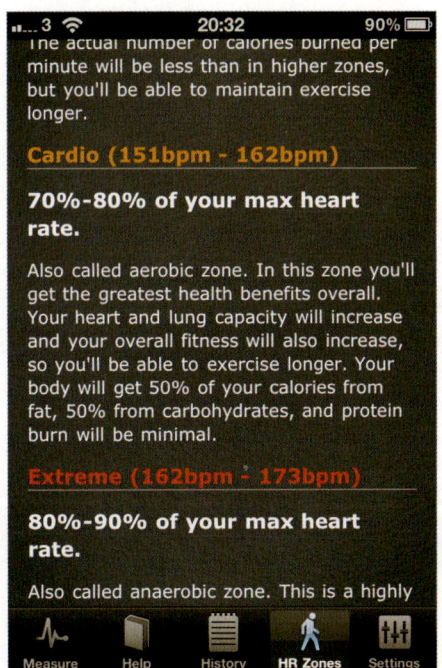

5: Proper exercising
It can also be used to check how hard you are exercising. It offers advice on how fast your heart should beat during different types of exercise.

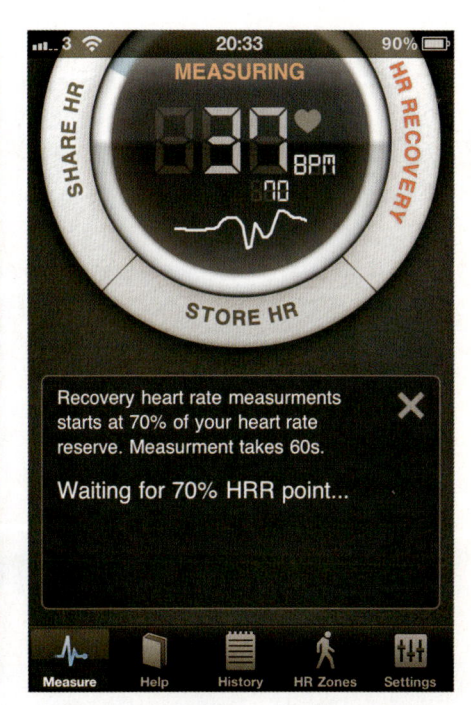

6: Time to recover
'HR Recovery' automatically records your heart rate when it reaches 70 per cent of your average heart rate, a quick way to test your recovery after exercise.

Tips | Tricks | **Hacks** | Apps

Hacks
Essential guides and features to help you get more from your iPhone

Features:

100 The secrets of jailbreaking
Everything you need to know about jailbreaking your iPhone

106 The benefits of jailbreaking
The best ways to extend the functionality of your phone

Tutorials

116 Reply to texts without exiting your current app
118 Move multiple applications at once
120 Learn to launch applications using gestures
122 Fit more apps into your on-screen folders
124 Shrink the icons on your iPhone's screen
126 Get Exposé-style tabs on your iPhone
128 Update your status from any app
130 Enjoy Flash-based content on your iPhone
132 Copy files and connect to your local network
134 Wirelessly transfer data securely over Wi-Fi

"Add extra functionality to your phone"

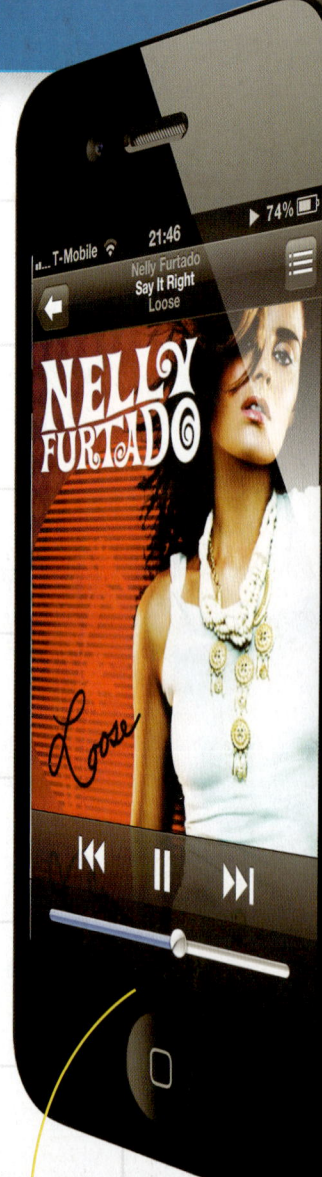

118 Learn to move multiple apps in one go

111 Control music from your Lock screen

98 iPhone Tips, Tricks, Apps and Hacks

Tips | Tricks | **Hacks** | Apps

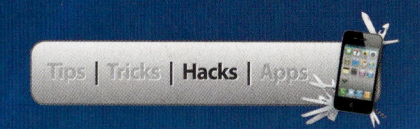

109 Access and explore your filing system

HOT HACKS
✔ View Flash
✔ Share files
✔ Tweet with ease
✔ Expand folders
✔ Share your 3G

114 Manage your iPhone photo albums

iPhone Tips, Tricks, Apps and Hacks **99**

Tips | Tricks | **Hacks** | Apps

Everything you need to know about **the benefits, pitfalls, delights and dangers** behind hacking your iPhone

The secrets of jailbreaking

100 iPhone Tips, Tricks, Apps and Hacks

What is jailbreaking?

Jailbreaking is the term used for hacking your iPhone in order to install applications and settings that aren't allowed natively by Apple. The perfect example of a jailbroken feature is the ability to change the icons that represent your apps. The reason that people have opted to break through Apple's control of the operating system is that they believe that as the owner of the device they have the right to do whatever they like with it. Of course, jailbreaking isn't as simple as making the decision. It involves seriously altering the software on your iPhone to accept jailbroken apps. There have been numerous ways to jailbreak and the system has to be fluid as with each new software update from Apple they plug any holes found by jailbreakers. The jailbreak community then has to find a new way to exploit the device to gain access to the operating system. There have been some incredibly inventive ways to do so, from the original jailbreak where users had to create their own, custom version of the software to load onto a device, to websites where you simply click a button and the jailbreak enters your device cleverly coded in a PDF document.

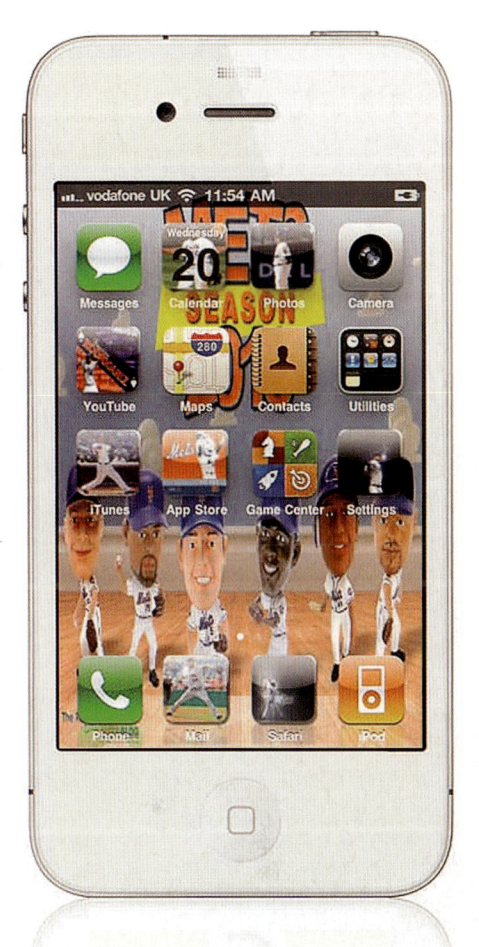

How do you jailbreak?

Jailbreaking is a process that is constantly changing and evolving. By the time this book is published the exploit shown here may well be patched and there will be another way to jailbreak a device. Each and every exploit comes from a developer who has constructed a system whereby the device can be jailbroken. This either involves visiting a website and following instructions or downloading software to do the same. The key factor is to ensure that you have the correct versions of the iOS software on your device, otherwise you could do irreparable damage to it. We cannot stress how important this is. If the jailbreak is for iOS version 4.3.3, you need to see this value when your iPhone is plugged in, with iTunes open and the summary screen showing. You can then jailbreak using the exploit available.

Jailbreak your iPhone

The JailbreakMe exploit is by far the simplest ever. There is no need for software, cables or even iTunes. This jailbreak was running iOS 4.3.3

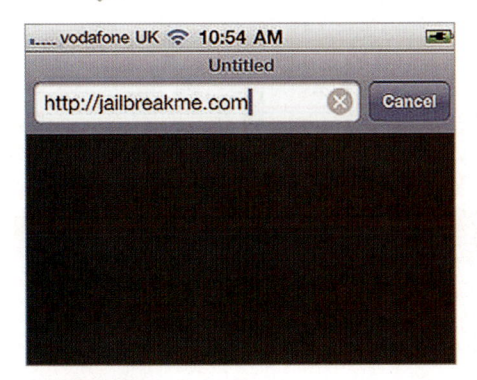

1: Navigate
On your iPhone, open Safari, type the address shown exactly as it appears and then tap the blue Go button on the bottom of the keyboard.

2: Tap it
When the site loads all you need to do to activate the jailbreak is tap the Free button which then turns into a green Install button. Tap that too.

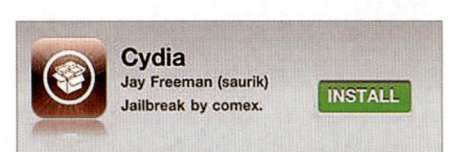

3: Watch in wonder
In just a few seconds your phone will be jailbroken and the jailbreak app store, Cydia will begin loading on your Home screen.

Is it illegal?

The biggest question that all would-be jailbreakers ask is whether or not they will be breaking the law if they hack their iOS device. This is a tricky question as there are different levels of legality that affect the jailbreaking ecosystem. First and foremost it *is* legal to jailbreak your device. In the eyes of the law you own the hardware and can put any software on it you like. In the eyes of Apple things are slightly different. It obviously doesn't view jailbreaking as an acceptable way to treat a product you've bought from it and, as a result, should it find out that you've jailbroken your device your warranty will be null and void. Beyond the obvious legal question there are some greater levels of legality that affect would-be jailbreakers. These questions apply to the apps that run on a hacked device. There are some jailbreakers that use the hacked system to pirate apps from the App Store, running them for free. This is totally illegal and should be avoided at all costs. For those who are unsure, if there is an App Store version of the app you've found on the jailbreak store without any new or different features then you should avoid it and buy the legal version.

Is it safe?

When you jailbreak your device you open up the safety controls that Apple has carefully laid in place. You have to therefore accept the risks that come with jailbreaking as part of the territory. There have been instances of jailbreak viruses which have been able to take information from hacked devices. These viruses work in a similar way to traditional PC viruses, opening a script, which talks to the owner of the virus presenting him or her with the opportunity to explore and exploit your device. If this happens, they will have complete access to all of your sensitive information. If you suspect that your phone has been infected, you will need to change your root password from Alpine (the default on every single iOS device) using the terminal app from the jailbreak app store, Cydia.

Where do you get apps?

In order to make any changes on your newly jailbroken iOS device you'll need to load an App Store that can place the new apps on your iPhone. This store is added to your jailbroken device automatically when you complete the process and is called Cydia. It works in much the same way as the regular App Store except that it's not quite as sophisticated. You can search for packages or browse through them by type and name. Despite the lack of Apple-esque finesse, Cydia is both fun and functional. The type of apps available are actually greater in range and scope than those present on the App Store, because of the lack of corporate control over the store. Hand in hand with this seemingly limitless scope is the unfortunate increase in the number of buggy and poorly coded apps – a direct result of the lack of policing that goes on. Fortunately the best apps are both extremely well made, very functional and easy to find with a bit of research online.

"Despite the lack of Apple-esque finesse, Cydia is both fun and functional"

Download an app

1: Open Cydia
Tap on the Cydia icon on your Home screen. If it is the first time you have done this, you will need to wait while the store updates.

2: User
Tap on User and then Done. This will take you to the simplest version of the store and the one that is most like the Apple App Store.

3: Browse
You can now browse the store. The featured section is a good place to start as the most popular and useful apps are here.

Tips | Tricks | **Hacks** | Apps

Does it affect your warranty?

Jailbreaking your iPhone invalidates your warranty from Apple. This means that should you experience any problems with the operation of your phone and take it into an Apple store in a jailbroken state, they will refuse to help you. Fortunately, you can avoid this by restoring your iPhone, iPad or iPod touch prior to visiting the Apple store. Restoring your device is the process of returning it to its brand new, factory settings. Do this in iTunes by using the Restore button. Be sure to backup your iPhone first so you don't lose any valuable data.

4: WinterBoard
If you want to customise your iPhone, you need to download the WinterBoard app. So tap on the WinterBoard button.

5: Install
Cydia isn't quite as easy to use as the App Store, so you have to tap on Install and then hit the Confirm button to get it.

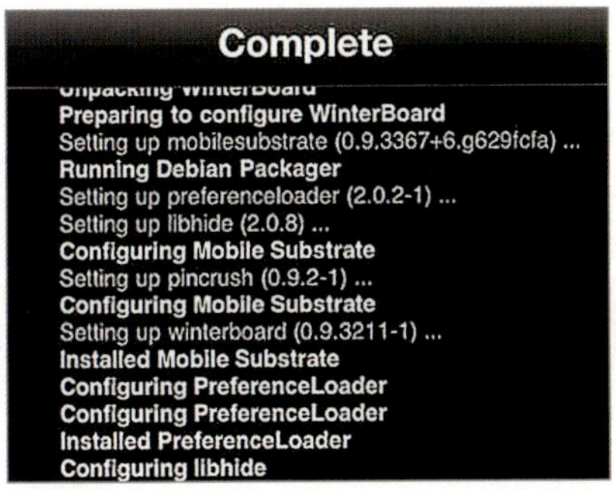

6: Code
As the app downloads, you'll see a lot of code being generated. When the app is done hit the Restart Device button.

iPhone Tips, Tricks, Apps and Hacks **103**

Tips | Tricks | **Hacks** | Apps

Can you still use the normal iPhone functions and apps?

Jailbreaking has no effect on your ability to use your iDevice as it was intended – unless you download an app that is designed to change those functions. You can still sync your device through iTunes, although any jailbreak data will not be saved or synced. This means that you can go about your normal routine with regards to iTunes, syncing music, movies, photos and backing up contacts, notes and other information. You can also browse and buy from the App Store in just the same way. You do have to be alert when syncing, however, as a jailbreak is only valid for one specific version of the iOS software, so should you unwittingly update your iPhone with new software you will lose the jailbreak and have to do it all over again. iTunes will alert you when new software is available and prompt you to download and install it. You just have to remember to carefully read all notices, pop-ups, menus and commands.

What do you do if you brick your phone?

The term bricking came about as the result of people's endeavours to hack their hardware. For those that were unsuccessful, their iPhones would become frozen and unable to function. As much use as a brick. This can happen to anyone while attempting to jailbreak for reasons too vast to enter into here. Should this happen to you, you can try and save the device by entering it into DFU mode. This is like a distress beacon which reaches out to iTunes and tells it to restore the phone. Activate this by plugging your bricked device into iTunes, holding down the Home and Sleep buttons simultaneously for ten seconds and then releasing. Eventually a symbol with an iTunes logo should appear and iTunes should alert you that it has found a phone in DFU mode. From here you should be able to restore your phone, although you may lose some of the data you had stored on the hardware.

Does it differ on different iPhones?

Would-be jailbreakers also have to be considerate of the type of device they are using as well as which carrier it connects with. This is all due to the type of baseband that the phone uses. The reason for the concern is that some people use jailbreaking to free their device from being locked into a certain carrier. This involves changing the baseband (which relates to the frequencies used by the carrier). Some jailbreaks have been able to unlock the baseband during the initial hack, but in most cases there has to be a second hack which frees the phone from the carrier, making it possible to insert any type of SIM card and enable the device to make calls and connect to the internet over the mobile network. In the US this situation is made even more confusing with the addition of different types of network. There are two global network types, CDMA and GSM. Care needs to be taken that the right hack is attempted to free the carrier lock otherwise you could brick your iPhone and render it useless.

104 iPhone Tips, Tricks, Apps and Hacks

Can you back up a jailbroken phone?

You can back up a jailbroken iPhone using iTunes as normal, however, the backup will only count and affect those things that are legitimately on your iPhone, so data from jailbreak apps will not be transferred. There are some jailbreak apps that offer the ability to back up the data so that should you wish to upgrade and then rejailbreak, the backup app will reload all of the data. This is a clunky workaround compared with iTunes but it does prevent the loss of data, which is useful. Check out Cydia for backup apps – the best free one is called AptBackup. There are paid versions which do a more sophisticated job, but free ones are ample for most needs.

1: Download
Search for AptBackup in Cydia and then install the free app using the Install button at the top of the interface.

2: Tap it
AptBackup will download and install onto your Home screen. Tap the icon to launch the app.

3: Read and digest
The app is beyond simple, just read the instructions and hit the Backup button. You can do this at any time.

Release of a newer version

As we've mentioned before, the jailbreak system is fluid. It has to be to survive all of the changes that Apple makes each time a new version of iOS is created to patch the old holes exploited by the jailbreak. Once you have jailbroken your device, that jailbreak will remain until you decide to either restore your phone back to the same versions of the software that you hacked or until you upgrade to a newer one. Should you wish to upgrade your device and then jailbreak again you can do so as long as there is a hack for the newer version. It's worth noting that the jailbreak community doesn't jailbreak each and every version of iOS, they tend to only jailbreak major revisions rather than every incremental change. If you want to become a jailbreaker you'll need to get used to following the Dev Team and keeping a close eye on which versions of iOS are available and have been hacked. You will find as you grow accustomed to the system that there are trends of popularity in types of jailbreak according to the iOS version that is available.

Restore the original settings

Going back to normal settings on your jailbroken device is always a possibility, and one of the reasons that people hack their iPads and iPhones. Nothing is totally permanent because each new version of iOS overwrites the last – you can always go back to the original version of the software you hacked or upgrade to the new one. When you go back to the normal version of iOS you will lose all of your jailbreak data and apps. Luckily, there are apps like AptBackup to take the stress out of returning to a normal version of iOS by storing your data.

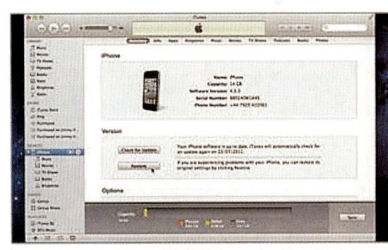

1: iTunes
Plug the iPhone into your computer, load iTunes and then click on the device on the left-hand panel. Now click on the Restore button.

2: Warning
You will now be prompted to back your device up before the restore takes place. This protects your data when the software is overwritten.

3: Confirm
Now confirm the restore. If there is a new version of the software available you will be warned that your device will be updated.

Tips | Tricks | **Hacks** | Apps

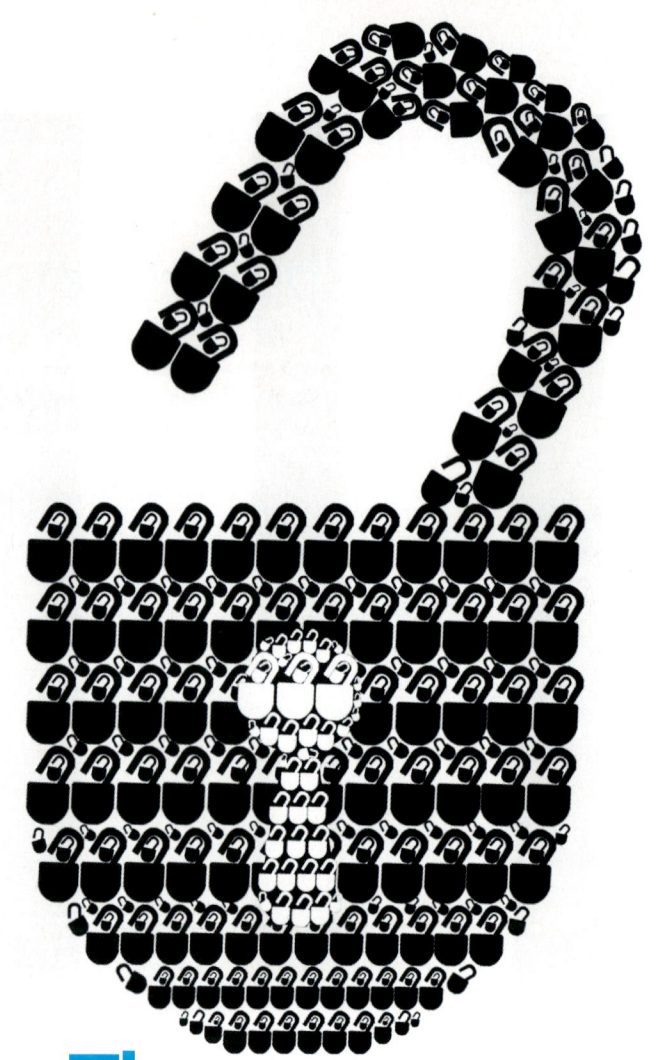

The benefits of jailbreaking

The iPhone is like a pocket-sized computer, but once it's jailbroken it can do so much more. Discover all the extra functionality it opens the door to…

If you were to sum up the world of jailbreaking benefits in one word, that word would be customisation. The obvious connotation is themes, app icons, backgrounds and sliders, but there's a lot more to it than that. The real benefit of jailbreaking is customising how the system works and there are a plethora of tweaks and hacks out there to do it for you. Rather than changing the way your iPhone works, they usually expand the functionality or just simply make it better. In this feature we're going to look at all the great apps and system tweaks that can bring those jailbreaking benefits to your iPhone and your life.

106 iPhone Tips, Tricks, Apps and Hacks

Tips | Tricks | Hacks | Apps

Apply custom themes
Change icons, backgrounds and sounds

Although background customisation is possible on non-jailbroken phones, the reality is that they are fairly simple and the SpringBoard icons remain unchanged. If you want to really alter the look and feel of your iPhone, from Lock screen to sliders, icons to themes and sounds to animations, then you need to jailbreak it. The good news is that there are thousands of themes readily available through the Cydia store. Themes can either directly replace what is already there or customise the display and functions. Most are installed using WinterBoard, but some require additional components such as Lockscreen Clock Hide and 60 Second Lock Screen, and for truly funky designs, you'll need apps like iBlanks, which is used to space out the icons into patterns.

Install a new WinterBoard theme

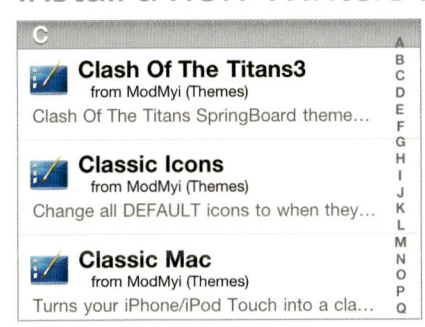

1: Find a theme
Launch Cydia and tap on Sections at the bottom of the screen. Scroll down the listing until you get to Themes. Tap on that and then look for Classic Mac.

2: Load Classic Mac
This theme changes your icons into those from an old Mac. Tap on the listing, then Install. Tap on Confirm to load them on return to Cydia.

3: Install with WinterBoard
Launch WinterBoard and tap on Select Themes. Hit ClassicMac then press the Home button to exit WinterBoard and load it.

Feature-packed texting
Like to text but despair at the built-in app?

Let's face it, the standard SMS app with the iPhone is rudimentary and there aren't a whole lot of alternatives on the App Store. Fortunately, there are no such restrictions in the jailbreak world, with the ability to send regular texts with video, photos or sounds to friends with any other kind of phone that supports SMS. You can create folders for draft messages, convert text to voice messages, attach contact pictures, use smileys and templates and forward texts via email. There's the option to use cheap networks for worldwide messaging, and you can hide texts and recipients with various privacy features. You can even send SMS using a web browser.

Send a photo attachment

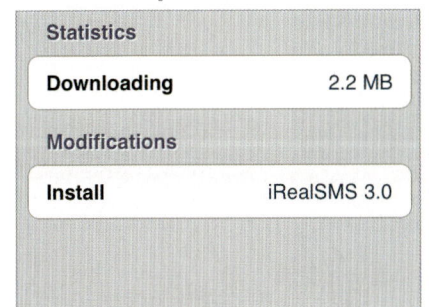

1: iRealSMS
One of the best jailbreak apps for SMS is iRealSMS 3.0. There's a free trial version so install it and then load the app.

2: Write a text
iRealSMS automatically imports your conversations and contacts. Tap on the Write icon then the plus sign to choose a contact and type your message.

3: Add media
The characters used are displayed next to the number of texts it takes to send. Tap on the camera/smiley icon and select a smiley, photo or contact.

iPhone Tips, Tricks, Apps and Hacks **107**

Tips | Tricks | Hacks | Apps

Internet music
Create playlists and download music for later

There are radio apps that stream music over the internet, but what happens when you are out of Wi-Fi or 3G range? That's right, nothing, because with no connectivity comes no music. Unless you've jailbroken, of course, because then you have access to services which enable the music to be downloaded for playing when you're way out of range. You can even create your own stations with music types, artists, eras and specific albums and records. Music can be queued up throughout the day for those times when you are going to be offline and you can set up storage for tracks to download to. Define how much space to set aside from what's available and fill it with great music that you can then listen to while out in remote countryside or on the tube.

Create your own radio station

1: Install Grooveshark
To create a customised radio station of your own you need an app like Grooveshark which has a free trial then a subscription. Download and install it from Cydia and then launch it.

2: Create station
Tap on Stations and then on Create a Station. Enter an artist or song name that you like, tap on Search and select a song. The app will start creating a station based on the music type.

3: Edit or play
The station will start automatically with a playlist of songs. Tap Stations to select a different one or on the right arrow to see details of the music, then tap to like or unlike this selection.

Downloading attachments
Get Safari to download attachments

Mobile Safari is fine for general browsing activities, but it has limitations that are tied into the way iOS works. It can't, for example, download embedded attachments in webpages or save images you find with Google. Not only are you prevented from doing this, but even if you could download those items, because there is no open filing system on the iPhone you won't know where they went or be able to access them anyway. Apps are sandboxed in to prevent viruses and malware infecting the system, but it also means you can't use the iPhone to its full extent. Fortunately there are system extensions for Safari that can get around this and enable you to download images, text, PDFs, ZIP files or anything that is stored on a website that can be accessed and downloaded. Depending on the file type you will need appropriate software to either use the file or access it. See the benefit on filing systems on the next page for more.

Download a background

1: Install Safari Download Manager
This is an app that lets you access and download all manner of files embedded or linked to in pages. Search for it in Cydia and install.

2: Look for backgrounds
Launch Safari and go to the Google homepage. Type in 'free wallpaper' and tap on Images for the thumbnails. Tap on one and then on View Full Size at the top.

3: Save it
Tap on Download To and use the file browser to navigate to where you want to save it. Tap on the down arrow to show finished downloads and where they are on the system.

Tips | Tricks | **Hacks** | Apps

Surf the filing system
Access and unzip, load and explore

If there's one thing you definitely can't do on a non-jailbroken iPhone it's rummage around the filing system. It simply isn't allowed. Once jailbroken though, you are free to go where you want, but do be careful where you tread. The benefit is that you open up the entire system of the iPhone so that you can do lots of different things. Having been able to download attachments with the Safari Download Manager in the previous benefit, a file viewer can now locate, open, print, email and save those files and attachments. ZIP files can be unzipped into folders, images can be copied and moved, documents can be opened and music dragged and dropped. A filing system viewer opens up the iPhone and turns it into a powerful computer where you are in control of the files.

View your downloads

1: Say hello to iFile
The best filing system package available on Cydia is iFile so hurry along to the store. iFile can access all areas of your iPhone, though, so exercise caution.

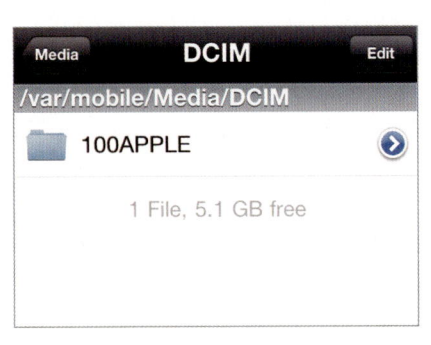

2: Locate the image
iFile is best used when you need to hack the system, but you can run the app by navigating to var>mobile>Media>DCIM>100APPLE.

3: View and copy
Tap on the folder and you'll see everything in the Camera Roll. Choose a file for the image previously downloaded then print, save or bookmark.

System shortcuts
Speed up your iPhone with shakes, taps and button presses

One of the main advantages of jailbreaking is that you can tweak your system to do things and work in new ways. One of the main proponents of that is a system app called Activator. This is used as a system shortcut to activate applications or specific activities. Whether you've downloaded it as part of something else or got it from Cydia directly, there are numerous ways it can be used. Taking photos is one example. How many times has a photo opportunity passed you by while you fumbled around switching the iPhone on, swiping the Lock screen and accessing the camera? On a jailbroken device you can set up actions like shaking to activate functions.

Directly activate the Camera app

1: Get activated
The first step is to make sure the Activator system is installed. In Cydia if it says Install tap on it, but if it says Modify you've already got it.

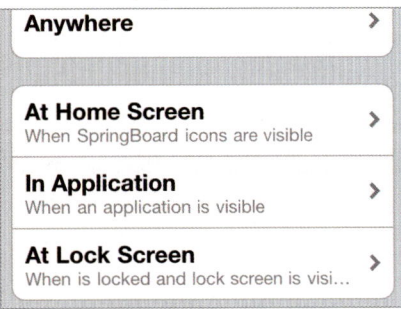

2: Set it up
Go into the Settings app and scroll down to Activator. Tap on this and then tap on At Lock Screen. Here's where you can define the action.

3: Assign the button
Under Home button tap on Single Press, then under System Applications tap on Camera. Turn the iPhone on, press the Home button and activate the camera.

iPhone Tips, Tricks, Apps and Hacks **109**

Tips | Tricks | **Hacks** | Apps

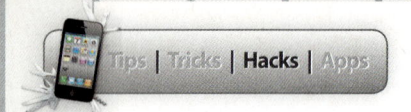

Information on tap
Increase the functionality of your Lock screen

So your Lock screen tells the time and date, but what if you could put more interesting and useful information on that initial screen? Of course you can, it's just part of the wholesale reconfiguration of what your device can do. How about adding calendar notifications of things coming up this week, the number of new mails waiting, notifications, missed calls, voicemail, SMS and icons for your favourite phone contacts? Want to get rid of the swipe bar altogether? You can do all of this. Remember, though, the Lock screen is only visible for a few seconds, so if you want access to all of this information you will need apps like 60 Second Lock Screen.

Load the Lock screen with info

1: Get the program
One of the best packages for reconfiguring your Lock screen is LockInfo, so search and install it. You will also need 60 Second Lock Screen installed.

2: Configure the app
Go into Settings and look for the entry for LockInfo. Tap on that then tap on Lockscreen. Enable this and then tap on Plugin Visibility.

3: Change the look
Still in Lockscreen, tap on Select Theme to choose a skin (there are third party ones available). Tap on Appearance and move the sliders left or right to change the opacity of the panels.

Configure settings quickly
Adjust, change and enhance in an instant

The Settings app is where all the action happens for people configuring their iPhone, but it has become a huge, sprawling industrial complex of options, and you need to exit whatever you are doing to access it. Getting to the Bluetooth on/off switch in particular is a pain as it's buried in the General settings. There are times when you need to be able to turn the 3G, Bluetooth, Edge data, Wi-Fi and Airplane modes on or off, or turn the Brightness down quickly as your battery power runs out. You can double-press the Home button to see what apps are running, but then it takes more presses to be able to get into Cancel mode. Fortunately there's an ideal jailbreak app, SBSettings, which can do all these things in one place and it's possible to configure it to pop up with a gesture, button press or tap combination.

1: Configure activation
To control your device quickly you need SBSettings. Search for it and install from Cydia. It doesn't have an icon so go to Settings and tap on Activator.

2: Tap to go
Tap on Anywhere, scroll down to Status Bar and tap on Hold. This won't be assigned to anything so scroll down and tap on SBSettings.

3: Instant access
Exit Settings. Now, at any time, tap and hold on the status bar to bring up SBS and toggle internet connectivity, brightness, processes on or off and check on available memory and storage.

110 iPhone Tips, Tricks, Apps and Hacks

Tips | Tricks | Hacks | Apps

Play music your way
Control your iPod music from the Lock screen

If you haven't already filled your Lock screen with diary appointments, contacts, the weather or other plug-in functions, we have another suggestion for you. Besides being a phone and all-round app-running powerhouse, the iPhone is also a music-playing iPod. You set it running, it plays the album, playlist or songs specified and it goes in a pocket. However, when you come to a track you don't really want to listen to, you have to switch the phone on, tap the iPod app and change it by either skipping or selecting another from your library. With a jailbroken iPhone you can shortcut that process by controlling the music directly on the Lock screen. You can adjust the volume with swipes, go back and forth between tracks on an album or individual songs, alphabetically. Double-tap on the screen to bring up the volume slider and forward and back controls. You can even get skins for the interface.

Control music on the Lock screen

1: Look for Snow Cover
The system tweak that lets you control music from the Lock screen is called Snow Cover 4. Search for it in Cydia and install as usual. The options are in Settings.

2: Load up your music
To see Snow Cover in action, go to the iPod app, select an album and set it going. Then hit the Sleep button to suspend the phone but leave the music playing.

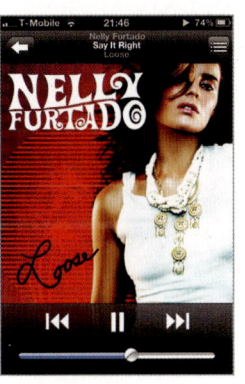

3: Control everything
Press the Home button to wake the phone up then swipe to move through tracks, up and down for volume or double-tap to bring up the media controls.

Fooling Wi-Fi
Make your apps think the 3G signal is really Wi-Fi

Mobile internet is great, but it's greater when it's a Wi-Fi signal, because not only is it faster and more consistent, there are some things that will only work with Wi-Fi. It's that big data stream guzzler – video – that is usually at the root of your Wi-Fi-only problems. Official apps like FaceTime also only work over Wi-Fi, not over the 3G signal. You can't watch high-definition YouTube videos over 3G and Skype doesn't want to know. Fortunately, a solution is at hand in the jailbreak community because we can fool apps into thinking that the 3G signal you are really receiving is actually a Wi-Fi signal, so they will then work. This applies to any app that will only work or offer specific functionality over a Wi-Fi network, and you can control which apps get fooled by toggling them on or off.

Turn 3G into Wi-Fi signal

1: Set it up
Go to Cydia and search for My3G (there's a trial version). Install it as well as the BBC News app. Run this and tap on Live. You'll get a Sorry message.

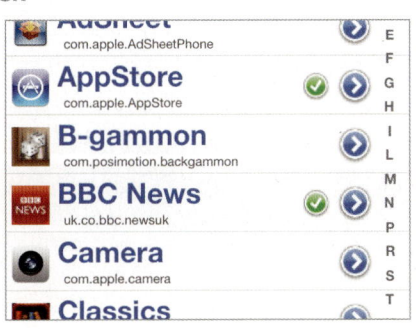

2: Configure the app
Exit the BBC News app and remove from the multi-tasking menu as well. Launch the My3G app and put a tick next to the BBC News entry in the app list.

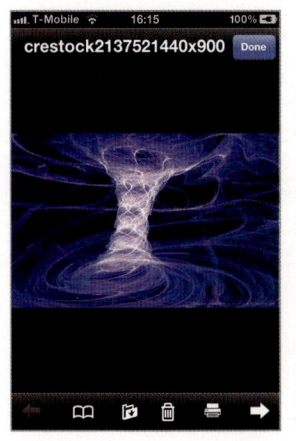

3: It's magic
Tap the right arrow next to the tick and move the Use Direct Flag toggle to the On position. Launch the BBC News app again and tap on Live to watch over 3G.

iPhone Tips, Tricks, Apps and Hacks **111**

Tips | Tricks | Hacks | Apps

The Lock screen office
Access your critical data the minute your iPhone is on

By now you should be getting the idea that the Lock screen, an open area of screen space, can now be turned into an information oasis. If LockInfo didn't give you enough then there are ways of delivering more information to your starting point in the iPhone experience. Firstly, as well as Mail, Calendar and SMS notices for both new items and missed calls, you can also feed in your must-have information. That starts with a seven-day weather report for your area and moves on to news feeds. Get fresh, breaking stories directly from the BBC, Reuters, ZDNet, CNN, Fox or any RSS feed. Want to keep up with news from American sports like the NFL, Major League Baseball, the NBA or the NHL? Add that to your sources then configure how your information appears.

Organise the information flow

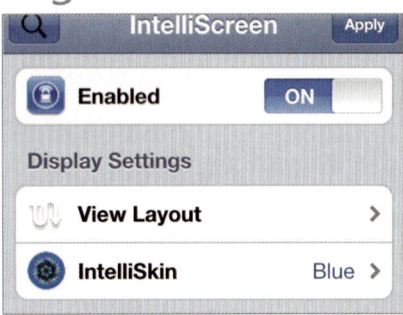

1: Get intelligence
Go to Cydia and search for IntelliScreen. Install it and then look for the IntelliScreen icon. Double-tap on this to run it and access the configuration screens.

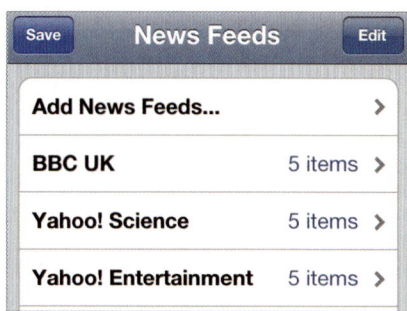

2: The info you need
Don't clutter your Lock screen with needless information, tap on each entry under Content Configuration and toggle them on or off.

3: Design the layout
Tap on View layout then double-tap on the 99:99 to toggle between two layouts. Grab an event panel and move it around, then add or remove.

Instant uninstall
The fast and easy way to remove your jailbreak apps

The next benefit for jailbreaking isn't really a benefit, but an essential system tweak. Confused? Okay, when you want to remove apps that you download from the App Store all you have to do is tap and hold them. They then go into wiggle mode with an X icon on the corner. Tapping on this uninstalls the app. However, any jailbreak apps that come with icons don't show this X. Normally you have to go into Cydia, tap on Manage, then Packages, find the one you want to get rid of, go to Modify and finally Remove. This is a cumbersome way of working, which is why this tweak is useful. Once installed it adds an uninstall X icon onto apps from Cydia.

Remove Cydia apps the easy way

1: Let's get CyDelete
Being a system tweak, this is very simple and easy to install and use. Go to the Cydia store and search for CyDelete. Tap on the entry and then on Install.

2: Install the tweak
Tap on Confirm and then install the tweak. There's a fair list of code to go through before you restart the SpringBoard to make it operational.

3: Delete away
Tap and hold on any app icon. All App Store apps will now show the X icon but so will ones from Cydia as well – like iRealSMS here. Tap on the X to uninstall.

112 iPhone Tips, Tricks, Apps and Hacks

Tips | Tricks | **Hacks** | Apps

Share your 3G
Allow other devices to use the internet

Are you one of those people who stayed on iOS 4.2.1, refusing to upgrade because there wasn't a simple jailbreak for 4.3.3? And then Comex came along with its JailbreakMe 3.0 exploit and you thought "great, I'll get round to that shortly". Well, it was short indeed because Apple patched the exploit within a week so if you haven't gone to 4.3.3 and jailbroken you've missed the boat. And that's why this next benefit is for your eyes only. Creating a Wi-Fi hotspot on your iPhone and tethering devices to it, or indeed tethering via Bluetooth and USB, was introduced in iOS 4.3 but isn't available in 4.2.1. Hence the need for a jailbreak solution that enables you to connect an iPad, iPod touch or laptop via Wi-Fi, USB or Bluetooth to the iPhone and share the 3G signal.

Create a Wi-Fi hotspot

1: Get the app
The jailbreak app that performs this function is MyWi 4.0 so go to Cydia, search for it and install. Double-tap on the app to see all the options.

2: Select the device
Out in the countryside there's no Wi-Fi connection, but you want to connect your laptop to the internet. Tap on Laptops then on WiFi Hotspot, which has the fastest setup.

3: Create the hotspot
Toggle the WiFi Hotspot to On to create the hotspot tap on Security to stop others connecting and on Advanced WiFi to select the radio channel and transmission power.

Sync over Wi-Fi
Sync your iPhone with iTunes wirelessly

The thing about iTunes is that it's great as a central hub for your music collection, but since you can browse and buy apps directly on the iPhone, get your mail over Wi-Fi and 3G, and do all the usual good stuff, it's a bit of a pain to have to manually connect your phone to the computer to synchronise it. This is especially the case when you are sat in one room and have downloaded an app but need to go to another to back it up into iTunes via the USB cable. Fortunately there is a solution that involves a jailbreak app and a small host program that has iTunes installed. With the two set up you can use your home wireless network to connect your iPhone to iTunes from anywhere within range.

Perform a sync without wires

1: Get the software
The first step is to look for Wi-Fi Sync in Cydia and install it. The next stage is to go to www.getwifisync.com and download the host program.

2: Set it up
This is available for Mac or Windows, so install it on your computer. Launch the app and then wait for the message about pairing to come up on your desktop's screen.

3: Perform a sync
You will get a message on the iPhone screen about pairing. Agree to it. Now when you run this app it will launch iTunes on your computer and automatically sync to it.

iPhone Tips, Tricks, Apps and Hacks **113**

Tips | Tricks | **Hacks** | Apps

Polite notifications
Get notifications of emails and texts on your status bar

By now you know all about the benefits of getting information onto the Lock screen, but haven't you ever looked at Android devices with a tinge of admiration over their notification system? In case you haven't seen it, whenever something installs, mail arrives or an app downloads, it posts a notification to a status bar along the top. To see what it was, you tap and drag the bar down to reveal a screen of information. Tapping on any event loads up the app that posted it, but a combination of Lock Info's InfoShade screen and Notifier+ can do the same on your iPhone. The events you can be notified of include calls, voicemail, messages, email, MMS, instant messaging and calendar dates. These can be displayed on existing status bar or a drag-down status bar, just like on an Android.

1: Which app is needed
There's two versions of the jailbreak app that offers this kind of functionality. One is Notifier, the other is Notifier+. The latter has more options, so download and install that.

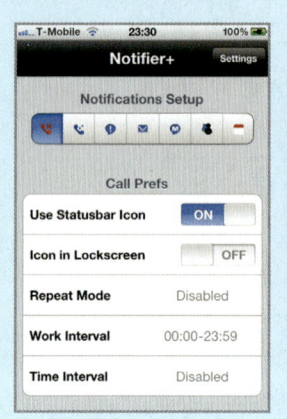

2: Tweak some of the settings
Notifier+ will post notifications onto the Lock screen that you can tap on to access the app in question. If you are using LockInfo, though, you may want to toggle this option off.

3: Check the events
When you get a notification an icon will appear on the Lock screen first. Tapping on this launches the related app. If the phone is on, notification icons will appear on the status bar for you to access.

Manage your photo albums
Create and manage new photo folders

One of the consequences of a sandboxed app system is that the Photo album app is pretty rigid. Want to create new folders within the Photo album? You can't do that. Want to delete photos in albums other than the Camera Roll? Nope. Want to move a photo from one album to another? You get the idea. Fortunately, with a system extension jailbreak you can do all of these things with new albums, though you can't change existing ones. Photos and videos can be moved around to new albums, entire ones deleted and folders copied from your iPhone to your PC via the USB cable. It's called PhotoAlbums+ for iPhone/Pod.

Create a new album

1: Create a new album
Run the PhotoAlbums+ app and tap the plus sign. Enter a name for the new album. If you also tap the lock sign you can add a password for this folder.

2: Copy pictures and video
Tap on Camera Roll, hit the right arrow at the top and tap to select the pictures to move. Hit the Move icon and they will instantly be moved over.

3: Manage albums
Go back out to the Album view to see your new album is now populated. Swipe left to right to bring up the Delete option, or tap to view the contents.

Tips | Tricks | **Hacks** | Apps

Light your way
Use motion-sensing activation to turn your phone into a torch

Ever since the iPhone 4 came with LED flash there have been apps that have utilised this light source. There are a few torchlight programs on the App Store, but they are all constrained by the same thing – they have to work the same way that all official apps work. You need to find the app icon and double-tap on it for it to work. That's fine in most situations, but after an evening at the local public house you might want something a bit easier to use. That's where the jailbreak Activator system comes in. We've already seen that this feature can be used to trigger apps and actions, with this ability to assign functions only available on jailbreak phones. For this benefit, we will assign a simple gesture or button click to a torchlight app so that getting the light to come on is as simple as using a real torch.

Assign actions to activating light

1: Find the package
The first step is of course to rummage through Cydia for the jailbreak app SpringFlash. You should also have Activator installed by now. If not, get it.

2: Assign the action
As you might expect, there's no icon for this, so go into Settings and tap on Activator. Tap on Anywhere so that it can come on even if apps are being used.

3: Make the motion
The default assignment is a short hold on the Home button to toggle on and off. Either keep that or try tapping on Motion and then SpringFlash.

Save YouTube videos
Download your favourite videos and view offline

Thank goodness for the YouTube app and the minimal ability to watch Flash videos. But what do you do when you are out of Wi-Fi or a strong 3G signal range? Well, most people will be sat there doing nothing, but the guy with the jailbroken iPhone will be watching all the videos he downloaded from YouTube when they were in internet range. Yes, you can download low, high or HD-quality videos from YouTube and watch them later. Also, YouTube only works over Wi-Fi, but with a jailbreak you can stream videos or save them to your device in low-quality over Edge as well. If there's a strong 3G signal you can get the hi-res videos too.

Find and save YouTube videos

1: Get the app
The app that performs this jailbreak benefit is MxTube. Install and run then tap on the Search icon (top right) and type the name of the subject.

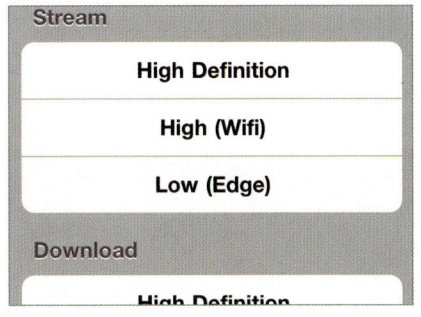

2: Select quality
You can stream to the app directly, but to save, tap on the Download option for your connection. There are versions for low, high and HD-quality downloads.

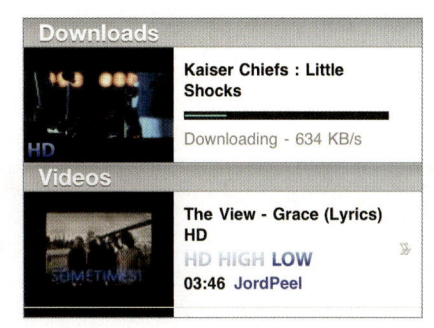

3: Download and play
Close Search to see the download progress. When it has finished it will appear in Downloads. You can then watch your videos when out of signal range.

Tips | Tricks | **Hacks** | Apps

Reply to texts without exiting your current app

Solve the issue of being interrupted by a text message when doing an important task and be able to reply without exiting the app

Task: Reply to messages with QuickReply for SMS
Difficulty: Beginner
Time needed: 5 minutes

The iOS notification system is not well known for its usability; it's fairly basic and doesn't deal well with multiple events or actions at once. For instance, if you happen to be writing a long email and then someone texts you in the middle of it, the notification will pop up in the centre of the screen, and there is no way of hiding it in the background. This means you either have to ignore it and risk the chance of forgetting to reply, or you have to stop what you are doing by clicking 'view' to open up the messaging app.

Thankfully there is a solution available for jailbroken devices that solves this; QuickReply for SMS adds in another option to the notification window – Reply. Hitting Reply will bring up an overlay of the text conversation, and you can quickly respond and get straight back to what you were doing before. Once you have this handy feature, you won't want to go back to a non-jailbroken iOS device. This tutorial will take you through all the instructions you need to easily reply to SMS messages from within another app, from installing it and what happens when you receive a text to uninstalling it if you don't want to keep it.

Step-by-step | QuickReply for SMS Replying from within an app

1: Cydia
You will need to have installed Cydia before starting. This makes finding jailbroken apps easier. Once installed, open it up to update the package list.

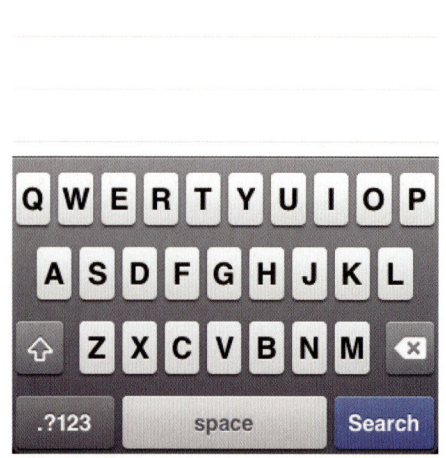

2: Search for the app
Click on the magnifying glass in the bottom right, and type 'QuickReply for SMS' into the search box. This will add it to your queue.

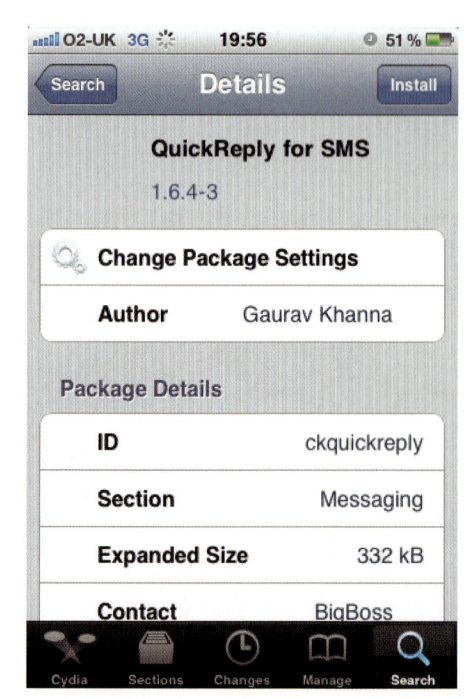

3: Confirm download
Click on the app to see more information about it; hit Install to add it to your download queue. Then press Confirm to start the installation.

Tips | Tricks | **Hacks** | Apps

Replying to SMS
Swiftly respond to a text message

Bubble icons
The speech bubbles are shown in the same way as normal, with yourself on the left and the other half of the conversation on the right

Background app
The app that you are currently using still remains visible in the background, slightly dimmed so you can read the text

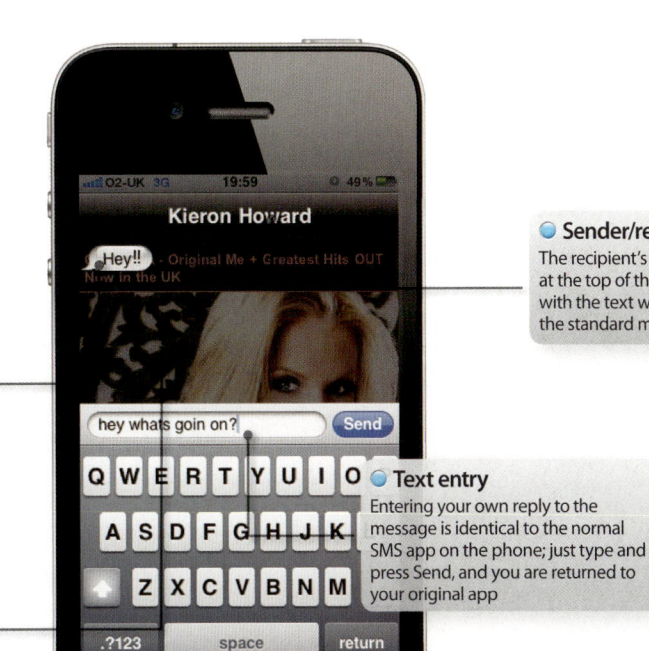

Sender/recipient
The recipient's name appears at the top of the screen along with the text window, similar to the standard messaging app

Text entry
Entering your own reply to the message is identical to the normal SMS app on the phone; just type and press Send, and you are returned to your original app

Knowledge base
Add a profile picture to SMS messages
QuickReply for SMS also adds in the ability to add an in-profile picture next to the sender of the SMS. Just add a profile picture to the contact and it will automatically appear in the notification.

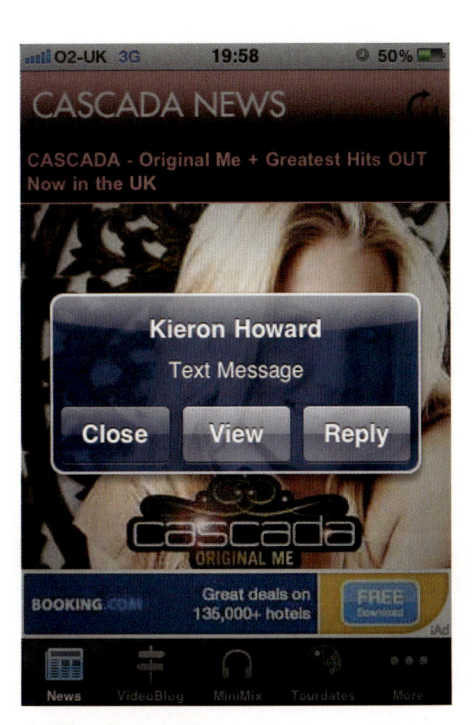

4: Give it a test!
Once it's installed, get a friend to text you while you are using another app. You should then see the Reply button added on the right.

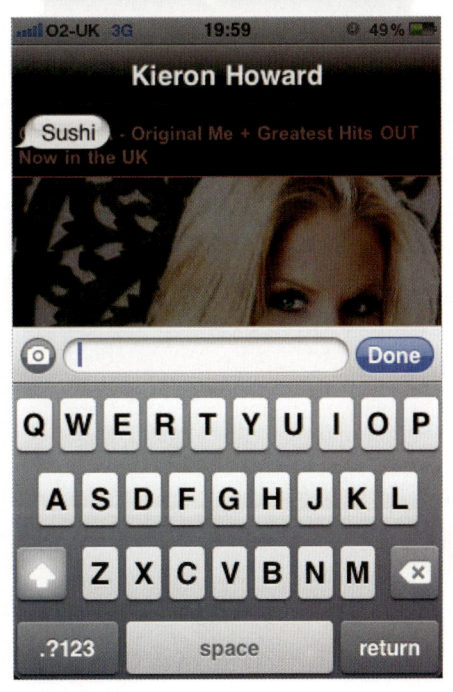

5: Reply to text
Clicking Reply will fade in a messaging screen overlay, you can then reply to texts as normal, then click on Send, and continue what you are doing.

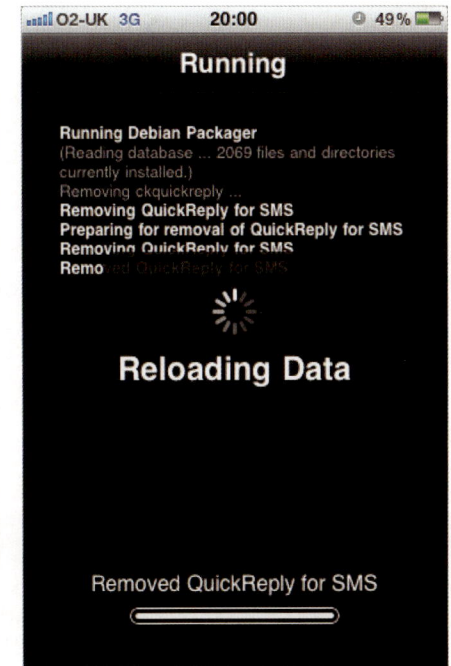

6: Remove the app
If you decide you no longer want the app, then just open Cydia and click on Modify, and then Remove. Restart SpringBoard and the app will be gone.

Tips | Tricks | **Hacks** | Apps

Move multiple applications at once

Moving lots and lots of apps to different folders can be a time-consuming task on an iPhone. Learn how to move groups at once

Task: Organise your Home screen icons with MultiIconMover
Difficulty: Beginner
Time needed: 5 minutes

The iOS Home screen is a very attractive looking place, it's clean, consistent and organised. Part of this consistency comes at the cost of the user being able to quickly customise the layout. Apple has not yet introduced a way of being able to move your app icons around in bulk on the device, although it is possible to move apps in groups from within iTunes when it is connected to your computer, but not while out and about.

With the largest iPhone capacity currently set at 32GB, there is a lot of room for apps, and it's possible to have hundreds or even thousands installed on a single device. Up until Apple introduced iOS 4 there was no real way to organise apps, but the update included the ability to store apps into folders, such as 'Games' or 'Tools'. This is great, but if you have filled up a lot of your phone's storage with apps and you want to recategorise them on the device then it means moving them one-by-one. In this tutorial, we will take you through installing an app – using MiltiIconMover in this example – that will enable you to group apps together and move them in a batch on a jailbroken device.

Step-by-step | MultiIconMover Organising multiple icons

1: Search MultiIcon
Once you have Cydia installed, open it and in the search box type 'MultiIconMover' and press OK. This will search for the app.

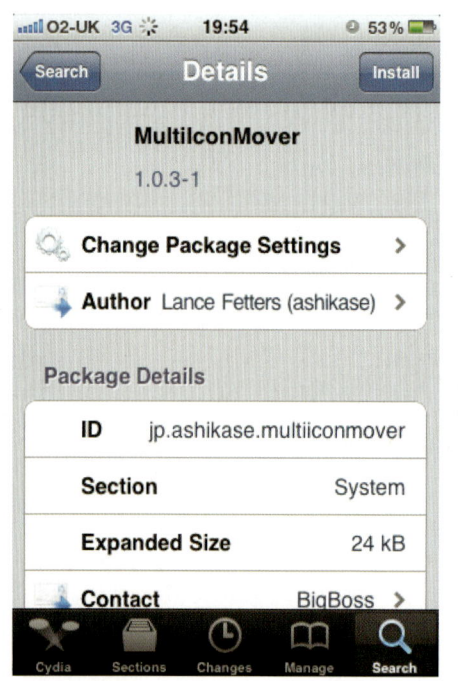

2: Install the app
You will then be presented with more information about the app. Clicking on Install will start off the installation process.

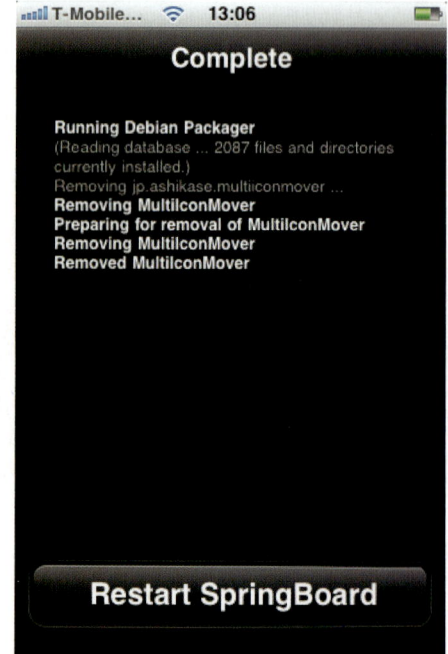

3: Restart SpringBoard
You might need to restart SpringBoard; click the Refresh button when asked. The app is installed, but there won't be an icon for it on your Home screen.

118 iPhone Tips, Tricks, Apps and Hacks

Tips | Tricks | **Hacks** | Apps

Shifting icons as a group
Speedy app placement

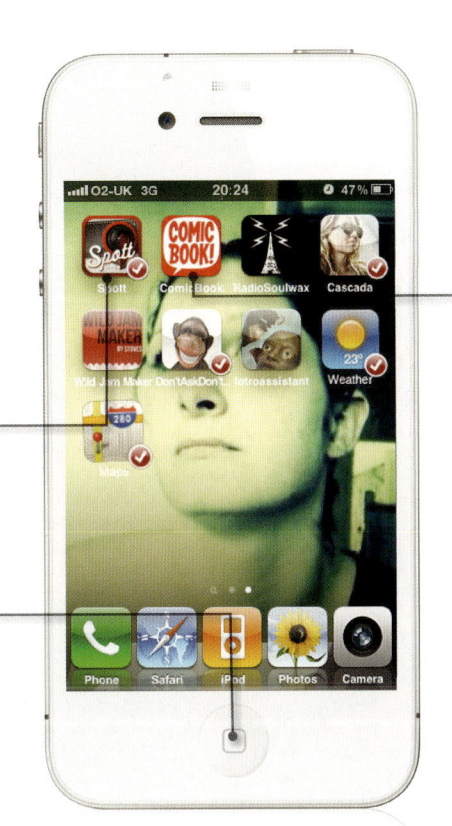

Icon selector
Application icons gain a small tick next to them once you have activated the 'wiggle' and pressed on them again

Group move
Once you have selected all the icons you want to move, just slide them across to the required Home screen, or press the Home button

Similar apps
A lot of people like to place all similar apps together in a folder or on a screen, such as all their games together

Knowledge base

Big Boss repository
If you don't want to get the app through Cydia you can also download the files from www.thebigboss.org. Big Boss is a repository for jailbroken apps that Cydia uses, but also enables you to download to your PC and install from there.

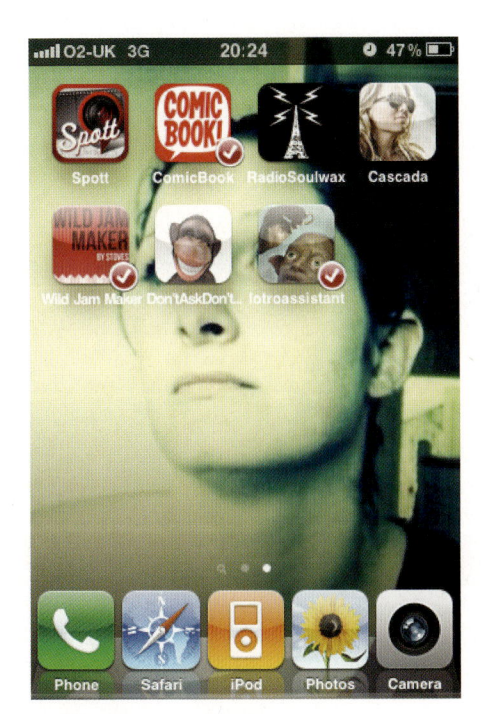

4: Move some icons
Long press on an app to start them wiggling, then tap others you want to move as well. Sliding one app will now slide all of them.

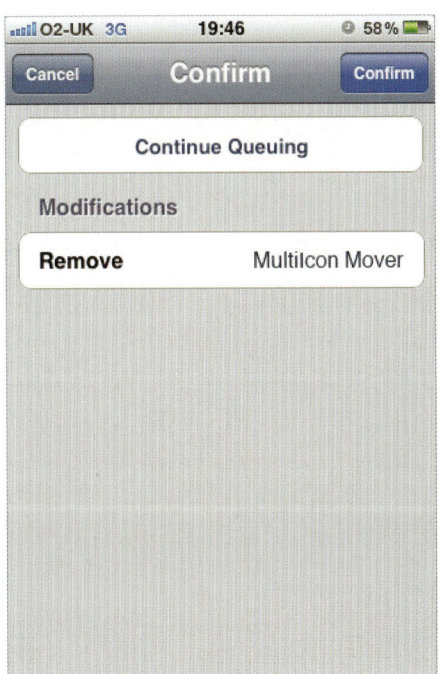

5: Remove MultiIconMover
If you have finished rearranging and don't want any clutter on your device, removing the app is simple. Open Cydia and click Modify on the app.

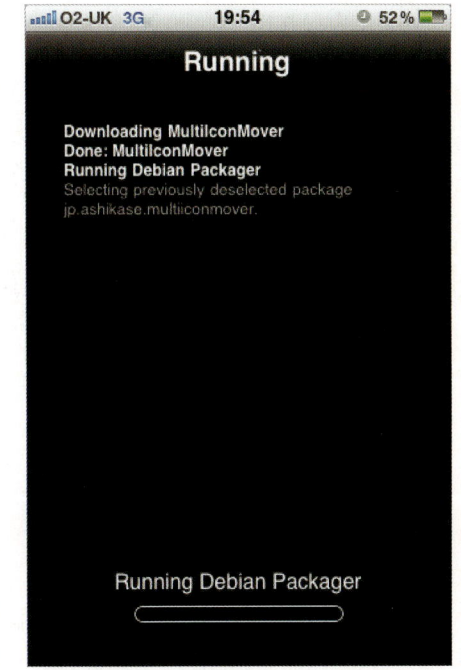

6: Removal complete
The package remover will run for a few seconds, and then you may be asked to restart SpringBoard again. Once this is done, the app will be removed.

iPhone Tips, Tricks, Apps and Hacks **119**

Tips | Tricks | **Hacks** | Apps

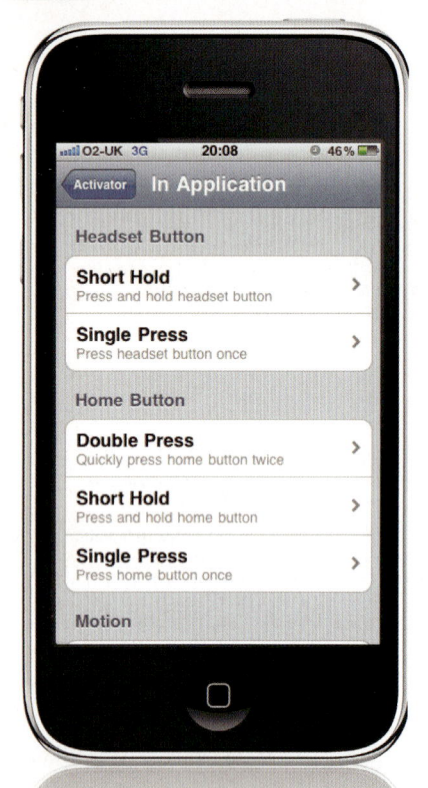

Learn how to launch applications using gestures

Speed up common tasks on your iPhone, such as launching particular apps, by using gestures to perform actions and shortcuts

Task: Set up gestures to perform functions with Activator
Difficulty: Intermediate
Time needed: 10 minutes

When Apple first launched the iPhone, one of its key selling points was the fact that it enabled a useable interface to browse the internet. Smartphones had been able to surf the web for years, but the fact that they lacked a trackpad or mouse in favour of a set of keypad cursors or small joystick meant that navigating pages was often cumbersome and frustrating. The iPhone had an innovative touch screen that made scrolling up and down pages quick and easy. The jewel in the crown of the iPhone's input control was the use of pinching to zoom in and out of webpages.

While there are a few other gestures used in iOS, it could be argued that there is room for many more to control the myriad of other tasks we all do, day in, day out. As with other jailbroken apps, this desire to build on what Apple has already made has led developers to produce a number of apps to achieve just that. This tutorial will walk you through finding, installing, and setting up some gestures for the Activator app, which is one of the popular famous gesture controllers available on the Cydia store.

Step-by-step | Activator Set up gesture controls

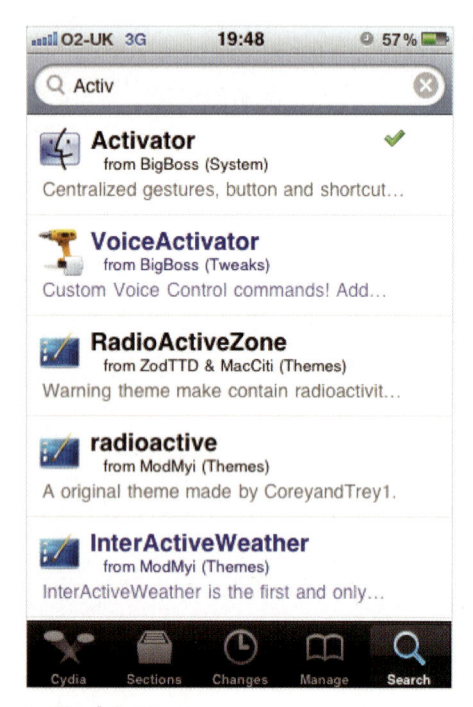

1: Find Activator
Open up the Cydia app store and search for Activator using the icon in the bottom right. Click on Install to add it to your download queue.

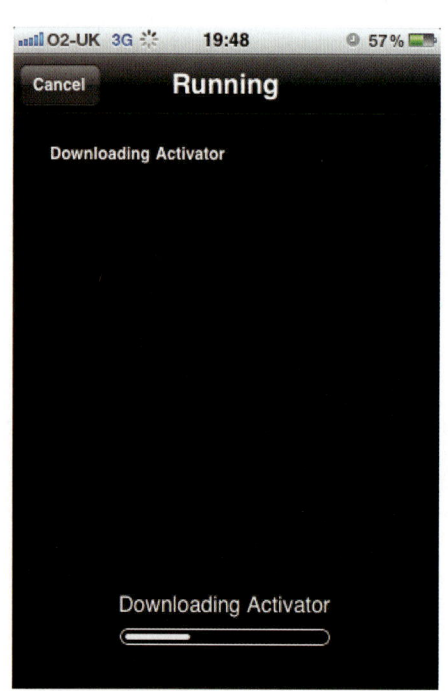

2: Install the app
Press Confirm and Cydia will start downloading the appropriate files and installing. This might take a few minutes depending on your connection.

3: Settings
Once the app has installed, open your phone's Settings menu and click Activator to enter the options for the application.

Tips | Tricks | **Hacks** | Apps

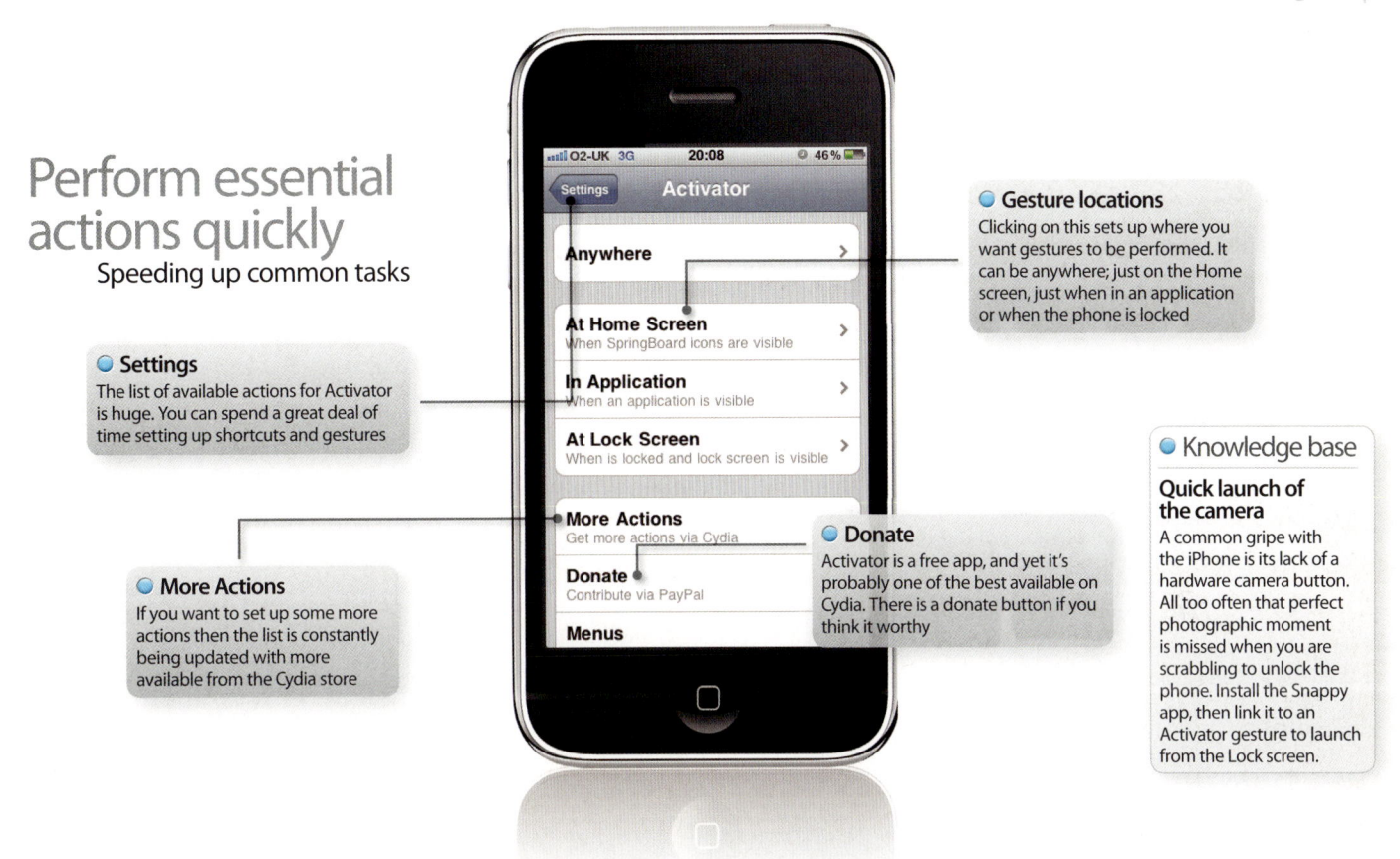

Perform essential actions quickly
Speeding up common tasks

● **Settings**
The list of available actions for Activator is huge. You can spend a great deal of time setting up shortcuts and gestures

● **More Actions**
If you want to set up some more actions then the list is constantly being updated with more available from the Cydia store

● **Gesture locations**
Clicking on this sets up where you want gestures to be performed. It can be anywhere; just on the Home screen, just when in an application or when the phone is locked

● **Donate**
Activator is a free app, and yet it's probably one of the best available on Cydia. There is a donate button if you think it worthy

● **Knowledge base**

Quick launch of the camera
A common gripe with the iPhone is its lack of a hardware camera button. All too often that perfect photographic moment is missed when you are scrabbling to unlock the phone. Install the Snappy app, then link it to an Activator gesture to launch from the Lock screen.

4: Setting up a gesture
You can set up when you want the particular gesture to be applied. You can set it to happen on the Home screen, in an app or the Lock screen.

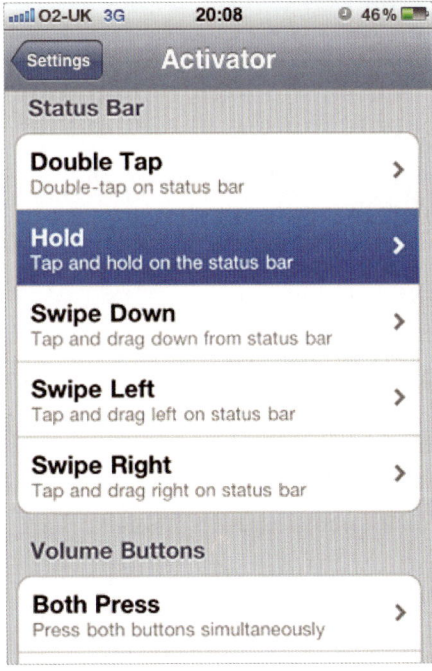

5: Example setting
If you wanted to long press on the status bar to switch apps, go into Anywhere>Activate Switcher and then just press the status bar.

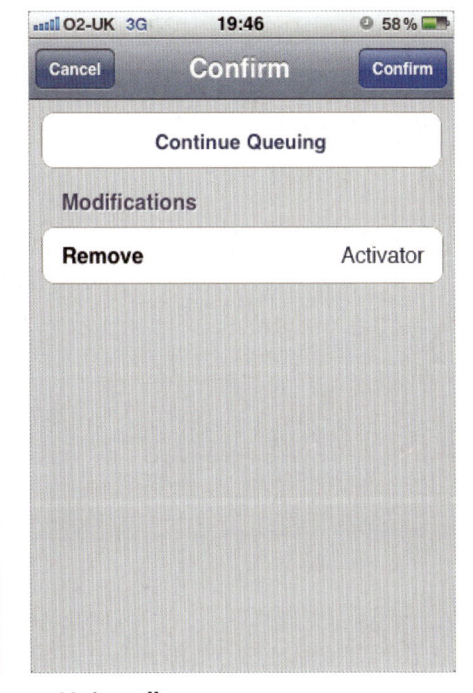

6: Uninstall
To remove Activator from your phone, all you need to do is open up Cydia and click Modify then Remove. Hit Confirm and it will be deleted.

iPhone Tips, Tricks, Apps and Hacks **121**

Tips | Tricks | **Hacks** | Apps

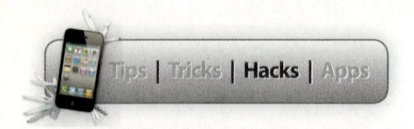

Fit more apps into your on-screen folders

If you don't quite have enough space for all of your apps, expand your folders using this helpful little extension

Task: Extend folder space with Infinifolders
Difficulty: Beginner
Time needed: 10 minutes

When Apple released iOS 4, the update brought with it a whole host of new features. One of these was folders, which gave iPhone users the ability to group apps together. The advantage of folders is twofold; first, it means you can put a lot of apps together and have them take up only the same amount of space as a single app on the Home screen. But more than that, it enables you to store apps that fit together in one place and give your folder a name, helping you stay organised. There's nothing worse than flicking through Home screen after Home screen to find the app you're looking for, after all.

But while folders are a great function, they're limited to 12 items each. This may be plenty for some users, but if you have a lot of games or productivity apps on your iPhone, it may not be. Infinifolders is the perfect solution. When you install it through Cydia on your jailbroken device you will be able to drag an infinite number of items into any given folder, just as the name suggests. Then you can scroll through your apps vertically in the folder, with the same bouncing animation as Safari when you reach the bottom.

Step-by-step | Infinifolders Make more folder space

1: Edit your settings
When you download Infinifolders it will instantly allow you to add more apps to a folder. Enter the Settings menu to configure the options.

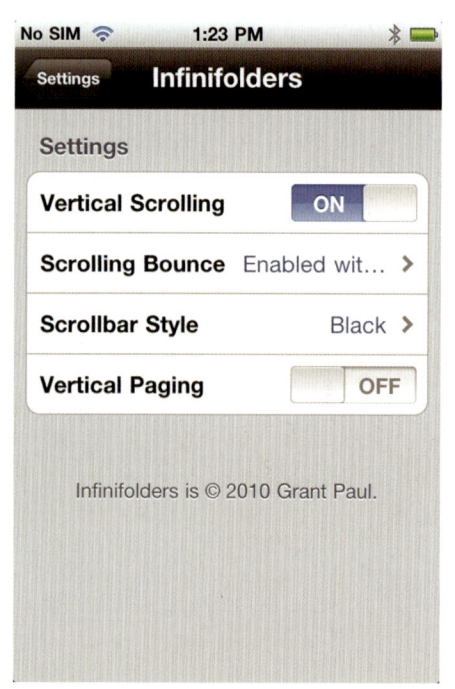

2: Choices, choices
You have four options. Make sure vertical scrolling is on so that the functionality is active from the off, then enter the Scrolling Bounce menu.

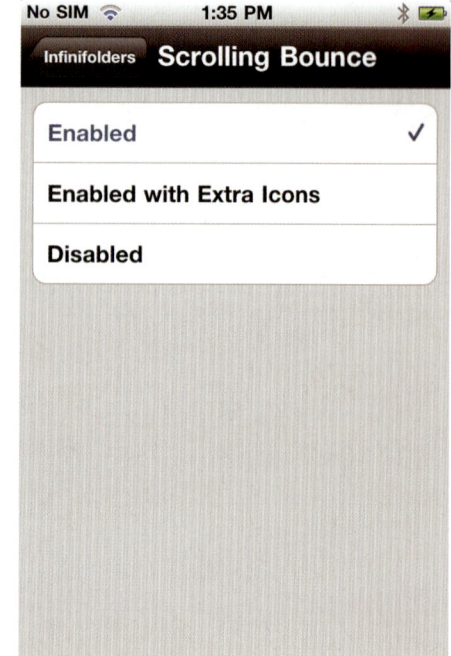

3: Bouncing
Here you can decide whether or not you want the screen to bounce when you reach the end of the list. Turning it off will help for older iPhones.

Tips | Tricks | **Hacks** | Apps

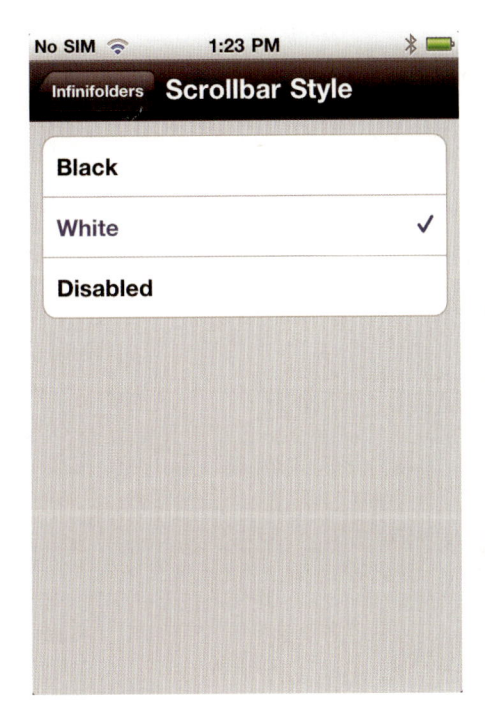

Your infinite folder
What a normal folder will look like

● **Notifications**
As with a normal folder, any notifications you get from apps will stack up. Here you can see a single Facebook notification, but two displayed on the folder icon

● **Other behaviour**
Other than the extended size of folders, their other functions remain exactly the same. You can still drag icons in and out of the folder, or rename it if you like

● **Scrollbar**
You can turn the scrollbar off if you want or choose between it being black or white. We like to leave it on, otherwise it's quite hard to know how far into your folder you are

● **Vertical paging**
If you turn this on and have 13 apps in a folder, the final app will be placed on a new page with the rest of the 4x3 grid blank. In this situation it may be worth turning the setting off to save space

● **Knowledge base**

Even more space
If you combine this app with one that shrinks your icons down, or allows you to have five icons on a line, you will have even more space in a single folder. A lot of apps from Cydia can be combined to great effect, so it's worth looking into what else is available and how it can work with what you already have.

4: Scrollbar
Next, choose your scrollbar options. If you disable it, it's easy to become confused regarding where you are in a folder, so we advise you leave it on.

5: Keep scrolling
When you're happy with your settings, drag your app icons into a folder. Open this and scroll your finger to see the rest of your apps.

6: Vertical paging
If you switched on Vertical Paging, your apps will be sorted into 4x3 pages. Scrolling down will then take you to the next grid of apps.

iPhone Tips, Tricks, Apps and Hacks **123**

Tips | Tricks | **Hacks** | Apps

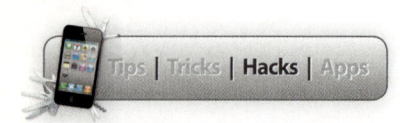

Shrink the icons on your iPhone's screen

Customise your Home screen to your liking by shrinking or growing your app and Dock icons

Task: Customise icon appearance with Shrink
Difficulty: Intermediate
Time needed: 10 minutes

One of the biggest problems with the iPhone is its lack of customisation options, and it's often this that prompts people to switch to another phone manufacturer, or look into jailbreaking their device. One of the biggest gripes is with the Home screen as Apple barely allows users to edit their main app screens at all. You are able to drag apps to different pages and into folders, but you can't edit the text under apps, you can't put icons on the right of a page without three more in front of it, and the icons are fixed at one size no matter where you are in the user interface. This might be fine for many users, but if you jailbreak you have a lot more freedom.

At its most basic level, Shrink gives you the chance to alter the size of your app icons. You can also change the colour of the text, decide where you want the page indicators to rest, turn on and off icon shadows and reflections, and generally make your screen look totally different. Combine this with some other Home screen-editing apps and soon people won't even know what type of phone you are using until you show them the logo.

Step-by-step | Shrink Alter your icons

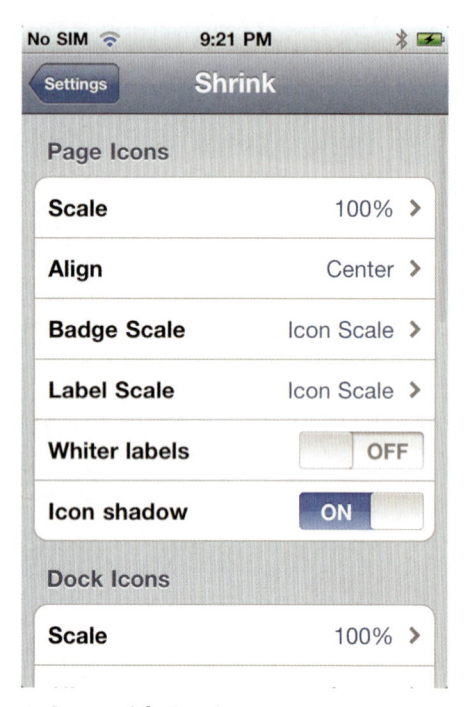

1: Start with Settings
Shrink will add a panel to the Settings app when you download it from Cydia, and this is where you can alter everything including size and colours.

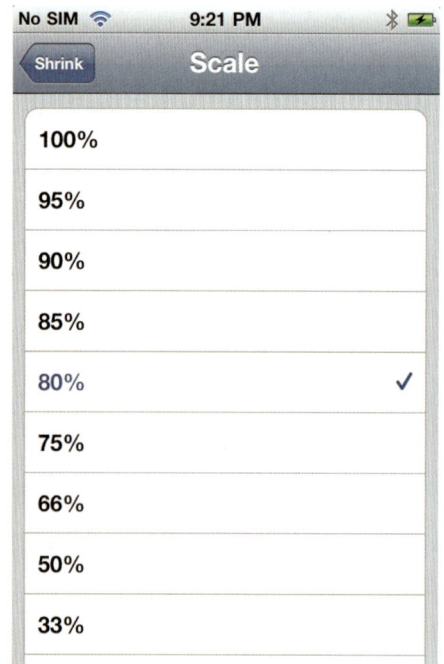

2: Scaling
You can set the scale of your app icons from this menu – the numbers go all the way down to 25% and all the way up to 300%.

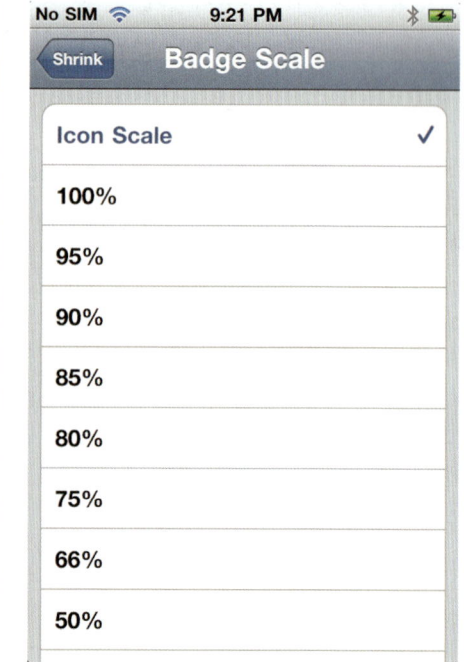

3: Badges
The app has thought of everything – you even edit the size of badges on your apps when you get notifications. Make them ridiculously huge for fun.

Tips | Tricks | **Hacks** | Apps

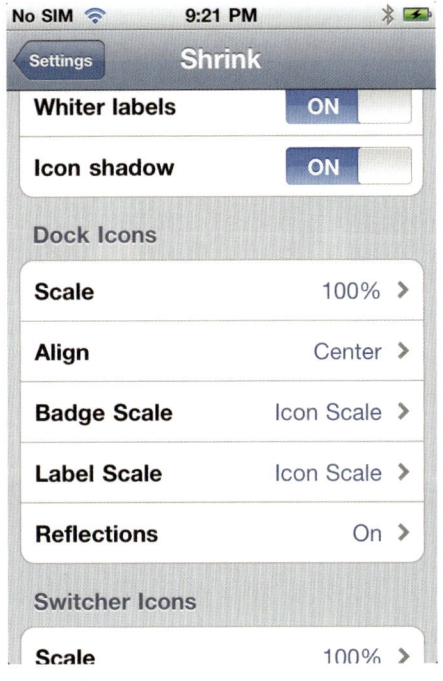

Big and small icons
A very different Home screen appearance

● What's in a name?
If the name of an app no longer fits in the space available, Shrink enables you to choose how it is viewed. You can cut off the text or add ellipses in the middle or at the end

● Notifications
You can change the size of the badges that sit on icons when you get a notification by entering the Settings menu, but these apps will always be pushed to the front if overlapping

● Going dotty
The page indicators just above the Dock can also be moved using Shrink. You can set them to hug the Dock, sit high on the screen or move depending on the size of the Dock icons

● Knowledge base
More apps per page
If you shrink your apps down, you might like to combine Shrink with another app from the Cydia store that enables you to add more apps per page. This way, your icons won't be too squashed together and you will have access to a lot more on a single screen, saving you the time you would spend swiping through Home screens.

● Spaced dock
As you can see here, the Dock icons are much smaller than normal. You can set them to be larger if you want to make them stand out more on each page

4: Docking
There is plenty you can do with the Dock, too. Turn on and off reflections as well as making the labels whiter, or changing the Badge Scale.

5: Off the scale
If you want huge Screen icons and tiny Dock icons you can, but apps will overlap. Those with notifications will be pushed to the front of the pile.

6: Text editing
You can also use Shrink to alter the size and colour of the text labels or remove them completely. Your phone will now have a whole new look.

iPhone Tips, Tricks, Apps and Hacks **125**

Tips | Tricks | **Hacks** | Apps

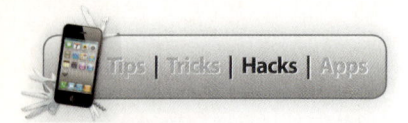

Get Exposé-style tabs on your iPhone

If you're sick of swiping through tab after tab, GridTab is the app you've been looking for

Task: Browse tabs quickly with GridTab
Difficulty: Beginner
Time needed: 5 minutes

Just a few years ago, the only way to browse the web was by using separate windows and then flicking between them to view different pages. The idea of having more than one webpage open in a single app or window would have seemed very strange, but now tabbed browsing is a huge feature of every modern browser, with multiple pages helping massively with users' workflows.

Safari for iPhone is no exception, and creating new tabs to view more than one page is quick and easy. Sadly, however, if you have a lot of tabs open at once, there are a few problems with the management system in iOS. If you're in the ninth tab, for example, and want to get to the first, you must swipe across the various others to get there. Thankfully, Cydia and your jailbroken phone offer you several solutions. One of the best is GridTab, a small add-on that gives you a grid view of your tabs that is similar to Apple's Exposé interface from the Mac. It makes tabbed browsing much slicker, and for such a low price it's certainly worth a download if you're a regular user of Safari on your iPhone.

Step-by-step | GridTab Browse and edit your tabs

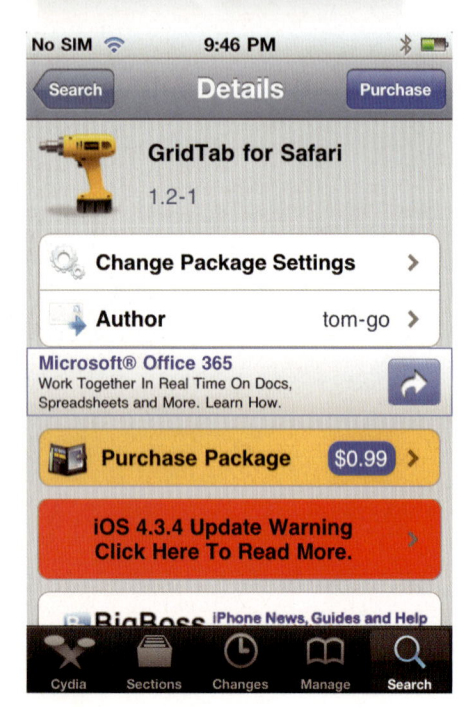

1: Compatibility issues
It's important to check that the app is compatible with your version of iOS. Tap in Cydia for more details, and check your version in the Settings app.

2: New tab
You can create a new tab just as you would without the package installed. Tap the New Tab button and a new page will fade into view on the grid.

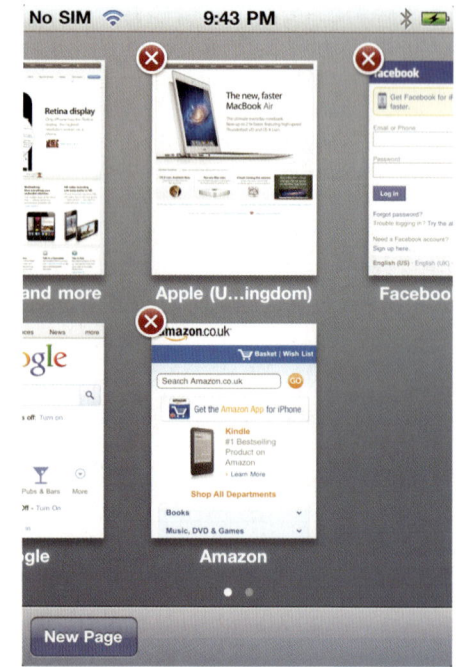

3: Turn the page
With GridTab, the only flick gesture you will ever have to make is a single one left or right to switch between the grid pages.

Tips | Tricks | **Hacks** | Apps

Your tab grid
A closer look at the GridTab interface

◯ iOS and Mac meet
The animations are stylised closely to the iPhone, but have a great deal of influence from the Mac interface, such as closing a tab and having it disappear into the X button

◯ Page preview
With GridTab it's true that you get a little less information than you otherwise would when browsing, but we think it's worth it for the increased functionality

◯ Editable options
There is no section in the Settings app for this extension because of its simplicity. What you see here is exactly what you get, and there's nothing you can change about it. Don't worry, though, it works brilliantly

◯ Two pages, not eight
If you're sick of swiping through pages and pages of tabs when browsing in Safari, GridTab is perfect for you. You'll only ever have a maximum of two screens, so switching tabs is quick and easy

◯ Knowledge base

Grids for apps
You can get a similar program for managing your apps when multitasking. If you don't like the icon drawer that a double-tap of your Home button opens up, search in Cydia for an app called Multiflow. It's a little more expensive, but the interface is slick, and – unlike Apple's multitasking solution – you'll see a live preview of your open apps before you switch to them.

4: Removing tabs
When you've finished with a tab, you can tap the X button in the top-left corner of it, just like with normal Safari. The tab will then disappear.

5: Reorganise tabs
One of the advantages that this extension has is the ability to manipulate tab orders. Touch and hold a tab to drag it into position.

6: Page limit
The extension can't change some things about Safari and you're still limited to eight tabs. This means a maximum of two grids to swipe through.

iPhone Tips, Tricks, Apps and Hacks **127**

Tips | Tricks | **Hacks** | Apps

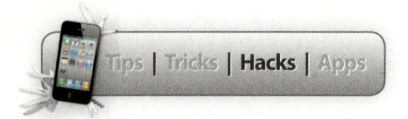

Update your status from any app

Using qTweeter, you only need a simple gesture to give you access to Twitter and Facebook, no matter what app you're using

Task: Install and set up qTweeter
Difficulty: Intermediate
Time needed: 10 minutes

One of the best things about owning a smartphone is that you are always connected to your social networks, so you can keep them all updated from one device. Sadly, though, the Facebook and Twitter iPhone apps don't make it very easy to update your status, with the buttons to tap out a few words buried deep in the interfaces. In the end it actually takes more time to get to the right page than it does to type and send your message.

qTweeter is the solution to this problem as this tiny app gives you the ability to update your status from absolutely anywhere on your jailbroken iPhone. Downloading it will put the invisible panel at the top of your screen. Swipe your finger down from the status bar and the interface will slide into view.

From here you can choose where to upload your status to, as well as adding things like photos, links and geotags with a simple tap. You can also choose to send a Now Playing message and edit the Twitter hashtag that it uses in the Settings menu. If you like to keep your Twitter and Facebook feeds up to date, qTweeter is a quick, simple and well-designed app that's worth a try.

Step-by-step | qTweeter Tweet from any app

1: Welcome to qTweeter
When you first download and install qTweeter from Cydia you will naturally have to sign into your Twitter or Facebook accounts.

2: Add and edit accounts
You can add and edit account details, the sound that will play when you receive an update and the background image on the qTweeter pane.

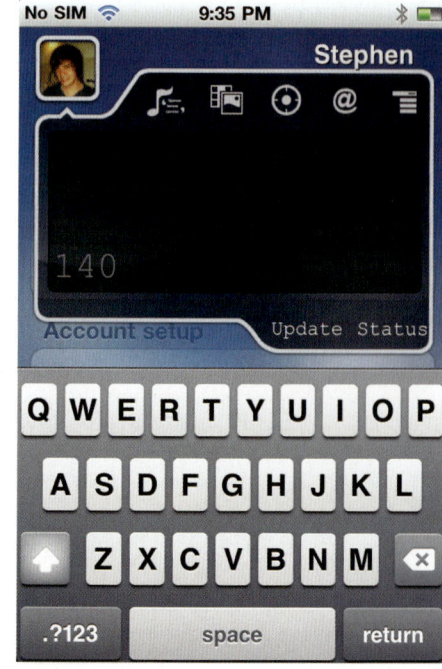

3: Status update
Drag your finger down from the top of the screen and this panel will slide into view, along with the keyboard to start typing.

Tips | Tricks | **Hacks** | Apps

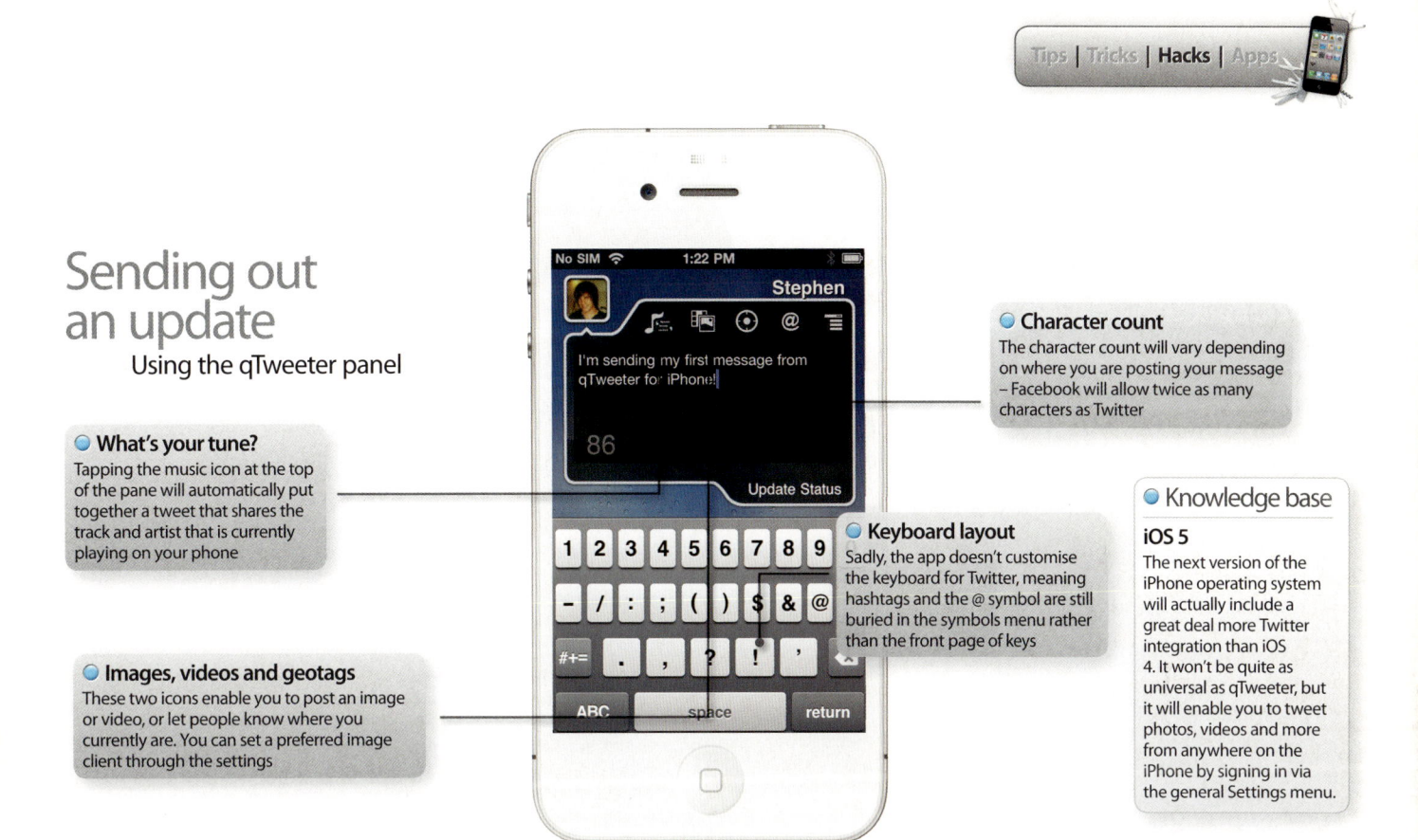

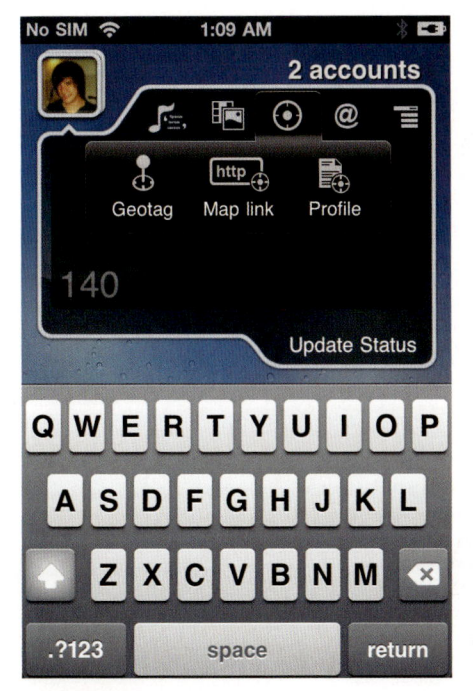

Sending out an update
Using the qTweeter panel

What's your tune?
Tapping the music icon at the top of the pane will automatically put together a tweet that shares the track and artist that is currently playing on your phone

Images, videos and geotags
These two icons enable you to post an image or video, or let people know where you currently are. You can set a preferred image client through the settings

Character count
The character count will vary depending on where you are posting your message – Facebook will allow twice as many characters as Twitter

Keyboard layout
Sadly, the app doesn't customise the keyboard for Twitter, meaning hashtags and the @ symbol are still buried in the symbols menu rather than the front page of keys

Knowledge base
iOS 5
The next version of the iPhone operating system will actually include a great deal more Twitter integration than iOS 4. It won't be quite as universal as qTweeter, but it will enable you to tweet photos, videos and more from anywhere on the iPhone by signing in via the general Settings menu.

4: Add options
Along the top of the menu is a series of buttons to share links, images, videos and more with a simple tap. The drop-down menus are simple and clear.

5: Multiple accounts
If you have more than one account set up, choose where your update is posted to. When you've finished your message just press Update Status.

6: qTweeter options
From within the application you can bring up a Settings menu. A tweet shrinker is built into the add-on, which is incredibly useful.

iPhone Tips, Tricks, Apps and Hacks **129**

Tips | Tricks | **Hacks** | Apps

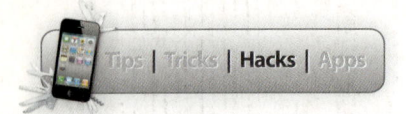

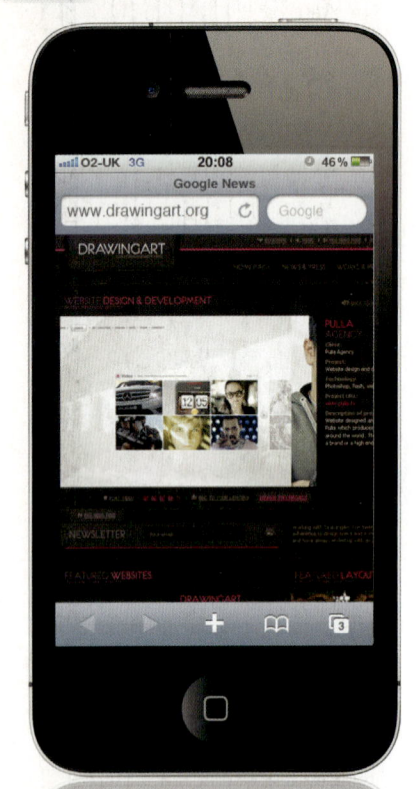

Enjoy Flash-based content on your iPhone

Apple has stuck to its guns with its decision not to allow Flash Player on its devices – find out how to get around that restriction

Task: View Flash using the Frash app
Difficulty: Intermediate
Time needed: 45 minutes

When the iPhone launched, a major gripe with it was its lack of support for Adobe Flash. Lots of websites use Flash to display dynamic content, and it's the most common method for sharing video on the web. Some suggest that there are performance issues or that it drains the battery quickly, and although there may be arguments to support this case, the fact that other mobile operating systems can use Flash does put a question mark over this.

There have been a few attempts at getting Flash running on iOS devices, including apps that route content through servers that convert the files into a format that iOS can play, but most have been unreliable and only support the basic Flash sites. However, there are a few apps available for jailbroken phones that can install Flash Player, enabling you to enjoy the full web experience in all it's Flash glory. You will need to be running iOS 4 for this to work, but it supports the latest Apple devices including iPhone 4, 3GS, iPad and iPod touch.

Step-by-step | Frash View Flash on your iPhone

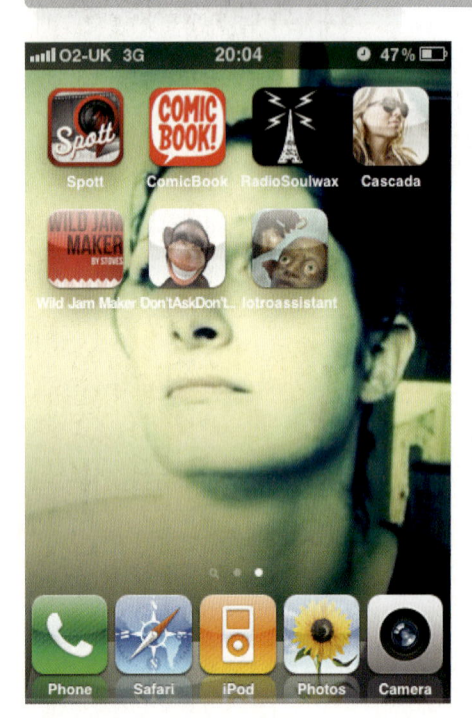

1: Jailbreak your device
First off you need to make sure that your device is jailbroken and that you are running the latest version of iOS. At time of the writing this is 4.3.3.

2: Open Cydia
The next step is to open up Cydia, the alternative app store, and search for Frash. If you don't have Cydia, you can install from www.benm.at.

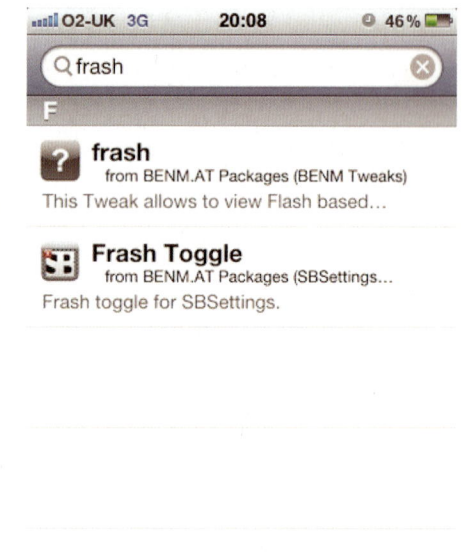

3: Install Frash
Once you have located Frash, click on it to start the install process. It will take a moment. Once done click 'Return to Cydia' and press the Home button.

130 iPhone Tips, Tricks, Apps and Hacks

Tips | Tricks | **Hacks** | Apps

Flash on iOS
What Flash looks like running on an iPhone

● Video content
A large percentage of video content is served up on the internet using Flash technologies. With Frash installed you should be able to view most of that content

● From mobile source
Frash was developed from the Android mobile OS version of Adobe Flash Player, so it maintains its mobile OS-based roots rather an than being a port from OS X

● Speed matters
Flash – depending on the content – can be quite intensive on your phone's CPU, and sometimes can make Safari run quite slowly, especially on an iPhone 3GS

● Text scaling
One complaint about Flash on small-screen devices is the lack of ability to scale text down very well

● Knowledge base

Frash limitations
Unfortunately, Frash isn't compatible with all Flash content. Flash is used for a wide variety of content on the internet, and although the developers have done well, some of the more complicated sites might not run perfectly.

4: View some Flash
You can now view Flash content on your iPhone. Frash works best with video content embedded on the web, but also for photo slideshows and galleries.

5: Changed your mind?
If you decide that you no longer want to see Flash content on your phone, just reopen Cydia and click on the Manage button at the bottom.

6: Remove Frash
Next click on Packages and scroll down until you see Frash. Next click Modify and then Remove. Click the Confirm button and wait until it has completed.

iPhone Tips, Tricks, Apps and Hacks **131**

Tips | Tricks | Hacks | Apps

Copy files and connect to your local network

Easily copy files to and from your iPhone without having to use iTunes, and connect your device to your local network

Task: Copy files and access your Mac's network using Netatalk
Difficulty: Beginner
Time needed: 10 minutes

It's possible to use your iPhone or other iOS device as a portable hard drive to move files from one place to another, but those files cannot interact with the operating system of the iOS device. For instance, if you wish to copy some photos from a friend's Mac to view them on your phone, you'll need to copy them to the phone in hard drive mode, go home, then add them to your iTunes sync, then sync your iPhone.

Clearly that is a clunky method, and a hassle if you are in a hurry. There are a few ways of transferring files to your iPhone from your Mac without having to go through iTunes, but lots of the apps are not free or not very feature-rich. This tutorial will take you through one method of copying files to the phone using Netatalk, open source software that has a long history, going back to way before the iPhone even existed. The interface is the familiar Finder for OS X or Explorer for Windows, meaning you can literally just drag and drop files to and from the phone. It also allows you to connect your iPhone to your Mac's local network for ease of use.

Step-by-step | Netatalk Copy files and connect to a local network

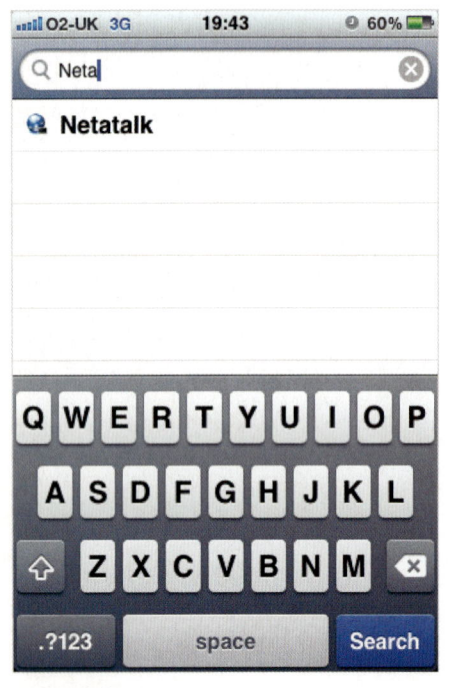

1: Find the app
Make sure you have jailbroken and installed Cydia. Open up the Cydia app store and, in the search screen, type 'Netatalk'. Then click Search.

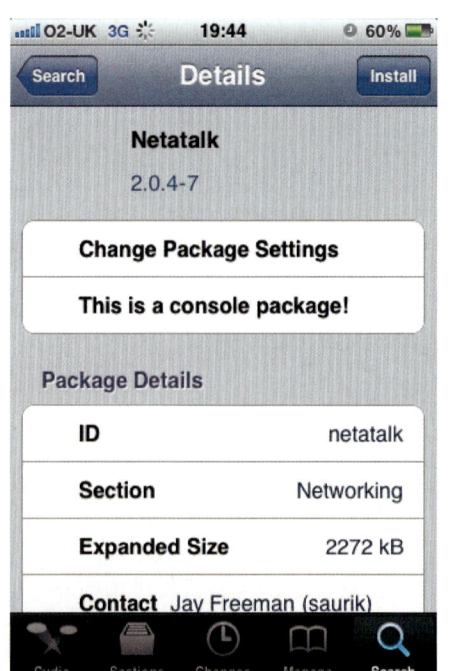

2: Install Netatalk
You will then see more information about the app. Click on Install to add it to the queue and then press Confirm.

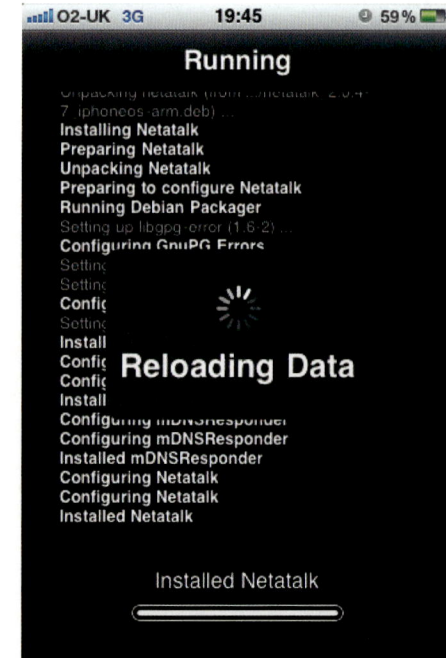

3: Restart SpringBoard
The app will then download and install onto your iOS device. Once this has finished you just need to restart SpringBoard.

132 iPhone Tips, Tricks, Apps and Hacks

4: Set up transfer on Mac
Once the app has installed, you will need to set up AppleTalk on your OS X machine. Open up Settings and then click on Network.

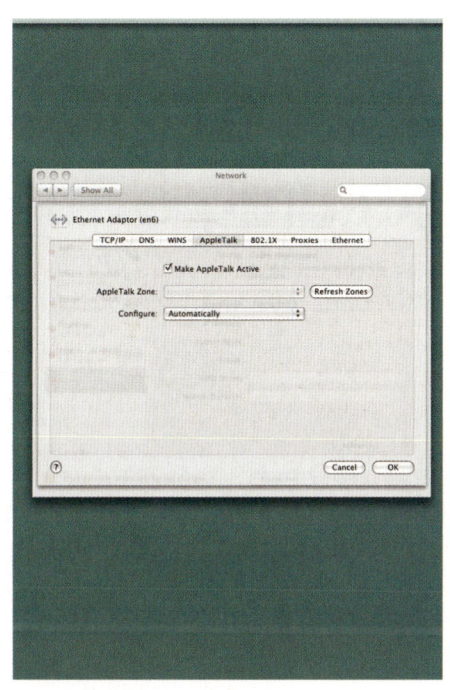

5: Connection options
Click on the connection you use for your local network and then click Advanced. Now click the 'AppleTalk' tab and click 'Make AppleTalk Active'.

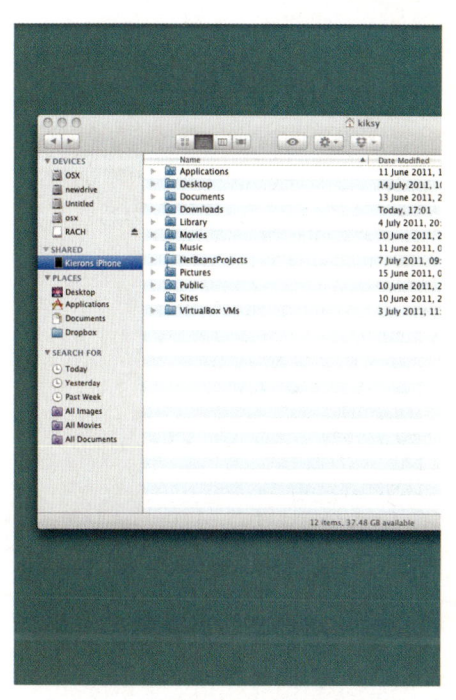

6: Connect iOS device to network
You now need to connect your iOS device to the network. Once it's on the same network as your computer it will show up in Finder's shared menu.

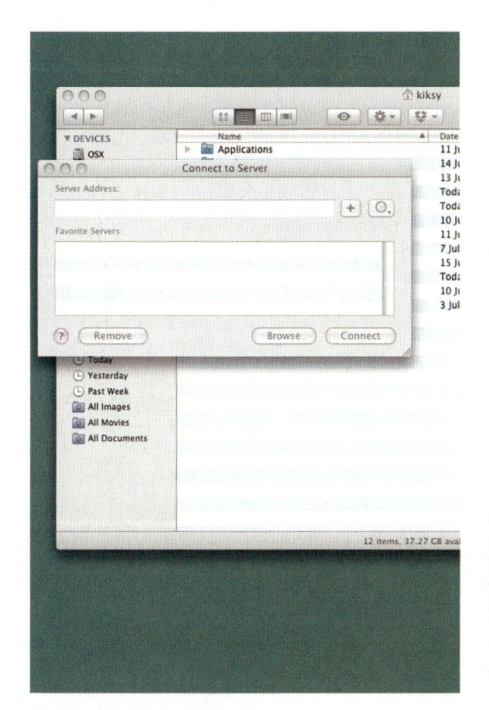

7: Connect to device
Choose 'Connect As'. When asked for a username and password, enter 'root' and 'alpine'. Your username might be 'mobile' if 'root' doesn't work.

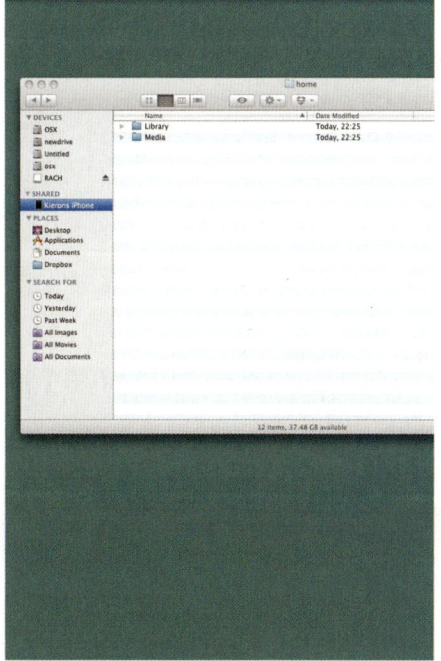

8: Drag and drop
You can now drag and drop files from your Finder window onto your iOS device. Be careful not to delete any of the OS or you might cause problems.

9: Uninstall Netatalk
To uninstall the app, open up Cydia again and then click on the app. Then click Modify and then Remove. Click Confirm and then it will be deleted.

iPhone Tips, Tricks, Apps and Hacks **133**

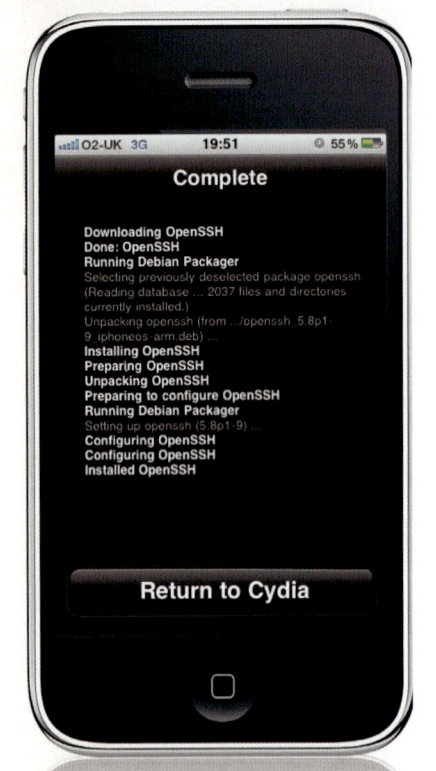

Tips | Tricks | **Hacks** | Apps

Wirelessly transfer data securely over Wi-Fi

You don't have to worry about USB cables to get data from your computer to your device

Task: An easy way to transfer files and data over Wi-Fi using OpenSSH
Difficulty: Beginner
Time needed: 10 minutes

One of the unfathomable aspects of iOS is the fact that there is no way of transferring files and data wirelessly to the device. Being able to transfer pictures, documents and more without the need for a cable can be very handy when around a friend's house, or if you're at work and there isn't a cable to hand. Of course, you'll also be concerned about the security of sending data wirelessly, but using this option you won't need to panic as all your data in encrypted to protect it from prying eyes.

After jailbreaking, it's likely one of the first things that you will do is to install some kind of access to the internal file system of the device. There are lots of ways of doing this, but the most common is by using SSH. SSH stands for secure shell and is a protocol that enables the remote transfer of information securely. There are lots of programs that support SSH such as Cyberduck on OS X, SCP on Linux and WinSCP on Windows. For this tutorial we're using OpenSSH, which works across all iOS devices and Apple operating systems.

Step-by-step | OpenSSH Securely copy files and data to your phone

1: Open Cydia
The quickest and easiest way to get SSH working on your phone is to download OpenSSH from the Cydia app store. Start off by opening Cydia.

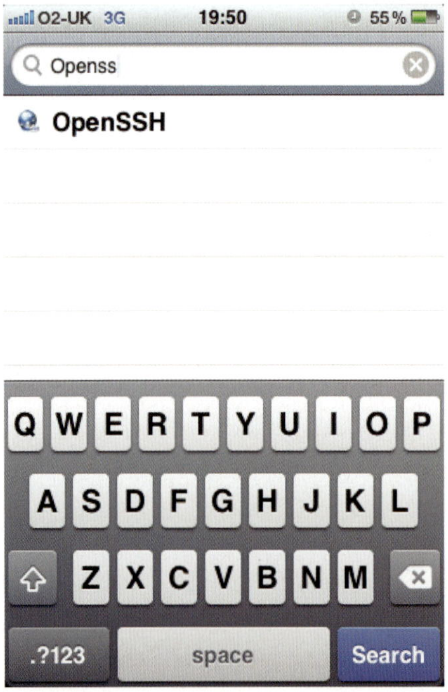

2: Search for the app
Once Cydia has finished updating the package list, click on the search icon and type OpenSSH. Click on this to bring up the installation window.

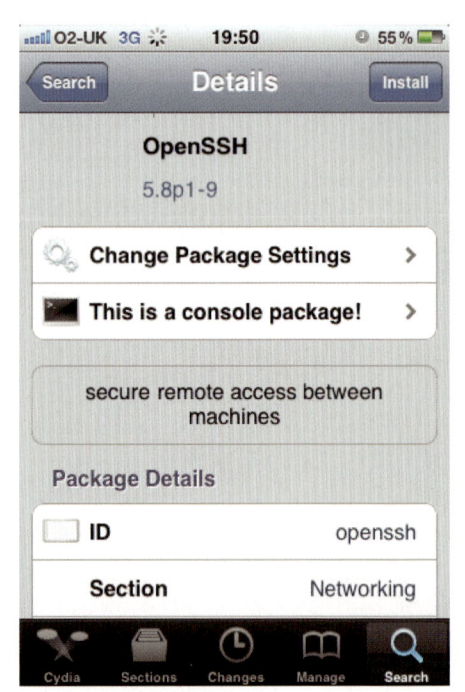

3: Install OpenSSH
Click on Install and then on Confirm to start off the downloading and installation the app. Once this has completed you might need to restart SpringBoard.

Tips | Tricks | Hacks | Apps

4: Get SSH client
You need a way of connecting to your phone via SSH, so download Cyberduck from www.cyberduck.ch or www.winscp.net for Windows.

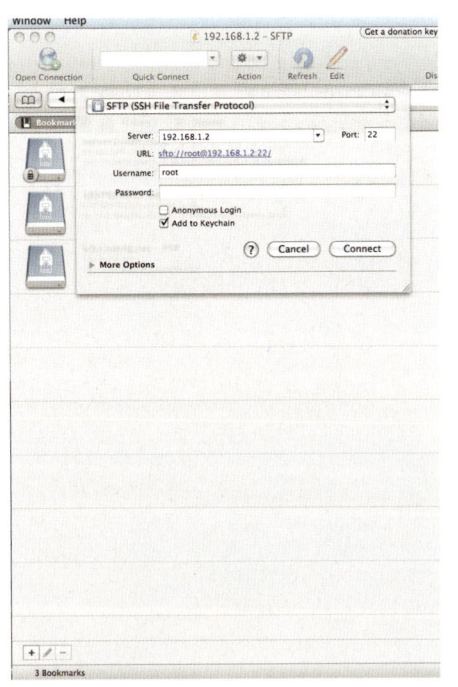

5: Install client
Install the chosen client on your computer and then open it up. Open up a new connection within it and enter the IP of your router, under the Wi-Fi settings.

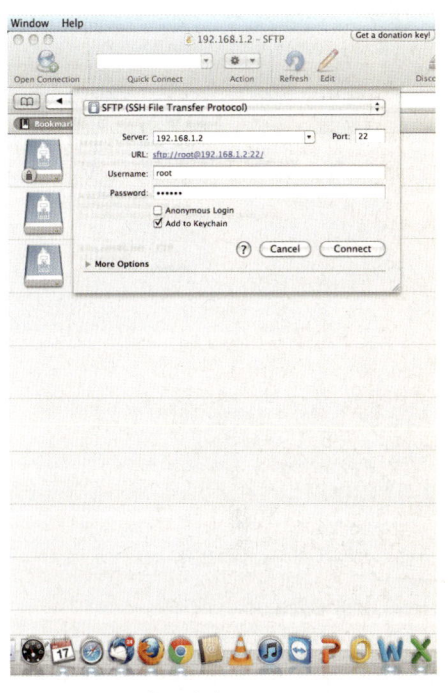

6: Enter credentials
In the Username field enter 'root' and for Password enter 'alpine'. The Port should be 22. Click on Connect and the computer will link to the phone.

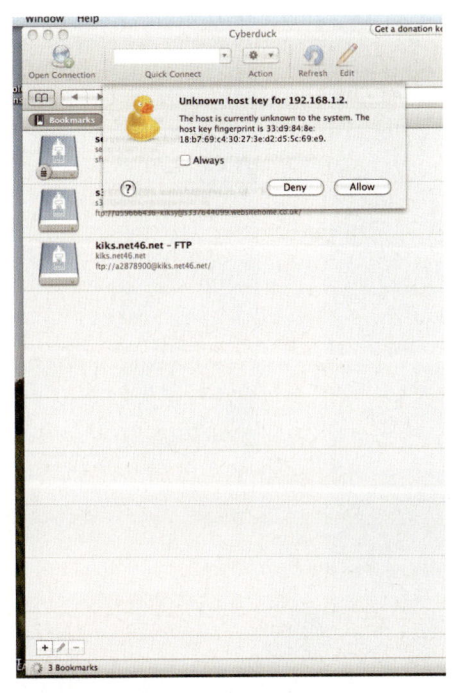

7: Allow key
After a few seconds of activity you may be told that the system doesn't know the key. Click Allow on this and then the connection process will be complete.

8: View connection
You will now have a connection to the phone. You can access your phone from anywhere if you forward the ports and all data will be sent securely.

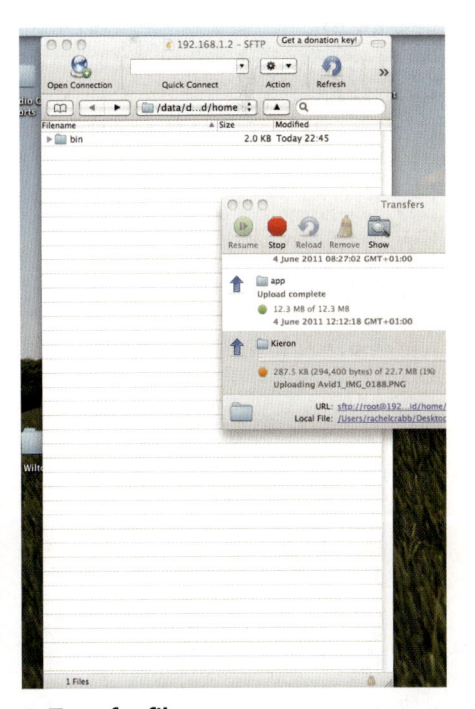

9: Transfer files
Transferring files is a simple matter of dragging and dropping to the correct folder. Transferring large files over Wi-Fi may take slightly longer.

iPhone Tips, Tricks, Apps and Hacks **135**

Tips | Tricks | Hacks | **Apps**

Apps
Discover the best apps to extend the functionality of your iPhone

- **138** Redshift – Astronomy
- **139** Thriller Books, Doctor Who Comics
- **140** Red Riding Hood Interactive Book, Deadline
- **141** Dragon Dictation, Audio Memos 2
- **142** Monarchy The Definitive Guide
- **143** 1400+ Dinosaur Handbook, SkyView-Explore The Universe
- **144** Beatles Diary
- **145** BEP360, AR Tattoos
- **146** PlayStation Official App, Spray Paint
- **147** Broken Sword – The Smoking Mirror: Remastered
- **148** Iron Man 2, Plants Vs Zombies
- **149** Angry Birds: Seasons, Pirates Vs Ninjas Vs Zombies Vs Pandas
- **150** Samurai II: Vengeance, Lara Croft And The Guardian Of Light
- **151** AmpliTube Fender
- **152** djay
- **153** Easy Food, Jamie's 20 Minute Meals
- **154** Amazon Mobile, In Your Dreams
- **155** David Gandy Style Guide For Men, Rate Your Life
- **156** MLB.com At Bat 11, SwingReader Golf

162 Add effects to photos with Color Splash

Tips | Tricks | Hacks | Apps

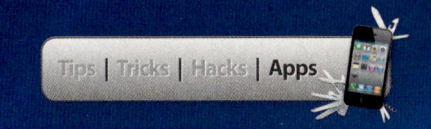

171 Get creative with the Adobe Ideas app

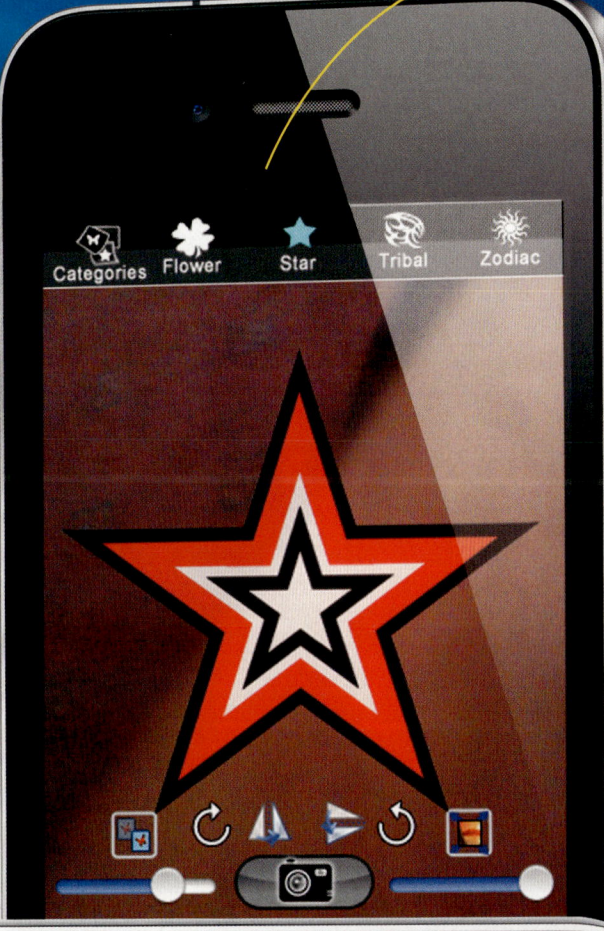

145 Plan your next design with AR Tattoos

157 Lewis Moody Rugby, Tennis Serve Technique and Tips
158 3D Animation Medical Videos Vol1, BMI/BAI Calculator
159 Human Anatomy Structures
160 Standard First Aid
161 Animation Creator
162 Trimensional, Color Splash
163 8mm Vintage Camera
164 LOVEFiLM UK
165 MyTrend, Facebook Photos Sync
166 Multistatus, Zwapp
167 Word Lens
168 Real Map Plus
169 eWeather HD
170 Ultimate Browser, GoDocs
171 Adobe Ideas
172 Speak It! Text To Speech, CamScanner+
173 Air Video

HOT APPS
✔ Easy Food
✔ Dragon Dictation
✔ Trimensional
✔ Word Lens
✔ Air Video

152 Create and mix top tunes with djay

iPhone Tips, Tricks, Apps and Hacks **137**

Tips | Tricks | Hacks | Apps

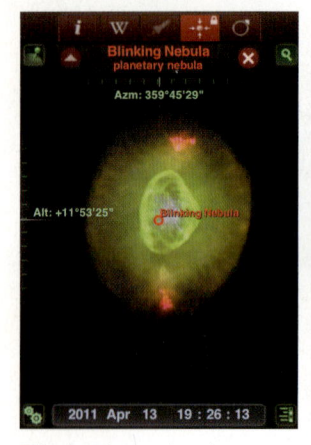

■ Head on a journey through space to a Blinking Nebula

■ Planets are beautifully rendered, and main features are highlighted

Price: £7.99/$11.99   Developer: United Soft Media Verlang GmbH

Redshift – Astronomy

Unleash your inner astronaut and take a journey into deep space

Never before has the night sky been rendered so beautifully, or in so much detail on a handheld device. This app is more than your regular stargazing companion, though. Yes, the heavenly bodies are represented in real-time. Yes, you can match their position in the sky by waving your iPhone upwards and using its position sensors and compass (on 3GS or higher models). And yes, there's detailed information including distance to mother Earth, size and other facts about the major lumps of rock and gas in our galaxy. All this is available in cheaper apps, so what's so good about this one?

Well for starters, Redshift – Astronomy charts more than any other app. With 100,000 starts, 500 'Deep Sky' objects, the 30 biggest asteroids, the ten comets that come close to the Earth, and not forgetting our own solar system, there is certainly a great deal to look at. The only way you'd normally get to view this much detail is by visiting the world's most powerful telescopes. Imagine this as your own private observatory.

Clever imagery lets you look in detail at star clusters, nebulae and more. Just click on a pinpoint of light, tap the 'i' button and learn more about it, such as name, type, magnitude, altitude, distance plus more scientific data. If that's not enough for you, if you have an internet connection, log onto Wikipedia through the app.

Not only are the heavenly bodies displayed in stunning 3D, it's possible to take virtual three-dimensional flights through space to any object you target, then orbit around it, just as if you were flying on your own personal spaceship. Tap on the menu on the bottom-right of the screen and pick where in the near universe you'd like to head to; stay close to home with a planet such as Mars, or go further afield and visit a star such as Polaris. Alternatively, take the 'Grand Tour' and the app flies you around starting from Earth, through the solar system, past constellations and out into deep space. Watch in 'Night Vision' mode and everything takes on a red hue, which is gentler on the eyes when out stargazing.

Make the most of your iPhone and show off its capabilities to your mates with this truly stunning piece of software.

Overall Rating ★★★★★

Tips | Tricks | Hacks | **Apps**

■ Page layouts are incredibly simplistic, but easy to read

■ Books have very little in the way of art, except front covers

Price: Free   Developer: Thu Ngan Bui

Thriller Books

Fancy a thriller? Check out this massive book collection

A free app from Thu Ngan Bui, Thriller Books offers a wide range of classic thriller novels as in-app purchases. Housing such classics as *The Phantom of the Opera*, *The Legacy Of Cain* and *The Insidious Fu Manchu*, the book store offers each text for £1.19/£1.79. However, if you would rather try before you buy, each novel can be previewed for free, which can grant you free access to the first three chapters or less. Each text takes mere seconds to download, and from the top menu, each book can be accessed with ease. Pages are presented in a simple black text on white background format, and can be scrolled through one at a time, or bypassed in chunks using a handy page slider at the bottom of the screen. Pages can also be bookmarked, and scaled down or blown up to help you read them better. Your favourite books can also be recommended to other users via the extras menu, and previews of novels can be mailed to your friends from within the app.

Overall Rating ★★★★☆

■ The storefront is chock full of new additions each week…

■ The art style is fantastic and as dark as the show itself

Price: Free   Developer: Idea and Design Works LLC

Doctor Who Comics

Tons of sci-fi adventuring in one handy app

Rich in side stories, lore and untold arcs, the Doctor Who franchise is ripe for the comic book treatment. The official comic series runs as a companion piece to the television show, and is well worth checking out if you're an avid fan.

The free Doctor Who Comics app serves as a digital bookshelf that can be populated with a wide range of comics, books and annuals. Texts come in full colour and are separated into both free and paid-for categories. Each paid issue comes in at around the £1.19/$1.99 mark and, given that each volume is many pages long, it actually works out cheaper than buying the physical comic itself.

Doctor Who Comics is a rare find in that the developers appear to have thought of every practical use possible. Professionally constructed, functional and slick, this is definitely a must-have companion piece for fans of the show.

Overall Rating ★★★★☆

iPhone Tips, Tricks, Apps and Hacks **139**

Tips | Tricks | Hacks | Apps

Price: £2.39/$3.99   Developer: Sleepydog Ltd

Deadline

A tense and enjoyable teen thriller

Deadline is an engrossing teen thriller from novelist John Townsend. Coming in at 72 pages long, this is a modern tale that focused on 13-year-old Barney, a schoolboy who happens to stumble across a deadly secret. Wanted, and on the run from hired assassins, his only hope is his best friend Laura and a plan to foil and diffuse a terrorist plot before it's too late. *Deadline* zips along at a cracking pace and is broken down into short paragraphs, which is perfect for reading in small chunks on the go. The occasional illustration helps break up sections and add focal points to each chapter, delivered in a neat manga style that apes the popular *Scott Pilgrim* series. *Deadline*'s best feature is that the publisher's books are all proof-read by kids to ensure that the flow and language holds their interest throughout. It's also very well written, ensuring there are absolutely no barriers to entry. Overall, *Deadline* is a superb book at an affordable price, and comes highly recommended for ages 9-12.

Overall Rating ★★★★★

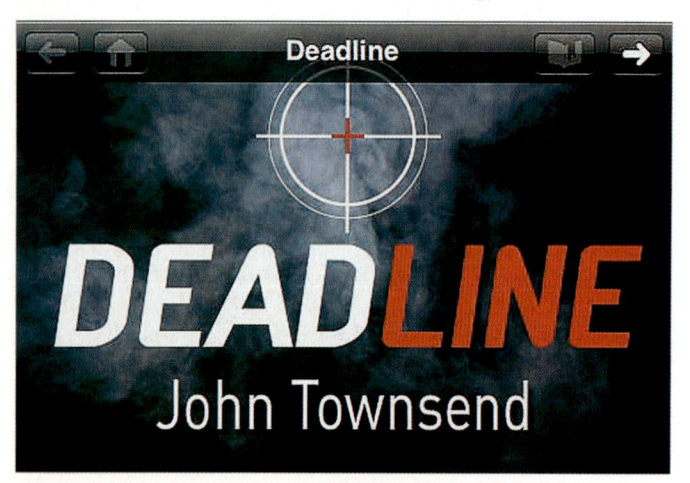

■ While the app options are slim, they perform their duties well

■ The art style has a Japanese vibe – perfect for manga fans

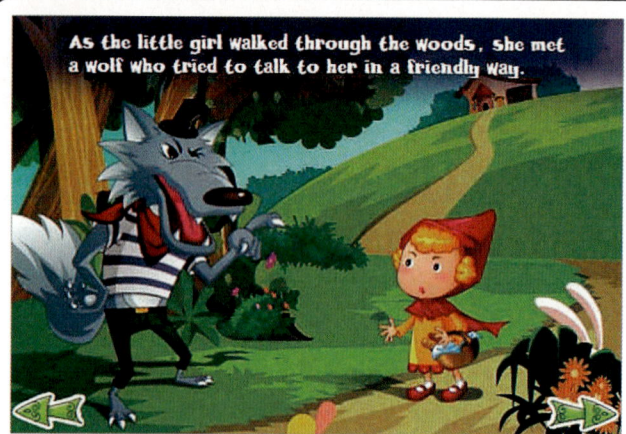

■ Character animation adds plenty of character to the story

■ The story's dark twist is handled in a funny manner here

Price: £0.69/$0.99   Developer: Ebo Online Entertainment

Red Riding Hood Interactive Book

A fresh take on an old classic

Some interactive storybooks can end up feeling rather scant in terms of options or actual interactivity, while others compensate for a lack of extras by simply being well-put together, enjoyable stories for kids. *Little Red Riding Hood* from Ebo Online Entertainment falls into the latter category by being a bright, playful take on the classic children's story, but without delivering much in the way of interactivity. What it does do, however, is present each page of the story in a simple animated format, that sees characters and other page elements moving around, making the story feel more vibrant as a result. Coming in at around ten pages long, this is a short offering, but it comes at a reasonable price as a result. *Little Red Riding Hood* is another solid kids book on iTunes, but apart from being a great story retold in a bright and engaging way, there isn't much to make it stand out.

Overall Rating ★★★★

Tips | Tricks | Hacks | Apps

■ Recording is done with a simple tap of a button…

■ See your spoken words transformed into flowing text

Price: Free   Developer: Nuance Communications

Dragon Dictation

Speak easy with this recorder

Dragon Dictation is a free app that lets users record audio, which is instantly converted into text. Simple is the best adjective to describe its inherent qualities; the opening screen offers nothing more than a three-word instruction and a button on a one-colour background. Tap, as instructed, and it's time to talk. When the talking is over hit the Done button and wait for the audio to be converted to text. This is where Dragon Dictation starts to show cracks. The conversion is often less than 100 per cent accurate. For a better success rate a user needs to speak clearly and precisely. For this very reason a keyboard icon is included. This offers the backup option of being able to edit text via the keyboard.

Completed text has several outlets, as it cannot be saved to the device itself. 'Text' adds it to the body of a message ready to send. 'Email' is pretty self-explanatory, while Facebook and Twitter lovers can post their message directly to an account. Its simplicity can be admired, but the same can't be said of its core feature, text conversion.

Overall Rating ★★★★★

Price: £0.69/$0.99   Developer: David Detry

Audio Memos 2

An essential dictaphone app for those who hate to write

The full title of Audio Memos 2 includes the extension 'The Voice Recorder', which perfectly describes what it's all about. The interface gets straight to the point with a red Record button, which you tap to start recording. It sounds simple and it is, but delve deeper and there's more than meets the eye. There's the date and time, a volume slider and a playback button. Tap the 'Add' button to start a recording and choose quality, volume and whether to use mono or stereo.

A completed recording makes its way onto the home screen list where users can take control of it. Delete with a single swipe and tap or simply tap to get a summary, and tap Send to email a recording. The fun doesn't stop there – tap the information icon to reveal an IP address. Add this to a browser and the iPhone is connected with all recordings listed in the browser. Click a link for playback or right-click to download and save to the desktop for future reference. Intuitive interface, good quality recordings, and expansive options make this app a winner.

Overall Rating ★★★★★

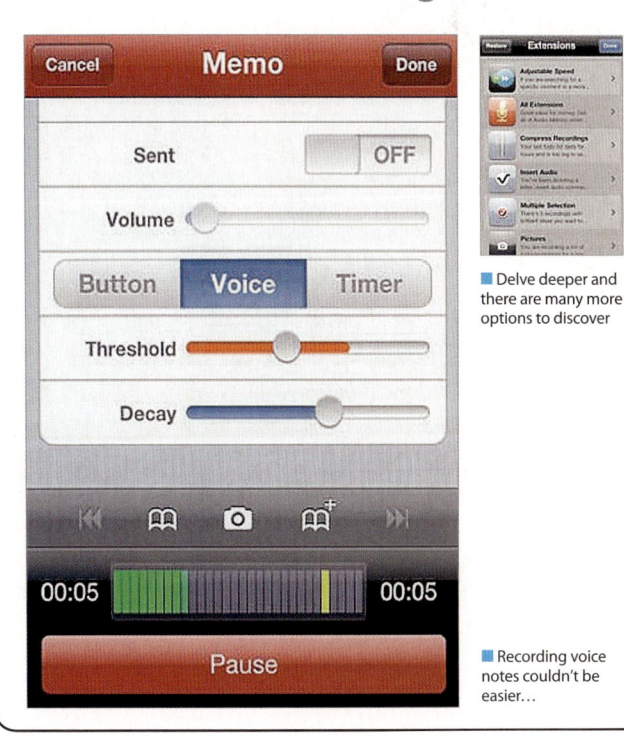

■ Delve deeper and there are many more options to discover

■ Recording voice notes couldn't be easier…

iPhone Tips, Tricks, Apps and Hacks **141**

Tips | Tricks | Hacks | Apps

Price: £1.49/$1.99 Developer: Daniel Dickenson

Monarchy The Definitive Guide

A complete guide to kings and queens of the UK

There's something different about learning history from your iPhone. When presented with a textbook, it's not long before your eyelids droop and you're yawning away. However, when we downloaded Monarchy The Definitive Guide the presentation of historical information seemed somewhat fresh and interesting, and soon we were digesting facts and important historical dates like never before.

Here you'll find a complete history of the British Monarchy spanning back 1,200 years. From King Offa of Mercia, right up to the UK throne's latest occupant, Queen Elizabeth II, you'll be presented with an image (painted portraits for the early ones, and photos for the most recent), the main facts such as date of birth/death, ascension to the throne, number of children, their coat of arms and a concise, yet informative, biography.

Take a look at the scrollable timeline feature for a quick reference, pinpointing who occupied ruled the kingdom and when. Viewing the monarchs this way – especially a lot of the early ones – is interesting as you can see how battles, wars and executions meant the royal turnover on the throne was pretty high at certain points in history. Go back to the main monarch menu and you learn how they lost their power.

Always closely related to the monarchy is the government, and included in this app is a chronological list of key politicians and Prime Ministers of Great Britain and the United Kingdom. Again you're presented with a portrait, key facts and information on how they supported the king or queen in power at the time. The Extras section includes brief histories of England, Wales, Scotland, Ireland and Northern Ireland, their flags and the national anthem. This app really is one of the best history guides available for your iPhone, it's a shame that it needs and iOS of 4.0 or higher, but with the volume of info it holds we can see why.

Overall Rating ★★★★

■ Right: Coats of arms for most monarchs can be viewed within the app

■ Far right: Famous politicians with biographies are also included

142 iPhone Tips, Tricks, Apps and Hacks

Tips | Tricks | Hacks | Apps

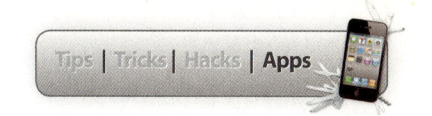

Price: £1.49/$1.99   Developer: Scott Hotaling

1400+ Dinosaur Handbook

A real beast of an app

Millions of years ago a plethora of big beasts roamed Earth. Now all we have left of them are fossilised remains and speculation as to how they walked, what they ate and how they looked. In this monster-sized 379MB app from Scott Hotaling, you'll find an comprehensive guide of over 1,400 creatures that were listed in the super order scientists call 'Dinosaura'. When looking at the list, dino experts will note that certain fossils that were once thought to be dinosaurs, but have since been disregarded are included.

Each entry is illustrated with an image of either the remains, fossil, skeleton or artists impression and a write up. You'll discover information on the common name, scientific name and other details in most instances, including who found the remains, where they were found and when they were found, as well as whether the remains are being exhibited.

Overall Rating ★★★★★

■ Details of each dinosaur are nicely presented with a well-rendered image

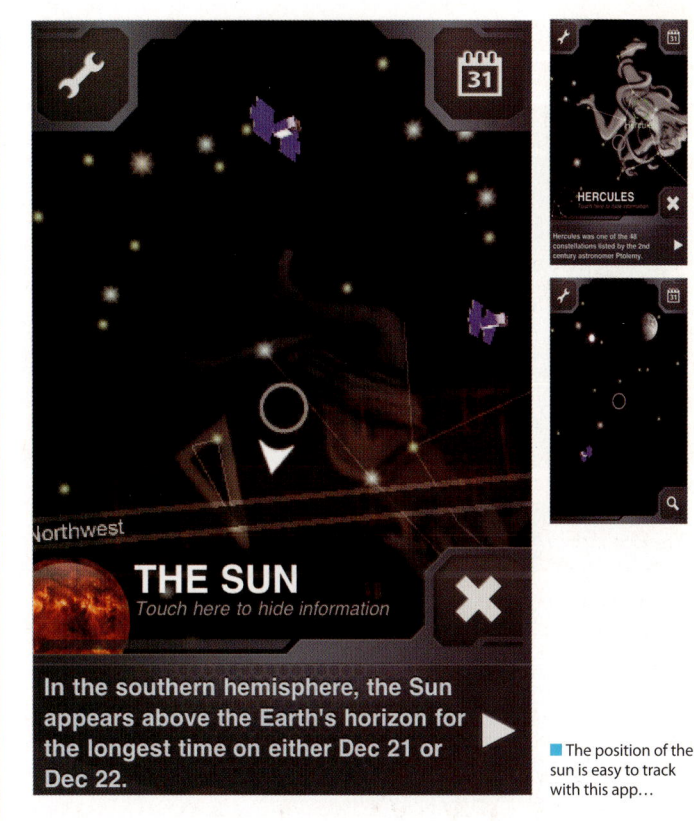

■ The dinosaurs on offer are listed alphabetically so you can easily find what you're looking for

■ The position of the sun is easy to track with this app…

Price: £1.49/$1.99   Developer: Terminal Eleven LLC

SkyView – Explore the Universe

For sun-seekers everywhere

Explore the skies from the comfort of your armchair, out in the garden or even when you're away from home. Activate this app, use your current location and as you move your iPhone around you can see a virtual representation of what would literally be in front of it. We first tested this inside, and a gentle pan around pinpointed that the moon would be opposite the front door, and there it was!

Other heavenly bodies you can locate are Earth-orbiting satellites, stars and constellations. When this app really comes into its own is when you take your device outside, point it up to the sky and track a particular pinpoint of light. Tap on it and you'll discover whether it's a planet, or what type of star it is, how far away from Earth it is, if it's part of a constellation and more. The internal gyroscope makes scrolling around smooth, fluid and responsive. This epic app is a must-have for your collection.

Overall Rating ★★★★★

iPhone Tips, Tricks, Apps and Hacks **143**

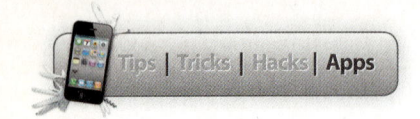

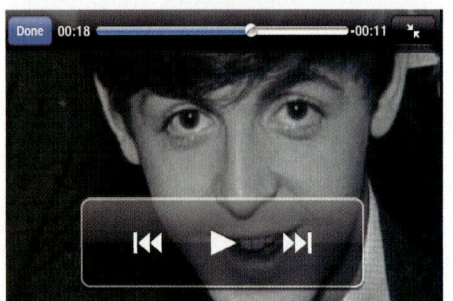

The app is packed with rare photographs, like this one showing the band going to a photo shoot

There is a decent selection of video footage included from the band's heyday

Price: £0.59/$0.99   Developer: DynaMedia Of America

Beatles Diary

It's the 'Fab Four' as you've never seen them before

So much has been written about The Beatles since they conquered the world back in the Sixties, so many photographs have been taken, and of course, so many recordings have been heard through the years that even die-hard fans may feel like they know it all. However, this expertly compiled collection of anecdotes, never-before-seen photographs and videos is a great app for fans to expand their knowledge of the band, and gain a greater insight into the various personalities in the planet's biggest band.

This app has been put together with the help of Alf Bicknell, The Beatles' former chauffeur, bodyguard and confidante from the mid-Sixties onwards, and is packed with insightful accounts, such as when he unwittingly destroyed George's famous '57 Gretsch Duo Jet guitar by not securing it tightly enough in the back of their car travelling from Blackpool to London, through to the sadly undocumented impromptu jamming session between the band and Elvis Presley that took place in Los Angeles.

The app is broken down into, fittingly, four 'fab' sections – a photo gallery, movies, rare documents and a 'bonus' section dedicated to Alf himself, which is full of cherished photographs of his years spent living in what must have been one of the most insane eras of British musical history in Beatlemania.

Alf himself, who presents many of the videos, comes across as instantly likeable. He recounts his memories with enthusiasm and clarity, often speaking from outside many of the buildings and establishments that played such important roles in the band's coming together and subsequent success, helping to give the app extra credibility.

Sadly, as charming as this app is, it isn't without fault. When browsing through the photo archives, your natural instinct is to hold your phone in landscape orientation, yet the photos remain rigidly in portrait, forcing you to scroll from one side to the other. Also, when viewing the annotations, there is no option to remove the text box from the screen without first opening up the picture, which is annoying if you simply can't remember which ones you've already viewed. Petty gripes aside though, *Beatles Diary* is a well-produced, app that fans of the iconic band will love.

Overall Rating ★★★★

Tips | Tricks | Hacks | Apps

■ The BEP360 game is a take on *Tetris*, the aim being to match up two or more icons

■ The augmented reality feature means you can position your favourite Baby Pea in the real world, and take pictures

Price: £0.69/$0.99   Developer: Talent Media LLC

BEP360

Gatecrash the Black Eyed Peas' party!

Presented in full 3D 360 degree-o-vision, this app comprises a special edition video of the Black Eyes Peas' recent single *The Time (Dirty Bit)* plus an addictive *Tetris*-style game, a photo session (that allows you to take pictures of the band), a Twitter link, and the augmented reality section itself. This works by allowing you to point your iPhone camera at one of the band's album covers, posters or a recently Googled image, and a Baby Pea will pop up and display their latest Twitter feed. You can also switch off the augmented reality mode, and have your favourite Baby Pea on-screen at all times, allowing you to take snaps of them in the real world and post them up to share with other fans in the 'BEP Earth' section.

It's a nicely put together app that allows fans to get even closer to their favourite hip-hop band, and paves the way for more artists to follow suit and provide more innovative experiences to capture the imagination.

Overall Rating ★★★★★

Price: £1.49/$1.99   Developer: Mobile Champs LLC

AR Tattoos

On the fence about a tattoo idea? Try this app first

Getting a tattoo is a hefty commitment, and anyone considering it has to make sure their chosen design is something they won't regret, especially considering the pain barrier that you have to get through to get the whole process done. Unfortunately, it's almost impossible to tell just how well a tattoo will look once the job is done, and the effects are almost impossible to reverse. So if you're considering investing in some body art, then trust the iPhone to have just the app you're looking for. AR Tattoos lets users map tons of brilliant designs onto their body by using their iPhone camera.

It's a simple process that involves selecting a design, scaling and rotating it to your specifications, and holding it over your desired body location. Once the pattern is lined up where you intend to have your tattoo, tap the snapshot button, and your would-be tattoo is then stored in your photo album. Each of the eight design categories are packed with colourful and greyscale designs that can be layered to create something more detailed.

Overall Rating ★★★★

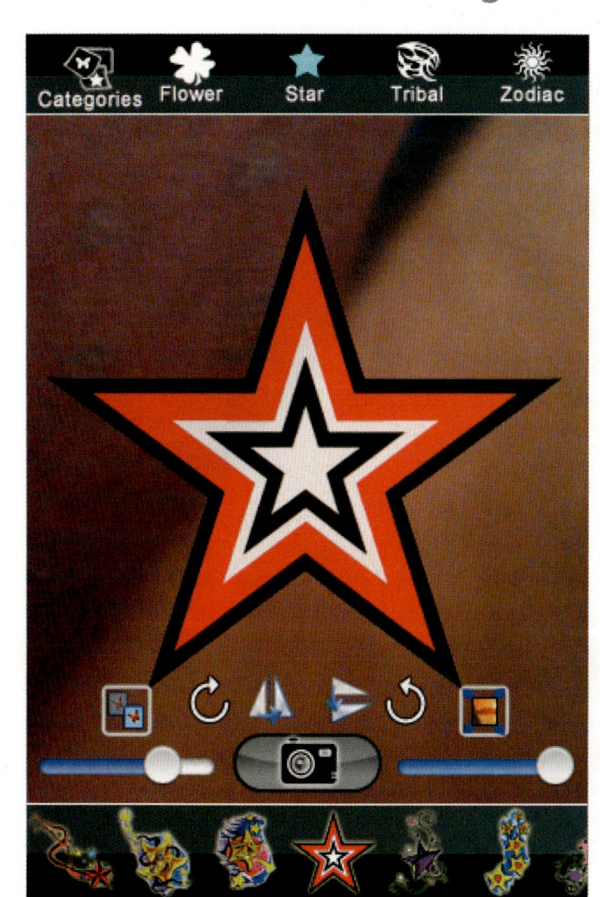

■ Floral images can be laid over tribal patterns to create multi-layered tattoos

iPhone Tips, Tricks, Apps and Hacks **145**

Tips | Tricks | Hacks | Apps

Price: Free   **Developer:** Sony Computer Entertainment Europe Ltd

PlayStation Official App

An app for PlayStation owners on the move

This official app from Sony lets users access their PlayStation Network (PSN) account, see the latest news, and also view games and peripherals. For a free app it's useful, with the same layout Sony has been using on its consoles for years.

The content is easy to read and quick to load, and you can search for relevant articles as well. You can also see the latest blog posts, which serves as a nice addition with some interesting content for PlayStation owners. There's also the opportunity to browse through the PlayStation catalogue and get info on any game, although you can't see any reviews yet. With the ability to log into your PSN account and view friends and Trophies, this is useful for PlayStation owners who want to be regularly updated. Future updates are said to include the ability to leave comments, but a 'Buy' option and some additional PSN functionality will hopefully be added as well.

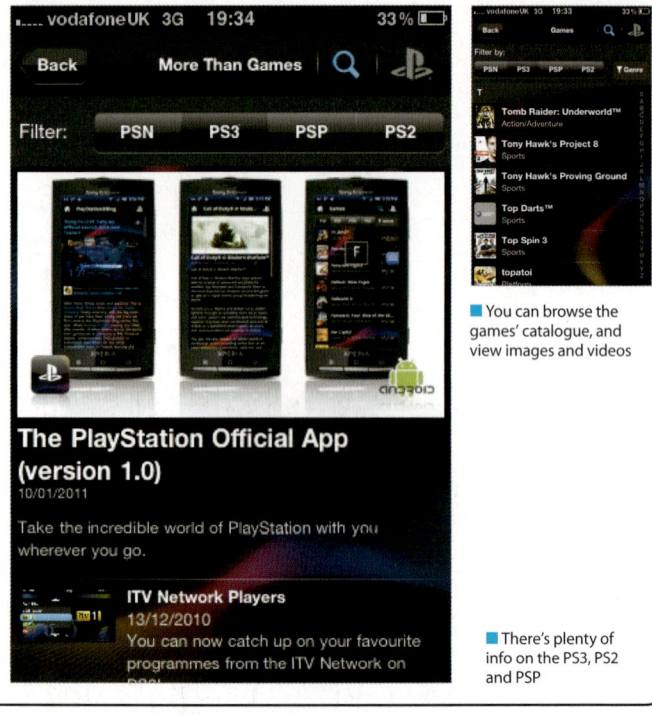

■ You can browse the games' catalogue, and view images and videos

■ There's plenty of info on the PS3, PS2 and PSP

Overall Rating ★★★★☆

■ You can edit your own photos with the in-built camera feature

■ There's an easy tool to get the exact colour you need

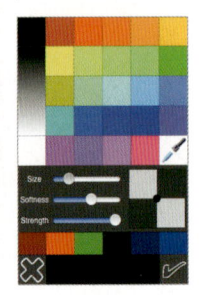

Price: Free   **Developer:** Daniel Cota

Spray Paint

The App Store gets yet another drawing tool

The initial impression that is given by Spray Paint isn't great; a bland white presentation screen with four options in blue text. The first lets you draw on 15 stock textures, ranging from a plain black screen to an image of the moon. The other three let you draw on images from photo albums and Facebook, or snap a new one with the camera, but that's it. Sadly there's no glittering array of features here, unfortunately.

Drawing is quick and easy, with two simple options: draw and erase. There's a pretty decent variety of colours to choose from as well, and quickly tapping them will let you create your own mixes, while a simple slide bar on the side adjusts the brightness. You can also change the size, softness and strength of your paint, and a zoom feature lets you finely adjust your paintings one square at a time.

Additionally, there's a few standard options, such as emailing the picture to a friend, or posting it on Facebook, which works swiftly enough, and without any problems. At the end of the day though, it's all been done before on numerous other apps, and in some cases better.

Overall Rating ★★★★☆

Price: £4.99/$6.99 **Developer:** Revolution Software

Broken Sword – The Smoking Mirror: Remastered

Unravel the mysteries of the Mayans in this classic point-'n'-tap advenure, with barely a mention of 2012

While *Broken Sword – The Smoking Mirror* has never been as good a game as the original released way back in 1996, what Revolution Software has shown is that it's now the developer to beat when it comes to porting classic point-'n'-click adventures to iOS. It's an understandably popular option for studios with such renowned games in their back catalogues, and while the quality of many of the games is undeniable, the standard of the Apple adaptations has fluctuated.

Here though, the port has clearly been given a great deal of care. This isn't a director's cut like the first game, so you won't find any new puzzles or added scenarios, but it borrows that version's excellent transposition of mouse controls onto the touch screen, making moving, interacting, and managing your inventory a snap. Also brought over are character portraits from comic-book artist Dave Gibbons (Watchmen), who contributes a new digital comic prologue as well, and a general cleaning up of the game's graphics, which largely remain detailed and beautiful.

This version brings plenty more to the table than that, though. It's now a universal app, so those with more than one of either an iPad, iPhone or iPod touch will no longer be forced to choose or buy it twice, and it actively encourages cross-platform play, with innovative Dropbox syncing for saving. In the absence of any official way to back up saved games and move them between devices, this feature could prove to be incredibly useful.

As a game, however, *The Smoking Mirror* simply isn't as good as the original. While it does have its own share of memorable moments, there aren't as many great characters to meet along the way, and to be honest it's a little too easy for experienced adventurers, who will breeze through without much difficulty. That said, it's still an enjoyable ride, made all the more pleasurable by some gorgeous artwork and characters who are still as entertaining now as they've ever been.

But even with our reservations, *The Smoking Mirror* comes highly recommended. This is a superb adventure that's been given one of the most polished iOS ports we have seen yet. All hail the iOS revival of the of point-'n'-click classics.

Overall Rating ★★★★

■ There are some genuinely funny lines, and the standard of the voice acting on display here is excellent

■ *The Smoking Mirror* comes with full Game Center integration for Achievements

Tips | Tricks | Hacks | Apps

■ Sky News is going to struggle tonight if Iron Man can't save the day!

Price: £2.99/$4.99 Developer: Gameloft SA

Iron Man 2
It's amazing what you can make with a few bits of metal!

The official game of the blockbuster movie puts you into the suit of Iron Man and War Machine and gives you immense firepower with melee combat, as well as the ability to fly, hover and pick up vending machines. Laid out in a very traditional 3D action game way, you stomp your way through each level, being guided by the suit's on-board computer and following waypoints and arrows to keep the action moving along. Complete a stage and you're rewarded with upgrades for all aspects of the suit, and more impressive weaponry.

Sadly, while everything certainly looks the part – with well-designed graphics and enhancements for the iPhone 4 Retina display – the game struggles a bit. Iron Man gets stuck in the scenery quite often, runs on the spot when he hits a wall and, while not many people will admit it, the iPhone screen is just too small to cope with displaying the action and overlaying a joypad and buttons. A decent effort but perhaps a little too ambitious for this platform.

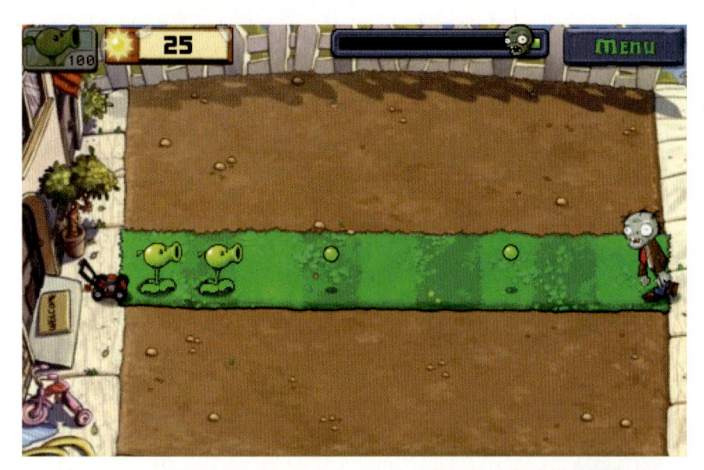

Overall Rating ★★★☆☆

Price: £1.99/$2.99 Developer: PopCap Games

Plants Vs Zombies
An essential app. End of

The tower defence genre may have skyrocketed in popularity in the last couple of years, spawning many games on many platforms, but only one title has truly captured the attention of both casual and hardcore players, turning 'a quick go' into a three-hour-long session. *Plants Vs Zombies* does nothing fancy with the basic defend-your-base formula, it just refines it slightly to such a degree that anyone and everyone can get involved.

Those put off by the insanely cheap price tag should worry not – if anything, *Plants Vs Zombies* has too much! By the end of its 50-level Adventure mode, you'll have amassed 49 plant units and yet the action still feels as fresh as ever. Utterly brilliant and if you only ever buy one game, make it this.

Overall Rating ★★★★★

148 iPhone Tips, Tricks, Apps and Hacks

Tips | Tricks | Hacks | Apps

■ Different birds offer auxiliary abilities, such as the laying of egg bombs or a diving attack

■ You'll have to plan your attacks carefully

Price: £0.69/$0.99 Developer: Rovio Mobile

Angry Birds: Seasons
Anger all year round

Angry Birds represents perhaps the biggest success story in handheld development. Add a price point everyone can afford, and solid (if not exactly original) gameplay mechanics, then sit back and watch the dollars roll in. And the pounds. And the euros, etc.

For those unfamiliar, *Angry Birds* borrows elements from just about every tank-based videogame ever produced – the player's job being to direct each bird using prehensile strength and angle to destroy a collection of pigs lying a distance away. Predictably, the porcine enemy has built itself numerous fortresses that each collapse under gravity should shots prove accurate enough.

All very delightful, of course – but we did have some issues with the seasonal version of the game, mainly that this compilation only represents snippets of gameplay from the main game, and the learning curve was slightly unbalanced. Otherwise, this joyful impulse buy was as delightful and addictive as ever, and with Halloween on the way there should be new levels coming soon!

Overall Rating ★★★★★

■ These giant pandas don't need to be killed, and can be used to your advantage

■ It's hard to bring down structures like this without crushing the friendly characters within

Price: £0.69/$0.99 Developer: PAN Vision

Pirates vs Ninjas vs Zombies vs Pandas
But none of them are angry…

It's inevitable that a game like *Angry Birds* will have some imitators, and this seems like a prime example. Look beyond the superficial similarities though, and you'll find some nifty ideas. For example, you can see the trajectory of your previous shot, avoiding the scattergun approach that could result on *Angry Birds*' more difficult stages. There's also more scope for more creative level designs, with touches like the ability to fire your variously skilled 'ammo', some of which have properties such as setting fire to wooden structures.

But even with these in its favour, the game lacks the immediacy of *Angry Birds*. It seems to have a much steeper learning curve, and is burdened by the presence of friendly characters who must not be killed. In a game that's built around randomness, such precision is frustrating. It unnecessarily complicates a formula that was nearly perfect in its simplicity.

Overall Rating ★★★★★

iPhone Tips, Tricks, Apps and Hacks 149

Tips | Tricks | Hacks | Apps

Price: £1.99/$2.99 Developer: Madfinger Games

Samurai II: Vengeance

So enjoyable your sides might just split…

Set in a vibrant Japanese feudal environment, players assume the role of a generic samurai character, destined to right a few wrongs using the pointy side of his blade. Combat is kept relatively simple down to necessity more than any other factor. Three attack buttons only are afforded to the player – two covering quick and more considered strokes of the blade, one used to evade. While some may conclude this is a scrolling brawler focused on combination attacks, in reality the truth is somewhat different due to the superiority surprise attacks give players against their foes, cleaving various parts away from various other parts in an instant.

Before you break out the Pop Tarts, though, be aware that *Samurai II* suffers from some perennial touch-screen problems. Too much of the screen can be obscured by the process of simply moving around, while puzzles must employ only one generic action button and are hence neutered. Such cel-shaded graphics, though, do play entirely to the device's strengths, giving many a reason to play on. So those in search of something a little different should give it a go, but be warned there is better stuff out there.

Overall Rating ★★★★

■ The look of the game is very distinctive…

■ Lara will be required to solve a variety of puzzles. Some of them involve lateral thinking, while others are more simple

Price: £4.99/$6.99 Developer: ideaworks

Lara Croft And The Guardian Of Light

Lara goes portable

After finding success on Steam, PSN and Xbox Live, it was somewhat inevitable that Lara's latest adventure would appear on Apple's machines.
Dispensing with the traditional adventures that were so popular on the PlayStation, *Guardian Of Light* instead takes a more arcade-style approach in the form of an impressive twin-stick shooter. There are still tombs to plunder and puzzles to solve, but the emphasis is placed firmly on action and destroying as many enemies as possible.

It's a concept that works well thanks to the solid controls, well-placed button layouts and some cleverly designed stages. Another huge bonus is the excellent multiplayer mode that can be played via Wi-Fi or Game Room. This adds massively to the core game, and having to approach puzzles with a second player in tow effectively gives you two games for the price of one. A bold new direction for Lara's adventures and a definite triumph.

Overall Rating ★★★★★

150 iPhone Tips, Tricks, Apps and Hacks

Tips | Tricks | Hacks | Apps

Price: £10.49/$14.99 Developer: IK Multimedia

AmpliTube Fender

Lighten the load with this app

Carting a huge, cumbersome amp around with you all the time is a guitarist's lot in life. It's better than being a drummer, hey? But it's still a pain in the neck and something that can now be avoided by IK Multimedia's fantastic iPhone app, AmpliTube Fender. Guitar amps can cost hundreds of pounds, whereas £29.99/$39.99 will net you the iRig lead to connect your guitar to your handheld device, and £10.49/$14.99 will open up a world of music with the AmpliTube Fender app itself. Simply plug the iRig into your guitar and you can play out loud or through headphones for the ultimate portable amp and recording suite.

While the output level of the iPhone is never going to be up there with the power of a 150W amp, using this app for practice could be one of the most liberating things you've ever done. Derived from the desktop software, the AmpliTube Fender app doesn't skimp on what's on offer, with five Fender amps available: the '65 Deluxe Reverb, the Super-Sonic, the '65 Twin Reverb, the '59 Bassman LTD and the Pro Junior. Whether you're seeking classic compressed, distorted, or gritty blues tones, there are a variety of sounds on offer. All amp tones have been scrutinised and approved by Fender itself, so quality is high, and the results are certainly impressive and very lifelike indeed.

It's not just a basic amplification app, however, as there are six Fender Stompboxes too so you can customise your sound. The stomps available are: the Fender Tape Echo, Compressor, the Fender Blender, Fender Phaser, Overdrive and Noise Filter. Each element of the tone is individually selectable and you merely have to tweak the dials like you would normally – it's a very user-friendly interface. You can even create up to 36 presets, which you can scroll through with a swipe of the finger, as well as having the option to rename them to make them easily memorable.

Overall Rating ★★★★★

■ You can get some great sounds through your pocket amp

iPhone Tips, Tricks, Apps and Hacks **151**

Tips | Tricks | Hacks | **Apps**

■ You can import tunes from your iTunes library…

■ The app comes packed with options to help enhance your sound

Price: £3.99/$4.99 **Developer:** algoriddim GmbH

djay

The premier mixing app comes to the palm of you hand

Could the iPhone be the next DJ turntable? With algoriddim's djay app, it's certainly an authentic-looking alternative. Its striking turntable/cross-fader interface reacts convincingly to touch input, but is it enough to substitute the unmistakable feel of working with 12" vinyl records? Perhaps not, but the cost and convenience of an iPhone-based DJ set-up certainly has its advantages.

Getting started is a breeze; simply open the app, and select a non-DRM track from your iTunes library. djay will calculate its tempo (or BPM – beats per minute), draw a waveform of the track, and apply any available artwork to the record on the turntable. From choosing a track until it's ready to play, the whole process takes about 15 seconds. The interface is intuitive, and within ten minutes of use it's possible for an experienced DJ to sound like they're performing on traditional DJ equipment. Novice DJs are also catered for within the app, with BPM sync tools that assist with mixing. Annoyingly, the BPM calculations can occasionally go awry, and we could find no way of manually correcting it.

Whatever your skill level, djay also includes some fun and easy-to-learn scratching tricks that could otherwise take years to perfect on traditional DJ equipment. Sadly, the Automix function doesn't always automatically 'beat-match' your tunes. Results appeared to vary from one record to the next, making it possibly more suited for background music purposes. AirPlay support is included, but our attempts to wirelessly broadcast music created a latency that made beat-mixing records incredibly difficult. You can also record your masterpieces within the app and have it saved in AIFF format. Recordings can be exported via iTunes, or played back within the app itself, which is a nice touch that will be appreciated by many.

Arguably, djay may lack the prestige of owning a proper turntable set-up, but it remains an accessible option for any wannabe DJ who hasn't got the money to splash out on the expensive kit. Alternatively, experienced scratch DJs, or those accustomed to feature-packed 'CD Turntables' may find djay slightly lacking in any of the advanced tools. Ultimately, it is best suited for enjoying at home, or for adding some excitement to a party. Either way you're going to have a blast.

Overall Rating ★★★★☆

Tips | Tricks | Hacks | **Apps**

Easy Food
A simple yet stunning cookery app

■ 'Perfect Match' will select a starter and dessert according to your main course

Price: £1.99/$2.99 **Developer:** Jakub Krupa

At first glance, due to its bright colours and simple menu design you could be forgiven for thinking that Easy Food is a basic recipe app – even one designed for children – with little depth, and overlook it for Nigella Quick Collection or Gordon Ramsay Cook With Me. However, not only is Easy Food considerably cheaper than these apps, but it also contains over 500 tasty recipes and a host of useful features.

Need some inspiration when it comes to what to make for dinner? Then why not add all the ingredients you have available to 'My Larder', and the app will attempt to find a select-ion of mouth-watering recipes that include them. It's not perfect by any means, but it does throw up some excellent ideas that you may not have thought of. For those planning a dinner party, the app's 'Perfect Match' function will come in very handy. Choose your main course, and it will select complementary starters and desserts to help you cook up the perfect meal.

All recipes come with a brief description, a list of necessary ingredients that can be easily added to the app's built-in shopping list, and some easy-to-follow instructions.

Overall Rating ★★★★★

Price: £5.49/$7.99 **Developer:** Zolmo

Jamie's 20 Minute Meals
Create 'pukka' grub

Adding to his range of hit cookbooks and TV shows, Jamie's 20 Minute Meals is the latest offering from UK chef Jamie Oliver. Offering 60 unique recipes, the app presents a summary, list of ingredients (in metric and US imperial measurements) and required equipment for each, with preparation detailed by a number of steps supported by high-quality photographs, and the occasional sound bite from Jamie himself.

The overall quality is exceptional, with a polished easy-to-use interface, and a design reminiscent of Oliver's cookbooks and magazines. Meanwhile, the 21 exclusive video clips cover general kitchen skills from preparing an avocado to honing your knife skills. Although requiring an in-app download, these vignettes are as professional as any of Oliver's TV shows, turning your iPhone into an indispensable cooking aid. The varied range of never-seen-before recipes takes in all manner of meals too, from soups and risottos through to pasta, meat, fish and puddings.

Overall Rating ★★★★★

■ Integrate a recipe's ingredients with your shopping list

■ The appetising photography is up there with any cookery book

iPhone Tips, Tricks, Apps and Hacks **153**

Tips | Tricks | Hacks | Apps

■ Amazon Remembers is a potentially revolutionary tool

■ The Amazon app's clean design epitomises its appeal

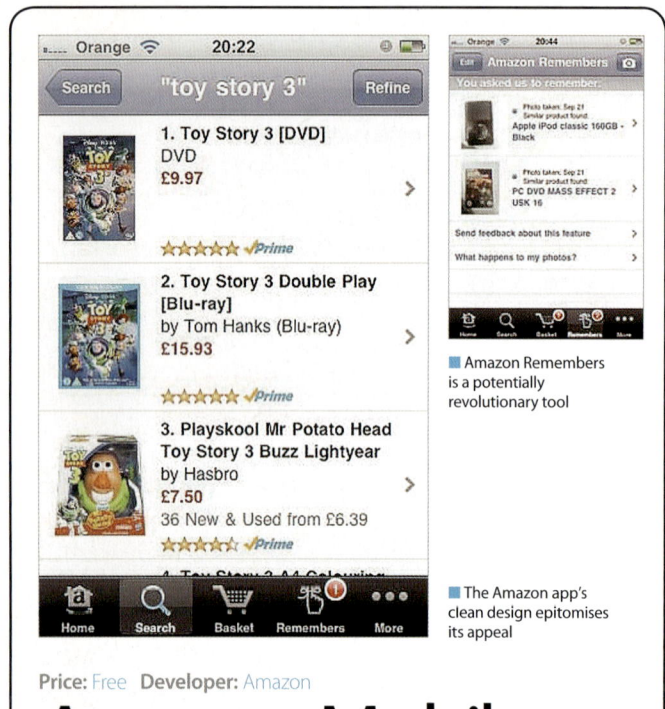

Price: Free   **Developer:** Amazon

Amazon Mobile
Retail heaven on iPhone

Considering Amazon's ubiquity with all things online, it comes as no surprise to learn that the company has its own iPhone app. An extension of Amazon's UK-specific web portal, the Amazon Mobile app provides an effective way to search, browse and buy all of the products that are offered on the website. Registered Amazon customers will benefit the most, with the app offering the same extras as the site. The app also enables you to track your packages, which is a particularly handy feature when you're on the move.

It's all extremely intuitive, and perhaps the only major difference to the website is the lack of screen space with which to bombard you with product recommendations and customer reviews, making for a refreshingly streamlined retail experience. If you're not sure what to buy, there's less scope for window shopping, but that's about as far as the criticism goes. Amazon Mobile UK also features an ingenious extra which the site doesn't – the 'Remembers' tab enables you to photograph products, before the app interprets what it is and links to the equivalent product on the site. We tested a videogame and an iPod and, impressively, it passed with flying colours. A great little app to ease your shopping experiences.

Overall Rating ★★★★★

Price: £1.99/$2.99   **Developer:** Belinda Recio

In Your Dreams
This is from which dreams are made

Many a time, you'll doubtless have experienced an acquaintance's need to wax lyrical about last evening's festivities. Rather than some drunken tale of woe, we're focusing here on the contents of their dreams, and the significance such imagery may hold for the rest of their lives. As most of us lack the financial clout to employ a psychiatrist, this app provides a cheaper alternative.

Divided into a number of sections, the app offers swift and ergonomic access to even the most odd of apparitions. Besides its diary feature that allows users to enter their thoughts via the usual text-based interface, there's also a nifty search function and various quick start guides. Though the information contained herein will doubtless prove useful for those of a more active night-time mind, the app's journal feature could have allowed for easier navigation. As cheap alternatives go though, this represents value for money.

Overall Rating ★★★★★

■ There's reference material for you to read through

■ Though the PDF material is nice, there's little to separate this from other dream interpretation literature

154 iPhone Tips, Tricks, Apps and Hacks

Tips | Tricks | Hacks | Apps

Price: £0.69/$0.99 Developer: Webdunia.com

Rate Your Life

Why bother to remember things when you have iPhone?

It's not often that when you review an app, you also get to review your life too; well, according to Rate Your Life, our lives are a mix of good and bad. If you, oddly, need an app to tell you this, Rate Your Life is a functional way to document your days.

The app lets you leave comments and notes about your experiences or feelings on each date, along with a rating from Excellent to Disaster. It then gives you verdicts and graphs about how your week, month and year have been. Using simple, touch-screen controls, you can scroll between graphs by swiping left or right, and touch the ratings at the top to make your decision. You can also set a password to keep out peeping eyes. You wouldn't be chastised for thinking this journal-style app would be aimed at the teen market, but with its formal, functional backgrounds and graphs, this doesn't seem to be the audience it's targeting. For adults, then, there's nothing major to fault with this simple app, but it's visually poor and basic in its functions. If you like the journal concept, though, it works well and could wake you up to the fact that your life isn't always bad. Hopefully…

■ The conclusions drawn are concise to say the least

■ The graphs are colour co-ordinated to match the rating you picked

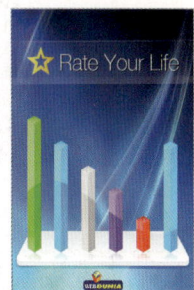

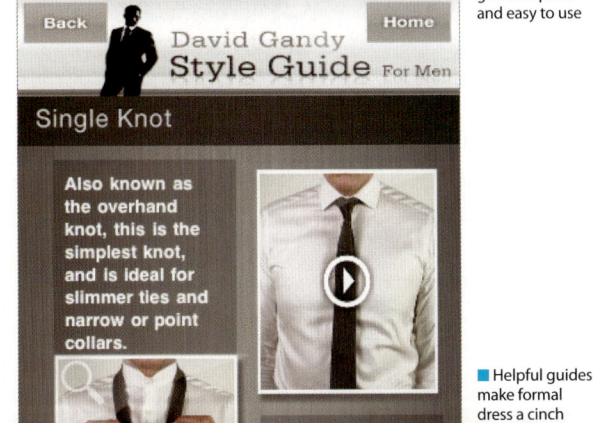

Overall Rating ★★★★★

■ The shopping guide is quick and easy to use

■ Helpful guides make formal dress a cinch

Price: £3.99/$6.99 Developer: International Celebrity Networks

David Gandy Style Guide For Men

It pays to look good

With this style guide, internationally famous male model David Gandy aims to demystify the world of fashion and equip the man on the street with the knowledge to look his best. Essentially a combination of informative guides, retail tools and interviews, the app takes a comprehensive approach to fashion with the bulk of the app's hefty file size housing 50 video interviews conducted with style experts.

Taking inspiration from current and classic style icons, with video comments from Gandy, the app also has plenty of substance to back up the style too. A retail guide enables you to search various online UK retailers, helping you find the clothes you want at the right price thanks to a slider that sets your budget. Meanwhile practical guides to suits and tailoring, as well as the 'Dress Code Cracker', provide you with all the tips you need for those formal occasions.

Overall Rating ★★★★★

Tips | Tricks | Hacks | **Apps**

Price: £6.99/$9.99 Developer: Major League Baseball Advanced Medi

MLB.com At Bat 11

Your handheld guide to the baseball season

It will comes as a surprise to anyone not a devotee of American baseball, that the teams play numerous times a week, day after day in fact. MLB.com At Bat 11 aims to keep the Major League Baseball fan up to date with constant score updates, news from your favourite team, regular season and playoff standings and, for MLB.com subscribers, live video from the games. There are also numerous extras like video highlights, find your nearest ballpark, details on all the teams, Twitter feeds etc. Clearly this is aimed at the fan who intends to go to games as in among the detail on each team is news about ticket prices and promotions, the schedule, rosters and stadium details for the next home game. However, £8.99 is a very high price since that does not include any live game commentary, either TV or radio. There are live score updates, live look-ins where key moments can be viewed from each game and push notifications for game starts and ends, and the availability of video highlights.

Overall Rating ★★★★★

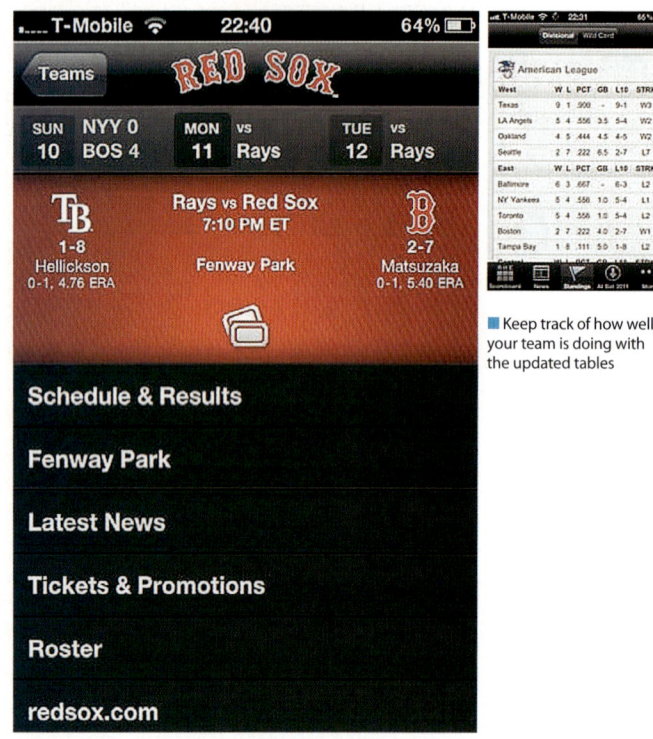

■ Keep track of how well your team is doing with the updated tables

■ Check out the schedule and results for your favourite team

Price: £1.99/$2.99 Developer: 11 Under LLC

SwingReader Golf

Lower your handicap by recording and assessing your swing

■ There are extra videos to view via YouTube

■ Use the drawing tools on the slow motion videos to check movement

As any golf instructor will tell you, it's all about the swing and that's what SwingReader Golf aims to help with. It uses the camera to record your swings – either with a friend holding the phone or using the timer countdown – which can then be played back in ultra slow motion. The clever part is that the app recognises and shows things like head and body movement with an overlay effect so you can see if you are moving around too much during the swing. Individual parts of the swing can be checked and also shared.

There's a library of grips and swings from golf pro Harry Rose, though these could do with some audio, which show how the basics should be done and there are links to numerous slow-mo clips on YouTube from the developer for comparison. Other clever aspects include the tempo analysis, text and audio notes and the ability to draw on the recordings to check head bobble, angle of swing and swing plane. If you are serious about improving, this is an excellent tool.

Overall Rating ★★★★★

156 iPhone Tips, Tricks, Apps and Hacks

Tips | Tricks | Hacks | Apps

Lewis Moody Rugby

Improve your rugby skills with the Bath and England captain

Price: £3.99/$5.99 **Developer:** International Celebrity Networks

Lewis Moody is the Bath and England captain, and this alone gives this rugby app plenty of gravitas. The main menu options offered up are split between the skill zone, the play book and nutrition and fitness.

The skill zone covers footwork, defence, handling, contact and decision making, backing up the written notes with video of Lewis delivering and practising his expert knowledge. The audio for some of these clips could be better but the video is clearly demonstrated. The playbook takes things back into the field of theory with front and backline specific areas. Each set of plays is illustrated in a step-by-step fashion that really shows how the moves are broken down and implemented. If you're a coach, you'll love this part.

The in-depth nature of the app continues when we get to the nutrition and fitness section. While the nutrition is a bit woolly, it does contain some important points and the fitness section has numerous activities for you to practice. Overall, this is an excellent app that would definitely be of interest to rugby fans and players alike.

■ There's copious video lessons showing the practical game…

Overall Rating ★★★★★

Price: £2.99/$5.99 **Developer:** Vook

Tennis Serve Technique and Tips

Get some better service

If you have just started to play, the hardest skill to get to grips with in tennis is serving. The aim of this app is to teach you the basics of grip and delivery, from throwing the ball to imparting spin. It's labelled as a video guide, yet there are only eight videos, one for each chapter, contained in it. In fact, it's more like a badly-formatted eBook. The main menu offers the following chapters: cover stance, the toss, the wind up, striking motion and follow through, spin, smart serving tactics, practice techniques and game-killing errors. Each chapter then has the information in text form, which doesn't scroll up and down as you might expect, but sideways, plus the video clip showing the lesson in action. The only other control is to activate a general page navigation system to jump from one chapter to another. Not well made, but useful enough.

■ The main menu offers eight chapters…

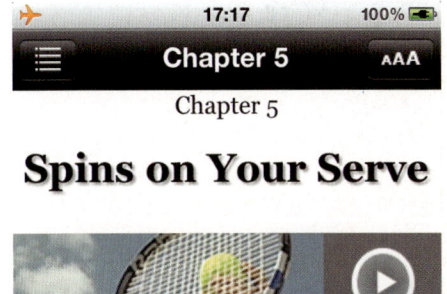

■ The overlaid navigation system makes moving around the app easier

Overall Rating ★★★☆☆

iPhone Tips, Tricks, Apps and Hacks **157**

Tips | Tricks | Hacks | Apps

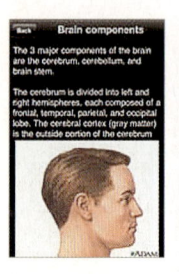

■ You can choose from dozens of topics…

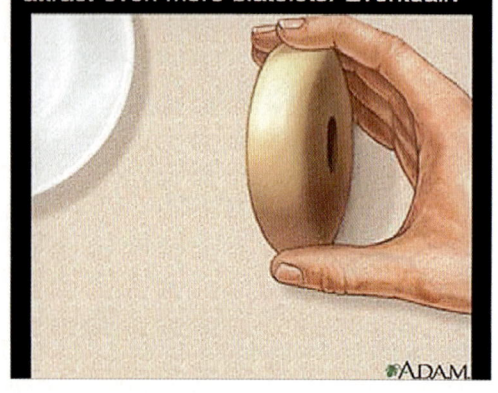

■ This app will certainly increase your knowledge of the human body

Price: £13.99/$19.99 Developer: voi nguyen

3D Animation Medical Videos Vol1

Learn about bodies on the iPhone

Words alone cannot convey the amazing nature of the human body and all of its nuances and complications. Our bodies are truly wonderful and they work in the most mysterious of ways. By grabbing your iPad or iPhone and this app you can explore the wonders of the body – and you can do it via glorious 3D artwork which brings everything alive.

Like a lot of apps, 3D Animation Medical Videos Vol1 starts with a list. It includes more ailments and functions than you could imagine, some familiar some not so. Clicking on one, such as blood clotting, displays some text accompanied by an automatically running video and the one thing that hits you is the quality of what is on offer.

Many of the videos are light-hearted in nature but they are full of information. Each one packs a punch, explaining things in an easy-going, accessible manner which really does enthral.

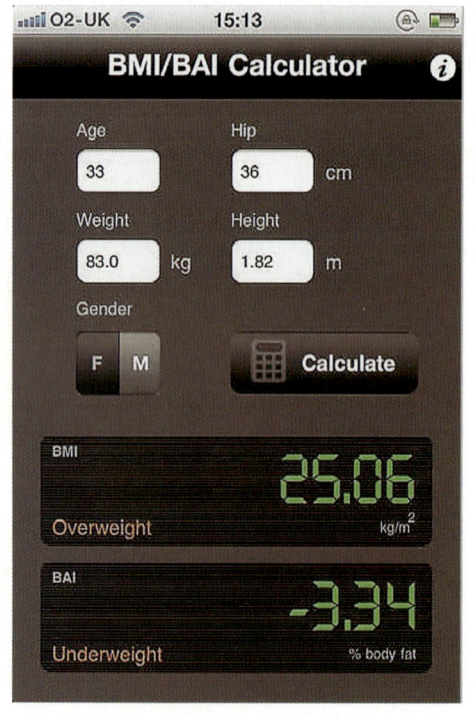

Overall Rating ★★★★★

■ The app explains how the BAI works

■ This app is packed with info…

Price: Free Developer: Juliana Apolo Da S. M. Lopes

BMI/BAI Calculator

Are you your ideal weight?

Many fitness experts will tell you that your BMI is not the only indicator of your health. BMI was developed in the late 19th Century by Lambert Quetelet as a way of assessing the level of fat in a person and yet it was fundamentally flawed. But not only does the BMI not take into account the person's sex, it also negates to factor in muscle mass. It is why some sports people are labelled overweight via the BMI method when they are anything but.

The BMI/BAI Calculator allows you to see your Body Mass Index but it also shows you your Body Adiposity Index which is a relatively new way of measuring body fat (so new that it was only published in March 2011). It takes into account the hips. This app asks just a handful of questions – age, hip, weight, height and sex – and from that it calculates your BMI and BAI, giving you a percentage of body fat. There are some downsides, but nothing to dissuade you from buying this very functional app.

Overall Rating ★★★★

158 iPhone Tips, Tricks, Apps and Hacks

Tips | Tricks | Hacks | **Apps**

■ This app is nothing is not comprehensive. It offers so much for users

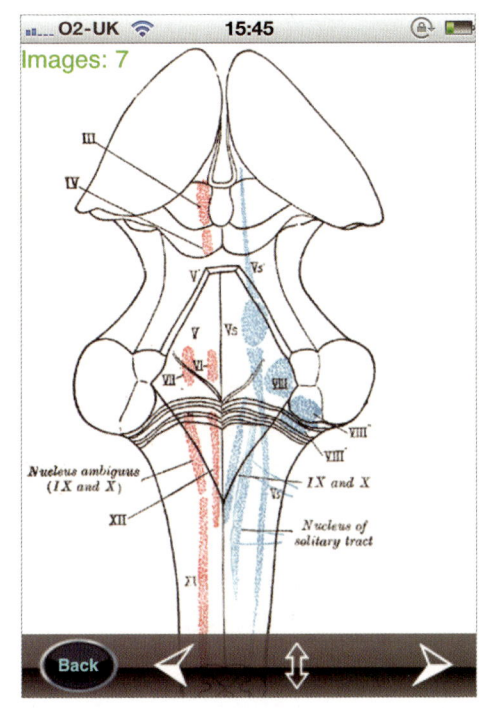

■ The app is packed with explanatory diagrams that are quite technical in nature

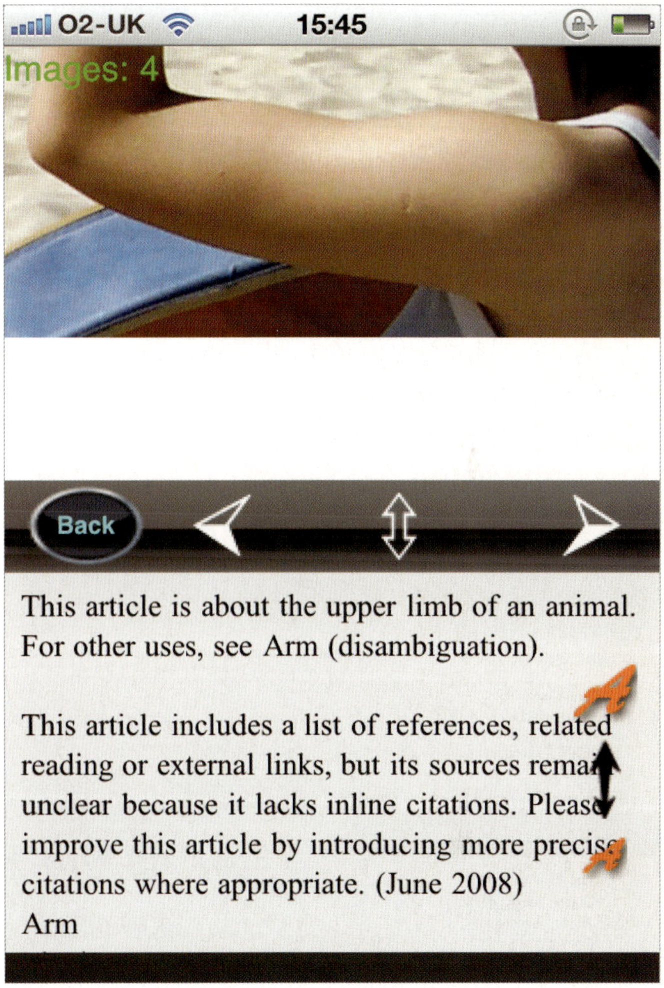

Price: £10.49/$14.99 Developer: Theo Harisk

Human Anatomy Structures

Explore your body in fine detail

When you start scouring the information within this most comprehensive of apps you realise just how deep and diverse the human body actually is. With more than 800 topics at your fingertips, it more than justifies the rather sizeable cost of this offering and given it has been put together with some care means you won't be disappointed.

Although you can flick your finger to scroll through the seemingly never-ending list of topics, it is far easier to do a search because otherwise you will be flicking for quite some time (the app definitely needs an alphabetic search option down the right-hand side of the main screen).

It's a shame that the app makers haven't categorised the topics to give you a helping hand when trying to find something of interest but it appears they assume you know what you are after (which is not always the case). To that end, however, they deliver.

All of the topics are accompanied by large, well-illustrated drawings. The text and image appear on the same page but you can move the text out of the way to see more of the picture and so you are able to get a better look at the descriptions. The app makes good use of the small iPhone screen in this respect (and if you want a bigger screen, it's also available on the iPad).

At times the text is rather dense ("Blood is a specialised bodily fluid that deliver necessary substances to the body's cells" and "the brachial artery is closely related to the median nerve"). There is a lot of technical information and it certainly would never get past the bods behind the Plain English Campaign. You get the impression this is not being aimed at the casual user but someone who has a good medical knowledge and wants some reference material handy on their phone. The annotations on the diagram are technical and non-descriptive and the actual images are text book in nature so it's not the most accessible app for many people.

But the sheer variety and knowledge that is on offer here and the fact that all of the information is stored on your device makes it an ultimate medical guide if this is your speciality. Anyone with a mere passing interest may find it a little bit too much.

Overall Rating ★★★★★

iPhone Tips, Tricks, Apps and Hacks

Tips | Tricks | Hacks | Apps

Price: £6.99/$9.99 Developer: Redivideos

Standard First Aid

Ensure you won't get caught out in an emergency

One of life's most useful and vital skills is first aid but we don't always find the time to go on a course. It is still a good idea to have some knowledge of what to do and that is where Standard First Aid comes into its own.

It is rather pricey but you do get a high-quality mix of text and videos that should help you through most situations. The app is only 0.8MB in size and that is because it pulls in the videos and text as and when you need them. It is not advisable to do this on a 3G or Edge connection because some of them are quite large and it will eat into your data allowance. The app also prevents you from accessing videos if your battery is low which is part-frustrating and part-common sense.

There is a long list of videos and text covering all of the main bases. They include amputations, burns, choking, cuts, eye injuries, heart attacks, nosebleeds, shock and spine injuries. The app splits everything up so that moving pictures are in one section and the written words in another. The app is also sectioned into 'Perform First Aid' and 'First Aid Training Course', the former directing you to exactly what you have to do and the latter giving slightly more of an explanation.

Both the text and videos offer solid descriptions of the procedures you need to follow. Everything is written in clear, non-waffly language which is just the thing you need when time is precious. The videos are well shot and demonstrated and the narration is also clear and concise. It is obvious that the filming has been done by a professional and so there is a greater tendency to trust the advice you are being given.

It is a shame given the quality of these videos and text descriptions that the overall app isn't more aesthetically pleasing. Other than the videos, this is an average-looking app but at least it isn't a case of style over substance like many of the other offerings on the App Store.

As a bonus, the app includes a quiz (but there is a definite North American bias and you probably won't spend too long on it, even if you are from that neck of the woods). Having to load text and videos each time you want something new is also annoying but the trade-off is a smaller footprint on your iPhone and you only view the items you want. Definitely a useful resource guide but there are better ones on the App Store.

Overall Rating ★★★★

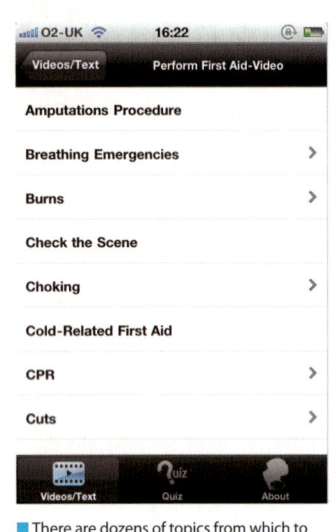

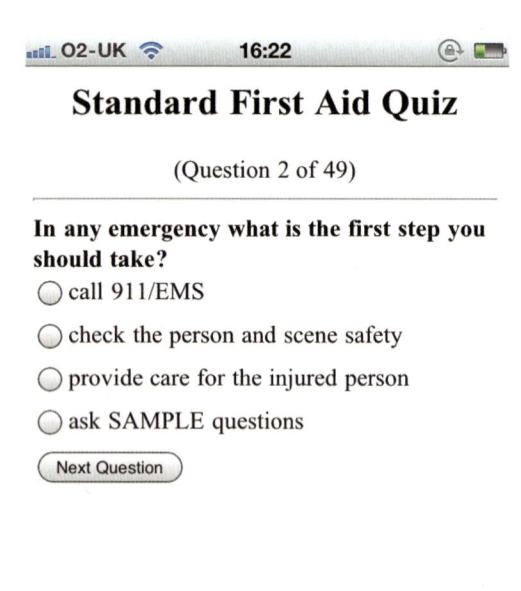

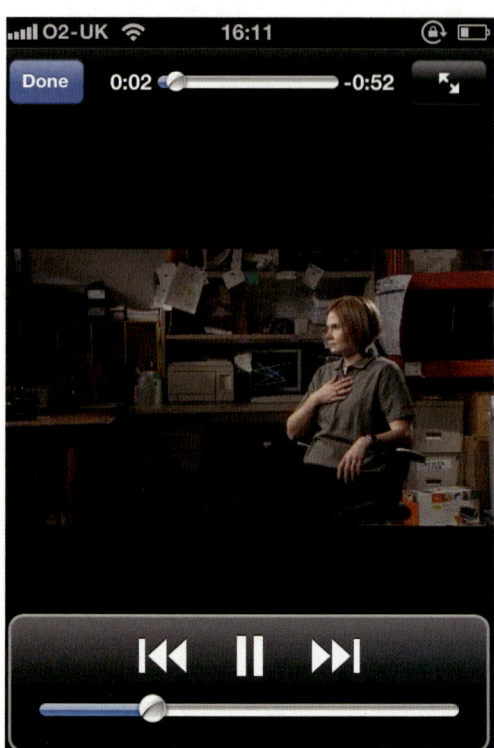

■ There are dozens of topics from which to choose, covering just about all situations

■ The quiz is for fun for a while…

160 iPhone Tips, Tricks, Apps and Hacks

■ Create satisfying animations in minutes…

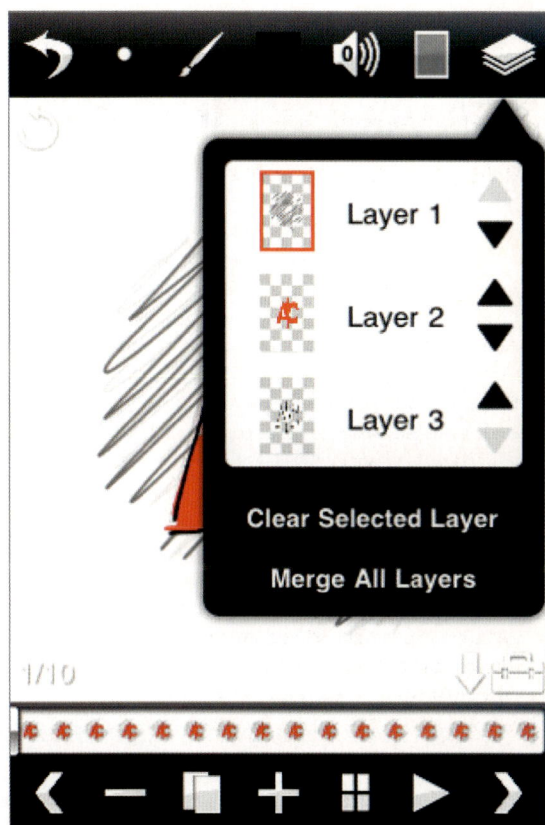

Price: £0.69/$0.99 Developer: Red Software LLC

Animation Creator

Create incredible animations on your iPhone with just a flick of your fingers

If you ever had any doubts about the potential of the software on the App Store then now is the time to cast them aside. We doubt even Steve Jobs himself could have envisioned a time where artists could create animations using their iPhones. And yet when you load an app like Animation Creator you almost feel as though the mobile phone was invented for this very purpose alone.

The purpose of this app is to act as a channel for your creativity. You are the director with a selection of simple, yet powerful drawing tools, layers and easy-to-use frame management at your fingertips. Also available on the iPad in HD, the app allows you to take a string of pictures and then transform them into instant stop-motion animation.

Once you've created a new project and tapped the toolbox button to show you the options you are ready to get cracking. You can select backgrounds, change painting/drawing tools and, of course, colours. Once you've started your animation you can use the plus button to add the next frame with onion skinning or you can copy the frame to add to it. For more ambitious users there is the option to add layers like a Photoshop document. The colour palette is a little disappointing but you can use a sliding scale of colours to create more desirable tones. The brush choices are cool, as is the ability to easily alter the brush size.

The latest version of the app also features a string of minor enhancements, such as a wealth of sharing options, plenty of toolbox additions, frame positioning and rotating options plus a great new interface that is more eye-catching and easier to navigate than ever. If you are artistic or just fancy something novel to play with for half an hour then you will undoubtedly get some enjoyment from this app. It's simple, easy to use and a great deal of fun, not to mention great value at such a low price point. So if you're after an arty app that can yield satisfying results quickly then you should definitely download this right away.

Overall Rating ★★★★★

Tips | Tricks | Hacks | **Apps**

Price: £0.69/$0.99   Developer: Grant Schindler

Trimensional
Scan in 3D, print and export

Trimensional is one of those apps that at first seems pretty frivolous, but could well evolve into something more significant with the help of future revisions. Described by some as the most innovative app to date, we're not sure we'd go as far in our own estimation.

It certainly is an entertaining scanner, showing aptitude when performing and detecting patterns of light to build a true 3D model. However, practice is recommended to get the best outcomes – with the Quick Start Guide advising to shoot in low light against a very dark background, and your iPhone brightness set to maximum.

Once you get the hang of it, your captures can be shared as a still JPEG or animated GIF via email. This is all a bit of fun, but Trimensional takes itself seriously. Advanced use of your scanned results are accessible through the 3D Model Export option – the privilege will cost you an additional £2.99.

Overall Rating ★★★★★

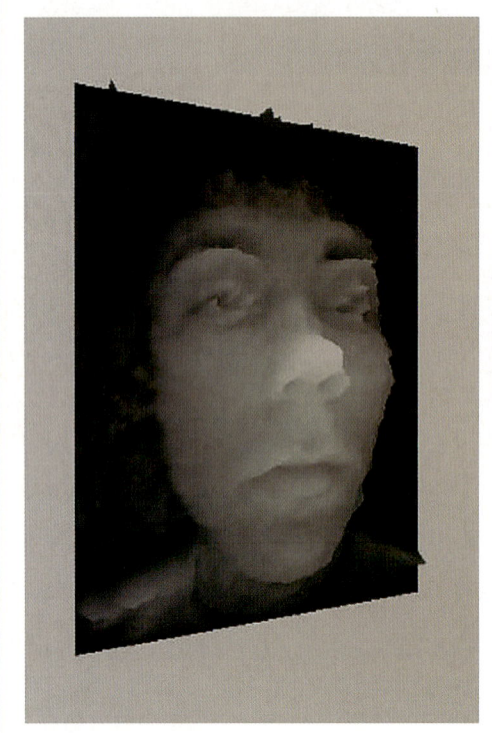

■ Build your own 3D model on your iPhone

■ An easy way to brighten up your pics

Price: £0.69/$0.99   Developer: Pocket Pixels, Inc

Color Splash
Helps to brighten up even the drabbest of photos

This is a very simple app designed with one purpose in mind: to allow users to select elements of a photograph and show them in colour with the rest of the picture being left in black and white.

The results can be effective and the app thrives on ease of use. Simply put, the app turns everything black and white by default and then you colour in elements of the picture with your finger. You are limited by the size of the iPhone screen but a pan and zoom button helps you get in close to areas. The main controls are a colour button and a grey button. If you change your mind after using the colour button you can use the grey button to reverse your colouring. Options to save sessions and save the final picture are useful, as is the Undo button, which can be used when you make a mistake. The interface is as simple as can be with big, easy-to-find and use buttons, and there are a host of other options available including sharing to social networks and inverting the colour to grey and vice versa.

Overall Rating ★★★★★

162 iPhone Tips, Tricks, Apps and Hacks

Price: £1.49/$1.99 Developer: Nexvio Inc

8mm Vintage Camera

Kick it old school with this vintage camera app

There are a large number of camera-related photography apps that do little more than provide an overlapping filter for your iPhone's five-megapixel camera. Such apps are obviously throwaway, providing a mild bit of fun before the inevitable regret over your sometimes-costly purchase starts to sink in. Thankfully, Nexvio's 8mm Vintage Camera app transcends the stereotype and actually adds genuine novelty value to the camera trickery it delivers.

It's still essentially a camera filter app at its core, but it also gives the user the option to record films in a variety of different vintage camera styles, complete with scratches, frame skips and blurred edges that have a raw, classic feel. Five filters can be applied to your camera, starting with a sepia-toned Siena finish, then moving through to Twenties black and white, the bleached colours of the Seventies, and the odd pink haze of Sakura lens mode. While the camera is rolling, each filter animates authentically as the image judders and skips erratically. However, if you just want a clear, normal image, you can also tone down these effects.

X-Pro is perhaps the most interesting filter of the lot, as it presents the camera view in full colour, but adds a smeared contrast that makes for some striking images. As we mentioned earlier, these tricks are more than aesthetic, giving users the option to record video clips set against their chosen filter. Recording uses a simple toggle process that can be started, paused and stopped all at the touch of a button. The final result is nothing less than superb, delivering the same quality that you would expect from your camera, but with tons of visual trickery overlapped.

While 8mm Vintage Camera has a comparatively meagre asking price, there's little need for such an app unless you genuinely like to snap films in vintage format. To the app's merit, iPhone owners shouldn't buy this expecting a cheap gimmick and a few laughs. Instead, there is real value here for mobile photographers who want to add a bit of creative flair to their phone snaps. We would like to see future updates help this app grow into a bigger, more powerful tool for photographers to use, but for just over £1 the tools on offer make this a very satisfying purchase overall.

Overall Rating ★★★★

■ Pressing the effect button can make images unrecognisable. Surprisingly, this makes the effect better

■ Recording movies is as easy and stress-free as you would imagine…

Tips | Tricks | Hacks | Apps

■ Switch off unused formats and games consoles to keep filter searches and help keep them relevant

■ Prioritise the films in a list by simply tapping the appropriate level button. Select a film and tap Delete to remove it from the list

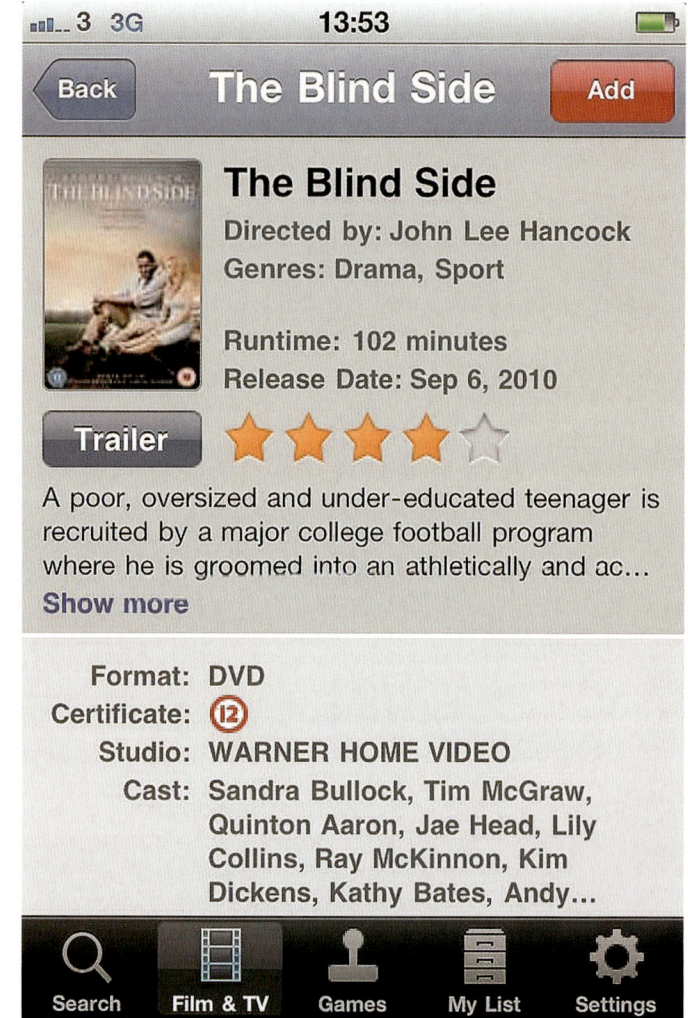

Price: Free   Developer: LOVEFiLM

LOVEFiLM UK

Browse over 67,000 titles and manage your lists on the move

LOVEFiLM is the UK's most notable, and usable, online movie rental service, and this app is almost the perfect companion. In what is surely a smart move, the app is not totally inaccessible to non-registered users. The app allows anyone to browse the LOVEFiLM library, tempting users to sign up. The initial interface is a typically text-driven list split across New Releases, Most Popular, Coming Soon, and a comprehensive list of genres. Flip up and down, find a genre and a single tap presents a list of relevant releases. The problem here is that the list doesn't seem to have any type of logical order and there is no option to filter anything except format. The options are Blu-ray, DVD or the default Show All, useful if you don't want a specific format. This can become a minor irritation when browsing regularly, but thankfully the Settings options resolves the issue. The Search & Browse Options enables the user to show results for a chosen format or a specific games console. The service offers games for all the major consoles including Wii, PS2/3, Xbox, PSP and DS. One tap switches off the unwanted option and, of course, narrows down a search. The alternative is to use the search facility, but this offers no more than the standard. It would have been nice to have seen alternative choices for misspelt titles.

Selecting a release reveals a mine of information, including director, runtime, release date and an expandable summary. Add in the format, certificate and cast and it's almost too much to take in. For good measure there are three reviews, if available, and a long list of recommended similar rentals. Finally, a trailer is available to help sway opinion and if you love a film enough, the option to add to a LOVEFiLM list. To connect to a LOVEFiLM account, users simply authorise the use of the app and take control and manage their LOVEFiLM lists.

Overall Rating ★★★★★

164 iPhone Tips, Tricks, Apps and Hacks

Tips | Tricks | Hacks | Apps

Price: £0.69/$0.99   Developer: Dev Round

MyTrend

View trends on Twitter

MyTrend is a very smart app that shows you trending topics, such as your favourite football team or a movie star, so you can quickly follow the stream on Twitter for that topic. What makes it smart is that you can first search for a term, like Randy Moss, and then see how many posts are on Twitter by date for that topic. That preamble screen is helpful for determining if you want to view that topic. The app runs fast once you find a topic, but searches can take up to a minute depending on your connection speed.

MyTrend shows you topics as either a list or a simple graph. For example, if you search for Obama, you can see which recent dates had the most activity on Twitter in discussing the American president. Each trend you type in stays on the list automatically. MyTrend uses a trendy interface itself – easy-to-use buttons, an orange and blue colour scheme, and no extra features to get in the way. That said, we'd like to see a few extra options for following a poster or clearing your search history.

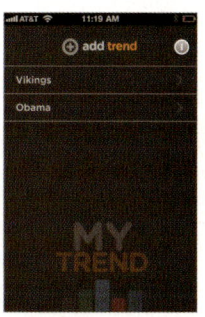

■ All topics you select are shown in a trend summary screen automatically

■ Searching for a topic is easy, but the results take about a minute

Overall Rating ★★★★☆

Price: £0.69/$0.99   Developer: iLegendsoft Inc

Photos Sync for Facebook   Manage and sync your photos

■ All your Facebook albums are shown in a clearly laid out screen

For most Facebook users, it's fun to upload photos and videos whenever you want. Managing them is not as fun. Facebook Photos Sync is a powerful tool that helps you manage your multimedia, including knowing exactly which albums you have, when they were uploaded, and which images and videos you have uploaded. The app has the rather amazing ability to let you manage this content even when you are not connected to 3G or Wi-Fi, and then upload the content in the background when the app is not even running (similar to how the iPod music player runs).

The app can auto-rotate your images before upload and works with Facebook privacy settings in determining who can see your content (just friends, or anyone). You can even set the app to sync when you want and to both upload new images and download images you have uploaded from a different tool, such as the Facebook app on your iPhone. A few handy little extras make this app one to buy: for example you can assign a password to the tool to lock out prying eyes, and the app authorises with Facebook quickly.

Overall Rating ★★★★★

iPhone Tips, Tricks, Apps and Hacks **165**

Tips | Tricks | Hacks | Apps

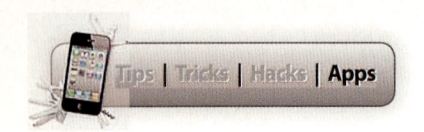

■ Post status updates simultaneously to both Facebook and Twitter

■ With more social networks to be added, this could become essential

Price: Free Developer: Yuriy Stelmakh

Multistatus

Facebook and Twitter combined

If you've ever found yourself repeating a status update on both Facebook and Twitter, Multistatus aims to make your life easier by letting you post to both at the same time, or just one of them if you want. Once you've logged in to both your accounts for the first time you won't need to again, and you can quickly update both without having to switch between two apps. You can also see the combined feeds of both Facebook and Twitter, which is again good and brings everything into one place.

However, while its basic layout is quick and easy to use, its lack of features is noticeably apparent. While you can post text updates, there's no option to upload photos or link to other people. There's also no option to reply to or comment on posts in your news feed, limiting the interactions on offer. While it's a good idea, the limited functionality means it isn't perfect yet. It's early days, and there's talk of allowing integration with other social networks in future, but for now it's just a bit too limited.

Overall Rating ★★★★★

Price: Free Developer: MillMobile

Zwapp

Turning app hunting into a social network

Zwapp aims to make the process of app downloading a much more social experience by allowing you to share your latest app purchases with friends and see what everyone else has been downloading. You can search via keyword similar to on the Apple App Store and you can also view popular paid and free apps among strangers and friends alike. You can also post your latest purchases to social networks such as Facebook and Twitter, to let people know what you've been splashing the cash on

At this early stage in its development Zwapp could really do with more users. There's very few people actually using the service yet and, until more people get on board, there's not enough user-generated content to make downloading it worthwhile. Of course, every app has to start somewhere, and there's no doubt that if Zwapp takes off then it could be a great app for people unsure of what to download next.

Overall Rating ★★★★★

■ Hopefully some more users will get on board…

■ If the App Store isn't user-friendly enough for you then you might want to check out Zwapp

166 iPhone Tips, Tricks, Apps and Hacks

Tips | Tricks | Hacks | Apps

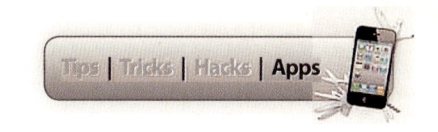

Price: Free   Developer: Quest Visual

Word Lens

Instant language translation, wherever you look

This app is somewhat revolutionary. Word Lens takes augmented reality apps to a whole new dimension by translating text via your iPhone's camera in real-time. You simply point your camera at foreign text – be it a signpost, book, noticeboard, absolutely anything – and the text will be magically translated into English as you stare at it through the phone's viewfinder.

The magic doesn't happen instantaneously with this free download, though. Once downloaded, what you essentially get is a demo that enables you to play around with the technology without utilising any useful features. The only features you are initially privy to in the free download are the 'Erase Words' option – which will remove chunks of text from whatever you point the camera at, and 'Reverse Words'. The latter is slightly more enjoyable to play around with, as you can point the camera at logos and suchlike, and marvel as it reverses the words in the viewfinder and presents them in a similar font style.

Where this app really excels though is in text translation, and for that you have to spend an additional £2.99/$5.99 apiece for the Spanish to English and English to Spanish add-ons. Though this feature doesn't tend to recognise many handwritten or stylised fonts, it does actually work by providing literal or rough meanings for whatever text you throw at it, making it rather handy as a quick reference guide for browsing menus or understanding danger signs. Also, if the camera doesn't convert the text in real-time, then you can access a separate manual feature to call up the on-screen keyboard, whereby you can type in a word and the app translates it for you. Remarkably, no network or internet coverage is needed to operate the app, so you can call on its expertise anywhere, which is very reassuring.

What with this being version 1.0, the options so far are limited, with Spanish being the only language downloadable at present. However, regular updates should see more languages added in the future, such as French, German, Italian and perhaps even Japanese – now that really would be amazing!

Overall Rating ★★★★★

■ If you're looking for a tasty lunch, this app will point you in the right direction…

■ The app itself is free, but you will have to pay additional charges to buy it in each language

Tips | Tricks | Hacks | **Apps**

■ The settings are easy to find and easy to use

■ The half map is a cool way to view the world making sure you don't get lost

■ The smaller map gives you more space to see your surroundings as well as your location

Price: £0.69/$0.99 Developer: Byungil Park

Real Map Plus

A great way to find your way

Getting to where you need to be has become significantly simpler since the advent of the smartphone and its ability to utilise GPS (global positioning satellite). Clever app makers have quickly grasped how to use the iPhone's many talents to glean even greater functionality from the raw data it is able to process.

Real Maps Plus takes your camera app and maps app and throws them together in a nicely designed, easy-to-use combo. The screen can be split a couple of ways and the idea is that you can look at both to see where you are going and the map at the same time. It's not quite augmented reality but it is clever enough that when you really are struggling to find which direction you should be heading in, it is a great help. The map overlay is simple and easy to read, if it had been too zoomed-out, as it were, you'd struggle to find your bearings. Too zoomed-in and you wouldn't get enough of a reading from moving around to ascertain if you've made steps in the right direction. If you are a fan of customising apps to suit you better there are a couple of cool options tucked away in the settings. You can alter the map display from mini, to a half page split-screen as well as changing the kind of map you see from satellite, to road, to a hybrid.

If you travel a lot and want an app that can combine your lust for knowing where you are with your inability to stop and work it out from a regular map, this hybrid option is going to be a total winner. The design is simplistic and easy to use and its main function is to use the camera to help tell you if you are in fact pointing in the right direction. As it is able to complete this task admirably without costing a fortune it deserves your attention. A well made, easy-to-use app with no bells and whistles but a solid engine that really works. Other app developers would do well to stick to the Real Map Plus philosophy. Doing one thing well is a thousand times better than doing 100 things badly. A great app that is well worth the relatively low asking price.

Overall Rating ★★★★

168 iPhone Tips, Tricks, Apps and Hacks

Price: £1.49/$1.99   Developer: Elecont

eWeather HD

Stylish, clock-based weather forecasting for your iPhone

A weather forecasting app that can deliver hourly forecasts for the next 12 hours and daily forecasts for the next ten days, at first glance eWeather HD appears a little complex. In actual fact though, it takes almost no time at all to become familiar with its layout, by which time you'll be appreciating the sleek interface design for its style and intuitive approach to weather forecasting. iPhone 4 users benefit from HD graphics optimised for the retina display, and the unique clock-based interface looks quite stunning as a result.

There are two distinct display modes in which weather data can be shown. On the first screen, the central clock displays the current time, date, air temperature and outlook while a separate segment for each hour contains a photo-realistic icon representing the weather forecast for that hour, over a period spanning the next 12 hours from the current time. There is also an icon within the clock face that, when tapped, selects between outdoor air temperature, perceived air temperature, UV index and precipitation probability as the data displayed in the hour segments.

The second screen, accessed by tapping a button, displays temperature and pressure information graphically with bars and trend lines that show the activity over the past 24 hours. This screen is also where you will find a full ten-day forecast, moon phase, set and rise times, sunrise and sunset times, UV radiation levels, relative humidity, wind speed and direction and an hourly rain probability forecast. There really is a wealth of information on offer!

Overall, the information in the forecasts proved to be towards the more accurate end of the scale, but the accuracy of the GPS locator could do with being narrowed down a little, as some locations in the UK were only able to be pinpointed to within a ten mile radius, and one slight interface niggle concerns the swipe feature that allows you to switch between days in the ten-day forecast. It somehow doesn't behave in the way you'd expect, but it's literally difficult to put your finger on why.

We're being extra-picky here though, because there is much to like and very little to find fault with here. eWeather HD is well-designed, well-executed and, well, very good indeed. If you're after a solid, reliable weather app then you could certainly do a lot worse than this one.

Overall Rating ★★★★★

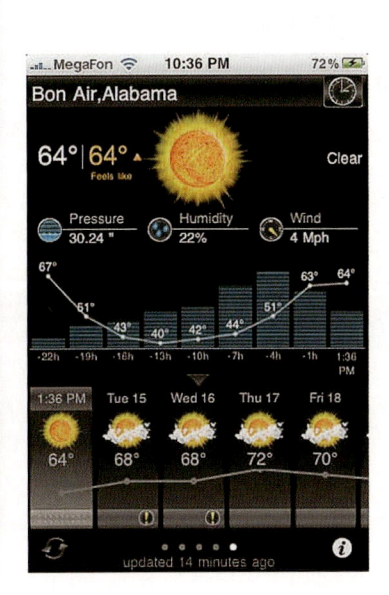

■ Impressive design cues, with HD graphics and trend lines

Tips | Tricks | Hacks | Apps

Ultimate Browser
Browse the web in style with this superb browser

Price: £1.49/$1.99   **Developer:** Lee Heap

Preloaded on every iDevice inluding iPhone, Safari is a solid app full of standard features you would expect from any good web browser. However, it pales in comparison when going up against a number of desktop browsers, specifically Google Chrome and Firefox, both of which offer a wide range of expansive bolt-ons and features.

Enter Ultimate Browser, a web browser that delivers all the features of a high-end browser for your iDevice. While the browser may look similar to Safari on start-up, a quick dabble in the top menu bar will reveal a wealth of features. For starters, you can open multiple tabs for when you want to explore multiple sites in tandem, as well as bookmarking favourites in a clear drop-down menu.

Underneath the hood lies a plethora of features, such as a cookie tracker, homepage settings, search engine preferences, ad blocking and even privacy options. The asking price is modest given how ultimately superior this app is over Safari.

■ This app comes packed with great features to discover…

Overall Rating ★★★★★

GoDocs
Price: £2.99/$4.99   **Developer:** Nikita Lutsenko

Bringing Google Docs and iPhone together

As the iPhone lets you sync email accounts from multiple service providers, it makes sense that Google Mail users can have access to Google Docs as well. Unfortunately this isn't the case. Enter GoDocs, a handy app from Nikita Lutsenko that gives you direct, secure access to Google Docs at speed. On downloading the app, all you need to do to sync accounts is enter your Gmail username and password, then you're connected in a matter of seconds. From the top menu you can browse your existing documents, open them, edit them and save them back on the cloud for retrieval later.

The app is well presented, giving you a basic list of existing documents to choose from, as well as a list of editing options. Each document has this sub menu of options, letting you edit docs online in real-time, download the source file, share with other users via email, rename and even upload new documents. It's an expansive toolset that delivers the features you demand.

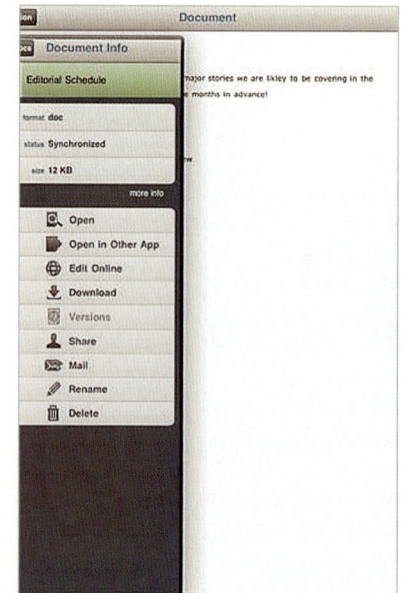

■ The app lets you sync up multiple accounts for ease of use

■ The app comes packed with features for the price you pay

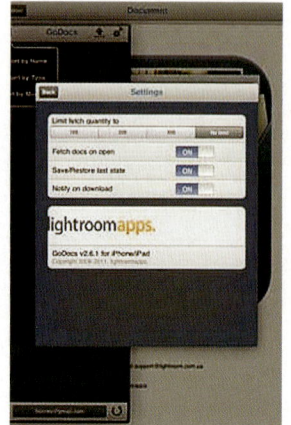

Overall Rating ★★★★★

Tips | Tricks | Hacks | Apps

Price: Free   Developer: Adobe

Adobe Ideas

Adobe needs to buck up those ideas before this app shines

Adobe Ideas is one of Adobe's two entries in the art app marketplace, and is aimed at digital artists treating their device as a sketchbook. Adobe's Photoshop and Illustrator are market leaders on desktop platforms, but despite some good functionality, this sketching program falls short of the brand's standards, and that of many other art apps too. If it's the first art app you've looked at, then initial impressions are pretty favourable. It has the bare bones you need for digital sketching, such as a brush, eraser, colour palette and opacity controls. Draw even the scribbliest of scrawls, and the app will snap it into a smoother, more vectored-looking line. This is great if you're noting down basic graphic design ideas, but less so for artwork, as the energy and uniqueness of line art is rapidly lost in favour of a homogenised smoothness. The single brush can be modified by size and opacity, but it's hardly the paintbox of tricks offered by SketchBook Pro or ArtRage. It's responsive to both your finger and a stylus, or NomadBrush, although the automatic line clean-up makes the latter somewhat redundant. The colour palette is excellent, with a full spectrum gamut, plus slots for five selected hues on the app's interface. You can import palettes from Adobe's Kuler website (kuler.adobe.com; a collection of user-generated palettes) to use here, or select your own. Again, this is ideal for graphic design ideas, but less relevant for digital sketching.

Where it all falls down is with its layering options. Most art apps will give you a couple, and in Adobe Ideas you can have up to ten, at a cost of £2.99/$4.99. Obviously, this is where you have to spend some money on this free app, but for many digital artists and designers alike, it's a turn-off. Layers are such an ingrained part of the digital art workflow that the lack of them makes the app feel lobotomised, and many people will balk at the comparatively high cost, especially if they're only after one or two, not the full ten-pack. There are better and more well-rounded art options out there.

Overall Rating ★★★★★

■ Layers are limited…

■ Sketch out ideas with ease…

■ You can create some decent artwork using this app

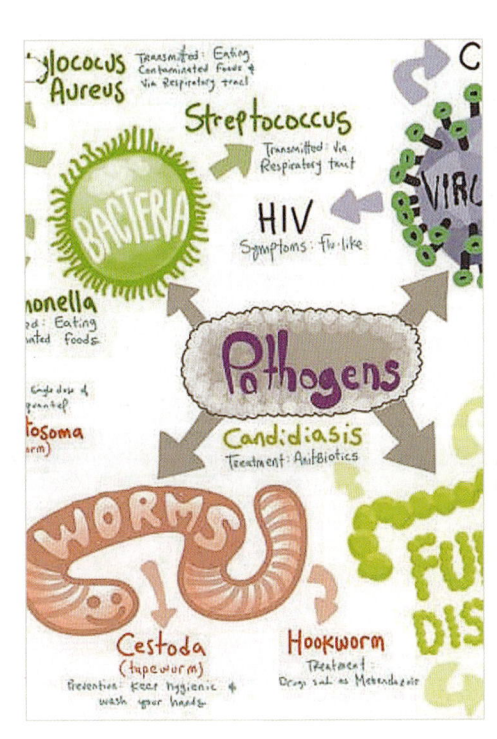

iPhone Tips, Tricks, Apps and Hacks **171**

Tips | Tricks | Hacks | Apps

Price: £1.49/$1.99 Developer: John Stefanopolos

Speak It! Text To Speech

Why write when you can speak?

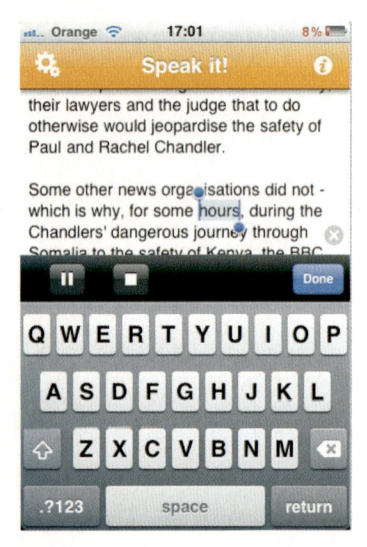

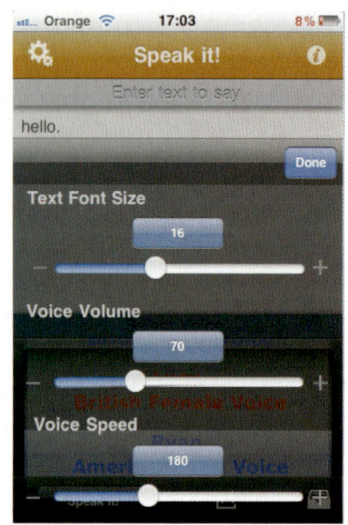

We suppose many aspects of modern life would have astounded us, ten or 20 years ago. Live online gaming, for instance, or how terribly expensive things are. Topping the list, though, come apps like Speak It!, which allows a device in the palm of your hand to speak for itself near-perfectly. It's not quite as simple as that, naturally. Though its sales blurb suggests the ability to read PDF files, it can only do this insofar as it can read any copied and pasted text from any document. So, before having the device spell out any text, users must delve into the source document as they would have done anyway, which is a shame but doesn't kill off the app's purpose entirely. It's possible, for instance, to send a spoken message to others via email, just through the entry of text. Naturally, too, it may prove of use to those unwilling to strain their eyes through the viewing of large text documents to have one of this app's four automatons speak it to them while either browsing other apps or doing nothing at all.

■ Emailed sound files are sent directly from within the app itself

Overall Rating ★★★★★

Price: £2.99/$4.99 Developer: Int Sig Information Co

CamScanner+

Need a convenient way to keep all your important documents close to hand?

Think of CamScanner+ as a portable scanner that lets you copy and archive reams of data and documents, and makes them available for use at any time. It's simple to use, and makes great use of the iPhone's camera function, capturing documents at a good resolution. All you need is a document ready to 'scan,' tap the 'add document' button on the app's home screen, then take a photograph as you normally would do. You don't even need to worry so much about the angle, shape or zoom of your capture, as CamScanner+ has a range of editing options that enable you to ensure your scan is as perfect as possible before saving. Everything we threw at the app was captured near-perfectly, from receipts and birth certificates to driving licenses; even scribbled notes on a scrap of paper. Once scanned, you are also able to tag and categorise your documents, and even upload them to your cloud storage facility, with Google Docs, Dropbox, Evernote, iDisk and Box.net all fully integrated.

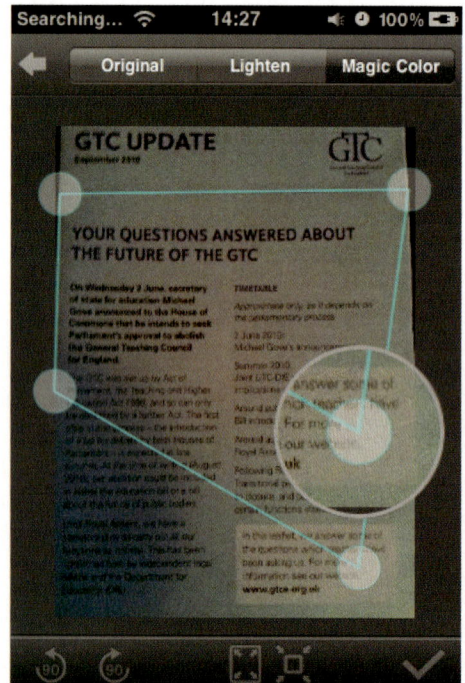

■ The picture editor gives you lots of options to ensure your scan is the best it can be

Overall Rating ★★★★★

172 iPhone Tips, Tricks, Apps and Hacks

Tips | Tricks | Hacks | Apps

Videos can be cropped, zoomed in, the audio increased, and you can even choose which streams to convert

The wonderful thing about Air Video is that if a file is in the wrong format for your iPhone it will convert it live so you can watch instantly

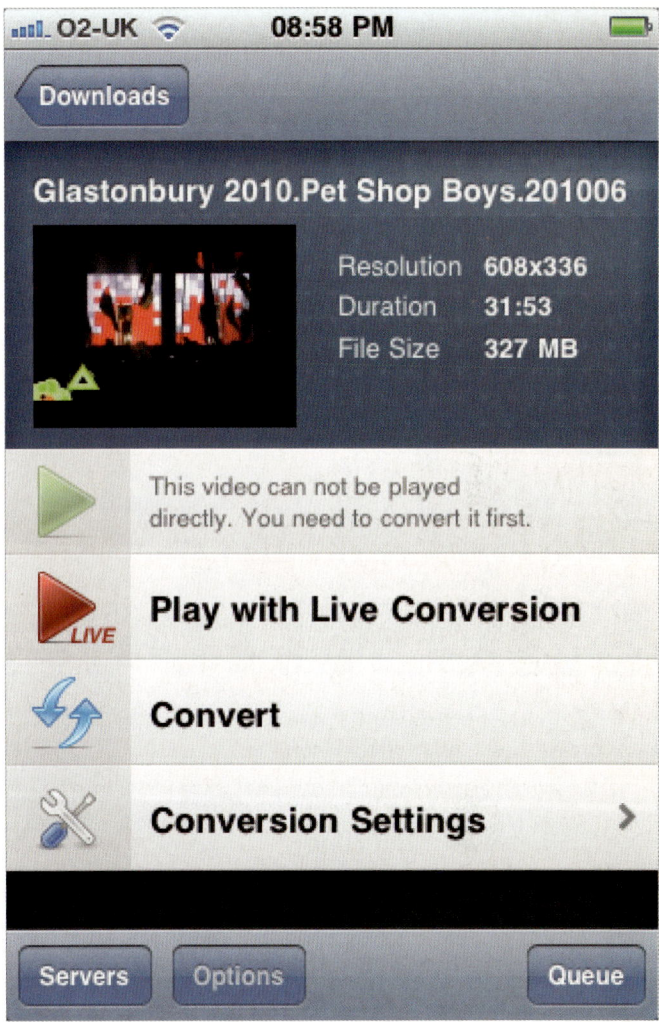

Price: £1.99/$2.99 **Developer:** InMethod s.r.o

Air Video

The conversion kit that does it all

No one watches television in the traditional way any more, right? We download episodes of our favourite programmes from BBC iPlayer, or catch a new movie trailer downloaded from the internet. But getting all these video files, with varying formats and bit-rates, on to your iPhone has been a bit of a faff – until now, that is.

AirVideo is the answer to all our prayers. With this app installed on your iPhone, and its server equivalent downloaded for Mac or PC, you can gain access to all the video you have stored on your computer from wherever you are. The server software sets up your computer for you, so you don't have to mess around with the technical aspects, and you simply point the program to your video folders. You can also point it to your iTunes collection of Video Podcasts, Trailers and TV episodes (although it won't play DRM-protected videos). Then you're all set to go roaming.

The system works a treat through a home Wi-Fi network. The AirVideo app finds your computer instantly, and brings up thumbnails of all the available videos. Some videos can be played instantly, while some need conversion into the correct format for iPhone – and that's where AirVideo gets really clever. You can set up a queue of conversions that will copy the videos to your iPhone for later viewing, or you can have the app convert videos on-the-fly instantly. This is great news for users, as it means no more laborious waiting times, so you can access your content much quicker.

The app will also crop an image, and you can zoom in on videos and customise its conversion settings to suit your own tastes. Even more exciting is the fact you can configure the server software and app to share videos through the 3G network – which means you'll have access to your video collection, no matter where you are.

There are certainly some improvements that can be made to the app – a search facility would be useful for those with hundreds of videos on their computers – but the developer seems to be listening to all the feedback it gets, so that should only be a matter of time.

Overall Rating ★★★★☆

iPhone Tips, Tricks, Apps and Hacks **173**

Exclusive offer

Enjoyed this book?

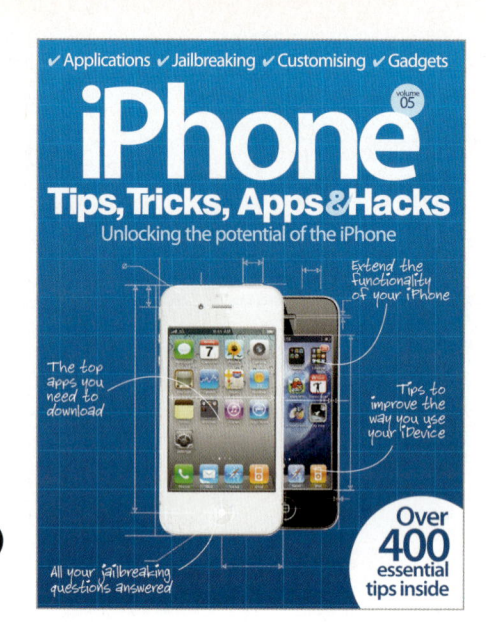

Exclusive offer for new subscribers to…

Pay only £3.50 per issue

Join the app revolution

Find the best iPhone & iPad apps
Every issue we review and rate over 400 apps that best fulfil your work requirements, indulge your hobbies and entertain you.

In-depth features
We give special treatment to the apps that excite us, like group tests for a particular type of app and face-off comparison pieces between two apps that share the same functions and themes.

Greatest Apps Ever section
A section to help ensure that you only download the best that the App Store has to offer

About the mag

iPHONE, iPAD & ANDROID
Apps magazine
www.knowyourapps.com

Pay only £21 every six issues (saving 30% off the newsstand price)

For amazing offers please visit
www.imaginesubs.co.uk/apps
Quote code ZAGTIP5

Or telephone UK 0844 245 6911 overseas +44 (0) 1795 592 922

Go creative with Mac, iPad & iPho

Upskill today with the very best creative bookazines and DVDs

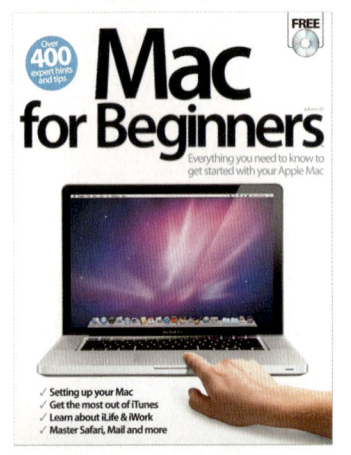

Mac for Beginners vol 3
Starting with the basics, this essential guide will teach you how to get to grips with every aspect of your Mac, from iLife and iWork to iTunes, Safari and Mail.
SRP: £12.99

The iPhone Book
This latest revised edition of The iPhone Book brings you a wealth of guides to help you get more out of your smartphone, from getting started to the must-have apps.
SRP: £9.99

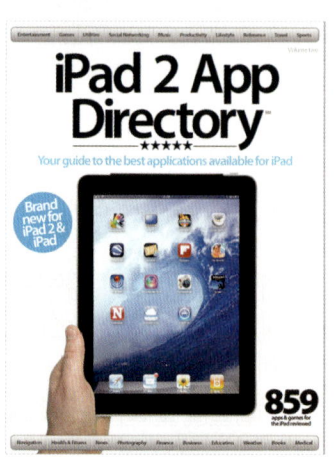

iPad 2 App Directory vol 2
With 859 reviews covering every section of the App Store, this Directory points you towards the very best apps and games out there for iPad and iPad 2.
SRP: £9.99

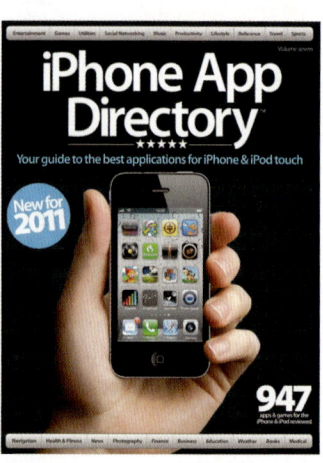

iPhone App Directory vol 7
The world's best iPhone applications are reviewed right here, including the very best for iPhone 4, with every App Store category featured inside.
SRP: £9.99

iPad for Beginners
Get to grips with your new tablet with these simple to follow guides. From setting up to getting to know the most useful features of your device, this is the ultimate guide.
SRP: £9.99

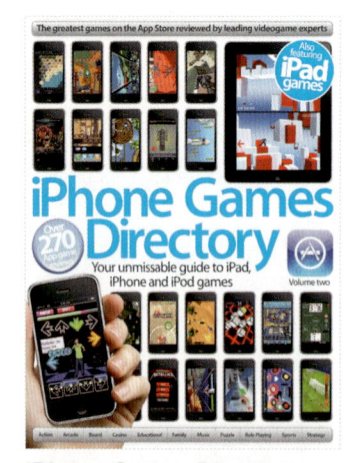

iPhone Games Directory vol 2
The world's most comprehensive guide to iPhone, iPod touch and iPad gaming apps, with all gaming genres reviewed and rated.
SRP: £9.99

iPhone for Beginners
Everything you need to get started on your iPhone. With step-by-step tutorials and a troubleshooting guide, this is a must-have for iPhone owners.
SRP: £9.99

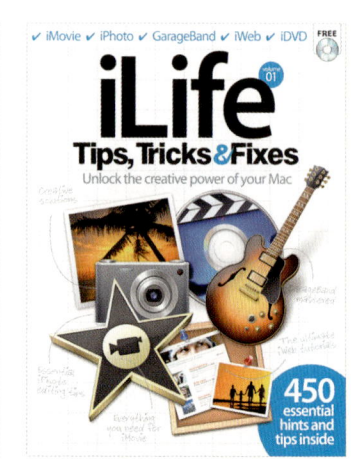

iLife Tips, Tricks & Fixes
Learn to master the complete suite of Apple iLife apps including iPhoto, GarageBand, iMovie, iWeb and iDVD with these in-depth features and guides.
SRP: £12.99

your
ne

NEW!

The iPad Book
The ultimate guide to iPad and iPad 2, this comprehensive book brings you a wealth of productivity, entertainment and lifestyle tips, along with all the top apps to download.
SRP: £9.99

Prices may vary, stocks are limited and shipping prices vary depending on destination

Order online now at:
www.imaginebookshop.co.uk

ip IMAGINE PUBLISHING

We don't keep secrets

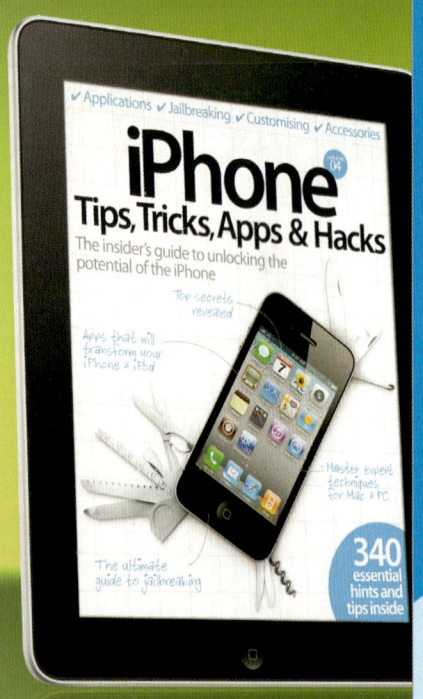

Tips & Tricks™

Learn the truth about iPhone, iPad, Android, Photoshop and more with the Tips & Tricks series' expert advice and tutorials

Also in this series

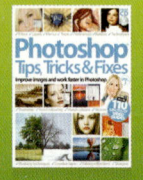

Bookazines
eBooks • Apps
www.imaginebookshop.co.uk

Now available on

High street — Kindle Store — ImagineShop.co.uk — App Store